LEEKS FROM THE BACK BENCHES

ALISON HALFORD

A FORMER WELSH ASSEMBLY MEMBER'S CANDID AND ILLUSTRATED ACCOUNT OF HER DISAPPOINTMENT AND DISILLUSION DURING THE FIRST FOUR YEARS OF WELSH GOVERNMENT

Published by Jeremy Mills Publishing Limited
www.jeremymillspublishing.co.uk

First Published 2007

ISBN 978–1–905217–72–4

Contents

About the author

Alison Halford was born in Norwich in 1940. After leaving her convent school, she served for three years with the Women's Royal Air Force and came to London, aged 22, where she joined the Metropolitan Police. After 21 years, she moved to Merseyside and took up her appointment as an Assistant Chief Constable. She was then the most senior woman in the British police service. In August 1992, having endured a gruelling battle for equality against her Chief Constable and the Home Office, the case was settled (that being the wish of the Home Secretary), and Alison retired from the police service, having served for 30 years.

She moved to Wales in 1994 and became a Flintshire county councillor, and councillor member of the North Wales Police Authority. In 1997, she won her 'phone tapping' case in the Court of Human Rights, Strasbourg and in 1999, having won by a handsome majority, she was elected the first Assembly Member (AM) for Delyn, North Wales, taking up her place as one of the 60 AMs in the first four year term in a long-awaited historic self-rule of Wales. As a non-Welsh speaking Englishwoman, she won her place against stiff opposition.

Alison served on the Local Government, Culture, and Economic Development Committees, but her true strength came into play when she sat on the powerful Audit Committee. Alison now lives three miles from the banks of the river Dee with more animals than she cares to admit to.

Foreword
by Swasie Turner MBE

The author is a lady of high integrity and does not suffer fools lightly. Her Parliamentary revelations make fascinating and most interesting reading. Miss Halford does not pull any punches as she reveals some of the niceties, and some of the not so niceties, of what goes on in the corridors of power.

She tells with complete candour what life is like for those 'powers that be' who either directly or indirectly rule our destiny. Some of her colleagues are responsible stalwarts who serve their constituents well, others are just members of the elite 'Chairbourne Infantry' who could be considered both parasites to the community or hypocritical, politically correct 'Jobsworths'.

I have had the privilege of not only knowing Miss Halford for many years, but also serving on the 'lower decks' for a lengthy period of Police service while 'Ma'am' was one of my Assistant Chief Constables. There is no doubt in my mind that it was due entirely to Miss Halford's dogged determination to bring about equality in what was a largely male dominated service, that we now have female Chief Constables.

Her determination to ensure fairness and equality prevails emanates from the pages of this, her latest, book (her previous book, *No Way up the Greasy Pole* is equally enthralling and informative).

Miss Halford doesn't shirk from drawing attention to those she considers 'don't quite come up to the mark', regarding their (privileged) membership of the recent, beneficial creation of Welsh Government in the name of the Welsh Assembly. She devoted all her time and energy as a member of the Assembly, but sadly soon became disillusioned and concerned at the antics and behaviour, and even the integrity, of some of its members.

Eventually, unable to stifle her deep concerns, and being a lady of strong principle and integrity due to an honest family upbringing which included her schooling at Notre Dame Convent Grammar School, Norwich, Miss Halford felt the honourable thing to do was disassociate herself from such 'below par' activity and step down.

Consequently, she changed camps and became an asset to the Conservative party by becoming an advisor to the Shadow Secretary of State for Wales on police affairs.

I will not steal her thunder by highlighting specific events or incidents among her scriptures, as I think the reader will be inspired by Miss Halford's candid record of events amongst the Welsh Assembly members throughout the book. I admire the author's detailed recollection of her four years as an Assembly member and respect her ongoing efforts to society immensely.

Swasie Turner MBE

'Politics is just like show business. You have a hell of an opening, coast for a while, and then have a hell of a close.'

Ronald Wilson Reagan 1995

'Politicians are the same all over. They promise to build a bridge even where there is no river.'

Nikita Khrushchev October 1960, press conference, New York

'The f★★★ing Welsh.'

Alleged to have been shouted by Tony Blair, following Labour's bad performance in the 1999 Welsh Assembly election

Dedication

The dedication of this book is split four ways:

To 'Team Delyn', Peter York, Leighton Jenkins and Glen Williams, who collectively worked tirelessly and loyally to fulfil my promise to those who entrusted me with their vote, namely that 'I was committed to doing my best for the people wanting the best.'

To Viv Williams, for freely giving of her time and total support when she ran my Delyn campaign office with spectacular efficiency.

To two dear friends, now sadly deceased: Peter Law AM MP, who was my partner in crime for voting against the Wales Millennium Centre, and, therefore, one half of the 'Millennium Two'. He gave so much to the Assembly and was given so little in return. And last but not least, to the wonderfully professional and caring Joy Jackson, who ran the Assembly Help Desk. Nothing was too much trouble and every problem solved.

From policing to politics in one big bound!

'Does the road wind uphill all the way? Yes, to the very end. Will the day's journey take the whole long day? From morn to night, my friend.'
Christina Rossetti 1862

I came to my new life in Wales on crutches having broken an ankle on a slippery slope, but I had lost my love of Merseyside and my career as a senior police officer had ended in tears. There was no way up the 'greasy pole' of the police promotion system for me. Having been denied promotion on nine occasions and with full encouragement from the Equal Opportunities Commission, I started an action for sexual discrimination against the Home Office, the regional Inspector of Constabulary and a couple of Chief Constables: the most important was Jim Sharples, my Merseyside boss. The Home Office finally offered a settlement after two years of stressful equality litigation and, having seen the darker side of life in the police service, I was not sorry to leave a profession I served faithfully for 30 years.

The European Court of Human Rights found that my rights had been breached in 1997, as my force had bugged my phones during my epic equality battle. My phone-tapping ex-boss kept his knighthood despite being judged as behaving unethically; British law had to be changed, and I retired to the banks of the river Dee without a Queen's Police Medal, despite my prestigious career. This is all history now. For years I had stared at Wales on the other side of the river Dee, and wondered about the ruined castle and the deserted cruise liner that hugged the Welsh riverbank. I could not have guessed, five years later, that I would be serving the constituency of Delyn as their National Assembly of Wales Assembly Member (AM), and Flint castle and the 'Fun Ship' would all be in my 'patch'.

Politics had not featured in my life. Police officers were not encouraged to be political, and apart from following my parents' political preferences and voting Conservative, my interest in Government issues was lukewarm. I disliked the sleazy antics of some Tories and related to former MP Matthew Parris's striking metaphor when he compared Government mistakes and deceits to rocks thrown into a bog: they vanish with a plop and are forgotten. But then the pile grows until finally the layer breaks the surface, forming a solid causeway that stands as a stark reminder that power corrupts. At that point, the public wakes up and demands a change. My protest at the causeway breaking the surface took the form of joining the Labour Party in the summer of 1994, and when I popped the Party card into my wallet, I intended to do no more than pay the annual subs and little more attention to the political pages.

I never considered I could reach the rank of Chief Constable either. No woman had ever been appointed to that rank and I confess I never thought the first woman to make that breakthrough was particularly equipped to make it to the top. How ironic that I had been her boss in Merseyside, and had pressed her case with the Chief Constable to allow her to have another crack at the crucial senior command course. She was facing strong competition from her male colleagues who had also flopped and wanted a second attempt. But as my luck ebbed, her luck flowed. The system propelled her through the ranks and the Home Office, desperate to show impartiality towards women as my equality case grabbed the headlines, gave the service its first woman Chief Constable. A clever move and one that is now quite commonplace!

My luck returned when I moved to Ewloe ward and Tom Middlehurst, the leader of the Labour-controlled Flintshire County Council, had other ideas about my retirement. As the Ewloe councillor he disliked sharing the ward with a Tory and wrote, suggesting I should attend party meetings. The Ewloe branch meetings were held in the Labour social club in Connah's Quay, where beer was cheap and everyone friendly. I slid into the room and was welcomed with 'here's fame' from the longest serving Party member. Buying the first round seemed a good idea, and the long serving Party faithful and I rather liked each other. I failed to see the elephant trap that Tom was preparing for me when he suggested that with local elections coming up soon, I should stand against the Tory. It's good fun and not much extra work, he cheerfully stated. My short Party membership was dismissed as not important, nor was Tom deterred when I confessed that I would be abroad for most of the time set aside for campaigning. 'I've paid the fare', I said mournfully. This too was dismissed as irrelevant, and my only contribution to my campaign was squeezed into a few days left before election day, when Tom dashed me round the area to belatedly meet the voters.

Waiting for the count to begin after the polls had closed, I wondered if I had been a complete fool to place myself back in the public eye. I had left the police force under a cloud, with my reputation torn to shreds. When you upset the police, the going gets tough and the battle for equality was vengeful and nasty. I feared that I would not get a single vote, but as Tom and I prowled around the trestle tables laden at the count, two piles were growing fast.

I arrived at the count, held in the local council office at midnight, and I noticed that officials were looking at me with interest. Entering the council chamber, I realised that the last time I had been in a similar room on the other side of the river was when Merseyside Police Authority was hell bent on disciplining me. I had won by a handsome margin for both positions of county and community councillor. I knew I had much to learn but I would not let my constituents down.

Events moved fast after that. Sworn in at County Hall the next day, official mug shot taken, and I was made vice-chair of the Personnel Committee, a post that attracted a £300 a year allowance. To give this paid position to a rookie councillor was a feather in my cap, and I was then voted to serve on the North Wales Police Authority as one of two Flintshire councillor reps. In hindsight I should have refused, as the next four years were both very hard work and totally frustrating, because I knew how a police force worked. My first meeting did not go well. A fax telling me how Merseyside Complaints and Discipline Department did things was handed to me by the Assistant Chief Constable (ACC). As I had headed that department for several years in the 1980s I really did not need this briefing. I assumed it a warning shot across my bows not to make trouble. That had never been my intention. Naively, I presumed that my knowledge would be helpful to the Authority and I had no desire to start yet another battle with another police force.

The Home Office changed the rules that governed how Police Authorities operated in 1994, because the Merseyside Police Authority, all 27 of them, were either elected councillors or Justices of the Peace (JPs), and the chair was always held by a member of the ruling political party; they were accountable to nobody. This political composition had irritated the Home Office when trying to terminate my protracted and police-image damaging industrial action, as the Police Authority's ruling Labour Group refused to accept their own Queen's Council's advice to drop discipline charges against me and end the legal battle. The Authority had already been criticised by the judge, Mr Justice McPherson, as having 'a smell of unfairness in the way the Police Authority had suspended' me, and the Home Office could not settle the matter unless the Police Authority co-operated. In desperation, the Home Office paid the Police Authority's share of my legal fees and compensation, as the Authority's intransigence knew no bounds. It seemed after that, rather than risk a similar stand off, it was easier to rewrite the rules governing Police Authorities.

The membership in North Wales shrank to seventeen. The Home Office dreamt up a new type of member, and the Home Secretary retained the right to approve the shortlist of people who could be interviewed by the Police Authority for final selection by Authority members. They were disparagingly known as 'Place People'. Home Secretary Michael Howard wanted to select the Chairs of Police Authorities but the House of Lords rejected this proposal, knowing it would politicise police forces. However, the elected members' wings (the councillor members) had been severely clipped and events would show that, in North Wales at least, the 'Place People' were indeed creatures of the Home Office and of the Chief Constable. Thus, political clout was diminished and non-elected members of the public worked alongside councillors and JPs, to ensure its police force was effective and efficient, to oversee complaints procedures and to operate as the discipline body for senior officers (the Association of Chief Police Officers ranks).

The first Chairman of the new North Wales Police Authority was such a 'Place Person', who had served as a North Wales police officer before leaving to practise in a local law firm. The chair rotated yearly and in 1997, Cllr E. Williams, an ex-detective from the North Wales force, occupied the position. The next chair was a Freemason, JP Charles Ley, who admitted his allegiance to the 'Brotherhood' during a heated debate over public office holders registering such an interest. Several members looked uncomfortably startled at this unsolicited admission, but none followed his lead.

Although my arrival as a Police Authority member must have been like 'manna from heaven' to many disgruntled citizens who had experienced rough treatment at the hands of their local force, and had no means of achieving redress, events would show that the 'Chiefs' were stunned by my arrival. Before long, my answerphone was taking as many as twelve calls a week, the record being four different callers registering their concerns over hapless policing behaviour in one day. The most time consuming of these was generated by 'Campaign for Justice', which had been set up in 1995 by two businessmen who had endured enormous harassment, and their numerous and serious complaints against the local police had been totally ignored.

A TV documentary, 'Rough Justice', told the story of one man being stopped 24 times, and his story in a Sunday newspaper made worrying reading. At first I tried to ignore their allegations, informing them that they should complain to their own local councillors, but their attentions persisted. I knew I would have to do something after reading a thick dossier of notes the pair had taken from other people, after Messrs Wilford and Hobson had placed an advertisement in the local paper, seeking out others who had similar grievances. It seemed that the Authority was not carrying out its proper function towards public complaints against senior officers, and I suggested that we needed data from the police to allow us to fulfil our function. My request for assistance from other Police Authority members fell on deaf ears.

In Merseyside, complaints files were available for inspection to Police Authority members. As the Complaints and Discipline boss in Liverpool, I entertained councillors for lunch on a monthly roster basis and afterwards, they were left to randomly inspect complaints and discipline files. Michael Argent had been the junior ACC in Merseyside, having worked for me in the Metropolitan Police, and should have known how I handled things. Nevertheless, he categorically refused to allow inspection of files to take place on the other side of the river Dee, and he stuck to his decision. This was one of the first indications that North Wales Police were prepared to give nothing away, and to be as obstructive as possible!

I was one of the four Labour councillors appointed to serve on the North Wales Authority, and we all became frustrated by the refusal of senior officers to give us the information we needed to do our job. As councillors, our duty was to speak up for the people who had elected us to office; we failed miserably because the Chief, his head of legal services, and the majority of members wanted everything kept under wraps and dumbed down. We were invariably outgunned by the rest: unhelpful Gwynedd and Conwy councillors, the five 'Place Persons', the three magistrates and, of course, the chief officers. It became clear that the Chief had to be protected, complaints closed down and no criticism of senior officers allowed!

Soon realising that the system was flawed, I somehow managed to insist that Police Authority meetings were taped, as minutes invariably bore little resemblance to my recollection of discussions and decisions made. Under invariably biased chairmanship, the three Labour councillors were powerless, and however much we pressed for fair play for people who paid the wages of a police force that some perceived as oppressive, we kept hitting brick walls.

Dennis Parry, my fellow Flintshire councillor, felt aggrieved that the Head of Legal Services, Mrs Jennifer Trigger and the Clerk, Leon Gibson, Chief Executive of Ynys Môn, were loyally committed to the Chief Constable rather than to behaving impartially and giving the public some chance of registering a complaint. The Clerk played a crucial part in Police Authority activities, as he gave us legal advice, and monitored our decisions to ensure we did not act improperly. As the force's Head of Legal Services, Jennifer Trigger performed two totally conflicting functions, a situation that would eventually come back to bite her badly. She handled all civil actions against the force, thus she worked for the Chief to defend these actions and complaints received against senior officers, and she was in the front line to inform and advise us on how we should deal with complaints and civil actions.

In my four years on the Authority, neither official once suggested that a complaint should be properly investigated, however compelling the evidence. Dennis Parry and I demanded that Mrs Trigger must obtain legal advice and establish a protocol as to how complaints should be dealt with, believing it was wrong for her to act as our legal adviser and look after the legal needs of the Chief Constable as well. Mrs Trigger's routine, when a complaint was received, was to collate papers and obtain statements from officers involved in the complaint. She was the lead figure in what was invariably a vigorous defence by the force who admitted nothing and never apologised, and yet she advised the Authority on how we should respond to complaints against the Chief Constable. A rape case became a watershed in the struggle to call the Complaints Committee and the collective Authority to account.

A young man, known to everyone in a tightly-knit farming community, was wrongly arrested for rape in February 1993, and suffered vilification by his community before he was proved innocent. The police investigation was flawed from the start and the man requested an apology, compensation, and proof that all his police records had been destroyed. When his complaint was ignored, he turned to the burgeoning 'Campaign for Justice' for help in 1995, and also complained to his MP, Dafydd Wigley, who wrote twice to North Wales Police continuing to seek an assurance that documents relating to his constituent's arrest had been destroyed. I wrote to Mr Wigley as I had been dragged into the affair by 'Campaign for Justice' after offering my help as a Police Authority member, and I was told that the complainant had been notified by two different senior North Wales officers that all his records had been destroyed.

Because the behaviour of senior officers had been challenged, the Police Authority's role was to deal with this complaint, as it was the Discipline Authority for senior officers. The civil action claim – the only redress the complainant had to seek compensation – landed on Mrs Trigger's desk as part of her job to protect the force from expensive settlements. Events unfolded and Dennis and I realised that far from the force destroying the rape documents as good practice, they existed and were lurking in Mrs Trigger's legal department ready to be used to defend the force against the compensation claim.

These documents were part of the process of discovery and Mrs Trigger would have known it – and yet, as the Police Authority's legal adviser, she tried to build 'Chinese walls' between these conflicting areas of responsibility. Discovering such duplicity towards the young farmer, 'Campaign for Justice' went into overdrive and a relentless battle ensued in an attempt to make the police act honourably. As the facts began to seep out of force HQ, they lodged a complaint to the Authority that the Deputy Chief Constable had misled a Member of Parliament over the destruction of the documents. This was a serious matter and it was the duty of the

Authority to hold an impartial investigation. Whenever the Chief had his back to the wall, he would offer to appoint an officer from within the force to carry out the enquiry, rather than consigning the investigation to an external police force: the proper way to conduct affairs. The enquiry was then quietly closed down and no criticism ever levelled at the police bosses. Even with my experience, and with the help of 'Campaign for Justice', it took many months to persuade the Clerk that the complaint against the arresting officers should not be ignored. Yet again, a fudge occurred and the matter was investigated internally. Although the young farmer won his civil action, full settlement details were not revealed.

The glaring conflict of interest that resulted in Mrs Trigger serving two masters, advising the Chief as his Head of Legal Services and being the Authority's adviser on how we were to deal with the man's complaint against the Chief Constable, was frankly iniquitous. She could never be entirely impartial, however honourable her intentions.

The Clerk enjoyed similar dual and conflicting roles. He was the gatekeeper through whom complaints had to pass and, although subtly done, his loyalty was for the chief officers, as he never once advised us to appoint an external investigator, even though numerous complainants called for this intervention. The problem did not end there. As Monitoring Officer, he had the statutory duty to ensure that our Corporate Police Authority actions and decisions were lawful. But we found it worked against the Labour Group because we were blue in the face asking just how he could hold both these roles. If he failed to give us the right guidance, who could challenge the man who had given us the wrong advice? He would hardly call himself to account and launch an enquiry into his own shortcomings!

In May 1997, I tested the weakness of the Clerk/Monitoring Officer fudge by writing to the Chief Constable asking for a copy of the Force Destruction Policy. On the 28th May, the Clerk wrote to me refusing any information on the grounds that 'the Chief

Constable was not prepared to commit expensive resources to the compilation of an exhaustive response to Cllr Halford's request for policy...' Backing the Chief, the Clerk wrote to me – 'He (the Chief Constable) considers it to be 'primarily an operational issue' and not one which is within the remit of the Police Authority.' This was just one of many classic 'catch 22' situations which occurred with regular monotony throughout my term as a Flintshire member of the North Wales Police Authority. Dennis Parry, and Wrexham councillors Malcolm King and Barry Williams, were appalled by this rebuff that was childishly illogical and silly. How could the Police Authority ensure that the force was effective and efficient if we could not examine the force's written policy? We had been refused access to complainants' files and now we were denied access to force's General Orders. On a genuine complaint against the Deputy Chief Constable, whose improper actions had led to a confidential settlement for which the public would stump up, the Authority were happy to sweep it under the carpet.

We needed an ally and turned to Andrew Loveridge, Flintshire County Council's Legal Director, for help. He wrote a stiff letter dated 8th July to the Clerk, firmly reminding him of his duty as Monitoring Officer and Clerk to adhere to the workings of the Complaints and Discipline Procedure, and that the Chief Constable does not have the luxury of declining to process a complaint. I was relieved to have won the backing of Flintshire's top lawyer, who had agreed with my interpretation of how to handle complaints. Andrew's letter worked and within days, the Force Destruction Policy was released to me. It was a small victory for common sense and made the hours of writing letters and championing 'Campaign for Justice' all the more worthwhile.

The next Police Authority meeting proved that senior officers had learnt nothing from this exercise in how the complaints procedure should operate. John Cooke, the ACC responsible for complaints, who always briefed us on the number and progress of outstanding complaints, was an experienced and professional officer.

Therefore, I remained worried when he continued to refuse to accept a serious complaint from a senior social worker against a Detective Chief Inspector.

She alleged that whilst visiting a client in the local prison, she and a woman colleague had been subjected to a humiliating strip search because prison staff had been given misleading information about them. She alleged that a Chief Inspector falsely informed the prison staff about her credentials, and in an attempt to call North Wales Police to account, she wrote to the chairman of the Police Complaints Authority seeking help. The Police Complaints Authority replied that it did not have the power to ask a chief officer to accept a complaint, and as that route proved abortive, I was the next person on her mailing list. Her complaint came to the Complaints Committee meeting on the 18th July 1997, and then I saw North Wales Police in its full, 'we are untouchable' glory.

John Cooke stated that he was again rejecting the social worker's grievance and he refused to accept it as a formal complaint! I was shocked as he was in contempt of statutory legislation. 'You don't have the power to ignore and write off the complaint without recording it and making some investigation', I challenged. He smirked confidently, airily waved a book at me, and bluntly told the committee, 'The Chief Constable has the right to veto what was a complaint and I have the advice of senior Counsel to make the same determination.' 'But you are failing to adhere to the requirements of the Police and Criminal Evidence Act and you must be acting without authority', I replied. He snapped back that it was me who was usurping my role. It was a nasty little spat and members' eyes rolled whilst this exchange took place.

After a further exchange of letters with John, the social worker's complaint was finally accepted, investigated, and officers were apparently disciplined. Both women won compensation from the force and from the Home Office. One nil to Cllr Halford! John Cooke was not amused. That heated exchange between the ACC and me finally proved to the Authority that as the ACC had ill-advised them over the social worker, it could happen again. My Authority colleagues agreed to instruct a barrister to draw up a protocol to advise us on how it should deal with complaints made to the Authority.

Dennis Parry and I were jubilant, as a clear code of conduct that members could understand had been long overdue. The barrister turned up trumps. He meekly chided the chief officer for 'trespassing' into yet another complaint that had been made against his deputy. That was a polite way of informing the Committee that the Chief Constable had been wrong to direct a Superintendent, a junior rank to his deputy, to investigate the complaint and then submit his recommendation, (or in his case, the lack of them) to the Chief Constable for directions.

This pretence of conducting an impartial investigation was the Chief Constable's ruse to keep control of the complaint, thus ensuring his deputy would be kept in the clear. In truth, the law had been flouted and the complainant cheated from the benefit of an investigation. The Authority had not realised it had been cuckolded and the barrister gave firm warning against the Chief Constable having control over an internal investigation in future. The 'protocol' became the bible that left the senior officers, the Clerk and the Head of Legal Services with a little less room for manoeuvre; unsurprisingly, our bible rules were frequently bent too!

The Labour councillors still had to battle for the rules to be obeyed and every victory was hard won. Having grudgingly agreed to tape each meeting, this simple procedure amazingly failed at what always seemed to be very sensitive stages of our discussions. For a force that prided itself on being modern and hi-tech, the failure to record all of the meeting on at least three occasions, because the tape recorder malfunctioned, was alarming, and of course denied us an accurate record of the meeting. The official minutes, produced by the officers under the control of the Chief Constable, contained minimal detail of our discussions and, invariably, the Chief preferred to brief us verbally without producing a written report, and so those recordings were really needed as it offered some chance of proving what had or had not been decided.

Campaign for Justice were pushing me hard to make progress on a variety of complaints they had been sent by the public, most of them seeming to have substance. By August 1997, worn down by the ever-growing list of people with grievances over how they had been treated by their local force, the Labour Group decided to ask for help from higher authorities than us, since the Police Authority's mode of operation was out of control. On the 23rd September, Dennis Parry and I met Malcolm King, a fellow Labour and Police Authority Councillor. He was the Mayor of Wrexham but had a slim majority; he knew he could not make a political mistake but supported the plan to ask the Home Secretary for help. He was in charge of the police and we felt he should be told how our attempts to fulfil our elected duties were being thwarted by the Chief and a compliant Authority. I felt encouraged that senior Labour Party members were willing to listen to me and to make a stand. I began collating the evidence and after a Herculean effort, a nineteen page report – thoroughly checked and approved, then signed personally by the four Labour councillors – was ready to be sent to the Labour Home Secretary, Jack Straw.

As I worked through the files and complaints, I realised just how little we were being told by the chief officer who continually tried to keep us in the dark. I outlined seven different reasons why the Chief Constable refused to give us the information we rightfully required as providers of an effective and efficient force. Accurate to the last comma, the impressive catalogue of the problems and difficulties we had encountered as members was posted to the Home Secretary on the 17th December 1997. Far from accepting this document as a tool to further better management of a Police Authority, we finally realised that this detailed document was not at all welcome in the lofty reaches of the Home Office and went down like a lead balloon. That leaden balloon landed heavily on us in a way we could never have guessed.

At first, the silence from the Home Office was deafening. We assumed that the Christmas break had slowed things down in the Home Secretary's department. As we did not feel we should send a long and complex document to all North Wales MPs, without warning, we wrote and invited them to ask for a copy. Several MPs took up the offer. Two MPs did not!

After Dennis Parry wrote to the Home Office asking for some feedback, Under Secretary to the Home Secretary Alun Michael broke ministerial silence on the 14th January 1998. He was 'very concerned by the extremely serious allegations in the report and the implications for the North Wales Police and the Police Authority.' He thought that the Chief Constable and the full Police Authority's comments would be useful and asked if we were 'content to disclose the report to these parties?' This skilfully crafted letter acknowledged that although he was very happy to meet with 'the co-authors, because of the serious allegations which it contains, and the need for proper investigation, it would not be appropriate to meet until the report has been given through the local process.' The final sentence assured us that the Home Secretary and he (Alun Michael) intended to follow developments closely. We were shocked by this clever ploy. Meanwhile, one of the Labour co-signatories got cold feet and wanted to distance himself from the report although he had willingly signed it originally.

Although Alun Michael had confirmed the seriousness of the report and the need for a proper investigation, he had pushed us into a corner by making us give it to other members; the worst of all scenarios, as they would regard our actions as both damaging and extremely disloyal. The Minister's letter mentioned that he had agreed to meet Barry Jones, my own MP, to discuss our concerns. Clearly, that meeting had not taken place either and the opportunity of seeking further help from our local Member of Parliament was shut. Malcolm King, Dennis Parry and I were concerned; as turkeys don't vote for Christmas, we knew that our Authority colleagues would not support our report. How could they? They were part of the problem. Had I written the document on my own, I may have understood the Home Office reluctance to get involved, but Alun Michael had failed even to support his own Labour colleagues, despite being long standing councillors and Authority members. To turn his back on a genuine cry for help and to dump us back into the arms of the 'enemy' was disingenuous and a bad case of ministerial issue-ducking. No external investigation ever occurred and our Authority colleagues took full revenge on us.

The Police Authority met on the 30th January 1998 at police HQ as usual and our report was an agenda item. Coffee and biscuits were laid out, but the biscuits seemed like cardboard and the coffee as cold as the reception we received from other members. Anticipating the pending storm, the media circus was out in force, their appetite whetted by our appearance on 'Week in Week Out' a few days previously. The first item welcomed back ACC John Cooke from a long illness. I mentally hoped that I had not contributed to his indisposition after our little disagreement last July. Then, 'Item 2 – Concerns by a Labour membership of this Authority' was reached. Dolefully, the Clerk read out the options. Should it be returned to the Home Office for their consideration, or should the Authority deal with it without involving the Home Office?

The temperature of the debate increased as various members wound themselves up into a plethora of righteous frenzy. The doctor member was asked if his Medical Complaints Committee would allow a doctor, subject of a complaint, to advise that committee; the curt reply was that the complaint would be delegated elsewhere for decision. No notice was taken of how the medical profession dealt with its complaints and then Michael Argent, my colleague from the Metropolitan Police and Merseyside, launched into a long, deeply insulting, and in my view unprofessional, tirade. He lashed into 'Campaign for Justice' and into the Labour councillors. His speech was interspersed with TV clips of news items and documentaries to make a particular point, and his particular point was to exact revenge and humiliation by rubbishing the co-authors and everything about my thoroughly researched 'Magnum Opus'. I learnt that I had arrogantly accused ACC Cooke of lying during the exchange over his failure to record the social worker's complaint. 'He considers the matter to be potentially defamatory and intends seeking legal advice as to how he might seek appropriate redress.' This was news to me and, as this 'potential defamation' had occurred over seven months previously, John Cooke had certainly taken his time to contemplate redress against me.

Michael Argent demolished the report, describing it with a clever quip as 'a personal initiative dressed up in an ill-fitting democratic overcoat.' His comments were so pernicious, I seriously wondered if I had a case against him for defamation. Dennis Parry was next in line to be humiliated. Michael Argent believed that Dennis had a 'most unenviable record of continually raising serious allegations against this force.' One related to a well-connected paedophile ring that Dennis thought was operating in the area, but no evidence had been produced. Dennis responded spiritedly, and explained that as an elected member it was his job to challenge potential wrongdoing. He hit back over the child abuse allegation by asking why Waterhouse was now investigating child abuse in North Wales? 'Because I listened to a complainant in Bangor and took instructions, and I took some names, and I had some phone calls, and I asked my Social Services to investigate them quickly, because I was worried', Dennis snapped back.

An engrossed public gallery learnt too that our report was 'inaccurate, ill conceived, malicious and detrimental to the well being of North Wales Police.' Not only was it 'long on rhetoric', it was 'short on evidence; it was launched as a secret report ignoring due process and seeking to approach Government on a Labour Party ticket.' The 'Campaign for Justice' was seated in the Public Gallery, and the Chief Constable ripped into the two men who had worked tirelessly to improve the complaints system in North Wales. When he named one individual as 'being branded by one of the area's most respected judges as a deliberately dishonest man,' I protested loudly as they had no way of defending themselves. I continued to protest that this attack was unfair and the Chairman, ex-detective Williams, now Cllr Williams, immediately threatened to 'name' me! Had he done so, I would have been forced to leave the meeting.

I bit my tongue during the rest of Argent's deeply hurtful tirade, but I felt sick with disbelief that the most senior law enforcement officer in the region could stoop so low as to ruthlessly abuse people who paid his wages and could not answer back. How could the Chief Constable make such allegations against me, a former colleague who had actively helped to secure his promotion to ACC in Merseyside? His damning words: 'Under the respectable banner of being elected members affiliated to a major party, the authors have associated themselves with a singularly unsuccessful and discredited pressure group who have attempted to blacken the name of a fine force.' We were accused of mounting 'a scurrilous, unjustified and unsupported attack on the force's professional track record' and we had 'launched a vituperative attack on its three officers of many years standing.'

We, the co-authors, were then asked to cast our minds back over the years of our membership and ask what contribution we had made to the betterment of policing in Wales. It was a masterful speech and I guessed that Kevin Fletcher, a lawyer from a major firm in Merseyside, had helped with the drafting. Ironically, Kevin had advised me on police complaints matters when I headed the Merseyside Complaints Department, and, in happier times, he had been welcomed to the Department's liquidatious Christmas bashes. Ironically, he had been the Equal Opportunity Commission's ruthless adversary when instructed to defend the Merseyside Chief against my discrimination action. He won no friends from my legal team over how he had conducted his brief. I wondered what fee he had earned for crafting Michael Argent's destructive rant.

Suddenly, our resignations were being demanded, the suggestion mooted by Glyn Bartlett, the former police officer now turned lawyer, who began to draft a resolution that would remove us from the Authority. Other members chipped in with various suggestions and we, the Labour members, sat mutely through the gathering head of steam to be rid of us. Words became muddled; the collective effort seemed not strong enough for the lawyer's precise mind. He preferred the resolution to say that 'not only' should we 'consider our position,' and 'in event of their resignation then nominating authorities be requested to nominate replacement,' but all this should be done 'at the earliest opportunity.' He had pushed too hard. A more cerebral member of the Authority objected and suggested that the Labour councillors should just 'consider their position.' 'But it doesn't add up to anything,' Glyn muttered plaintively.

The resolution shrank to: 'the members be requested to consider their position.' Full stop! The tape recording technician had excelled and that chaotic debate was captured for posterity. This was the second time that the Chief Constable had demanded our resignations! He had insisted upon instructing a barrister to provide the excuse for removing us from the Police Authority! I told him politely that he was wasting public money, as we had done nothing to warrant our removal. Compliantly, the committee agreed to Michael Argent's demand and a sum in excess of £48,000 was spent on the barrister who had been given the task of defending the indefensible! Tracking down force expenditure, legal advice had been my high priority, simply because the information was shrouded in mystery. A 'force legal fees' budget-line simply did not exist. After protracted probing, I established that legal costs were buried in the general expenditure under 'Sundries' in the balance sheet. Such accounting made it impossible to establish the true cost of the force and Police Authority legal fees. A small and seemingly niggling point maybe, but when a force and Authority can bale itself out of impropriety by employing ruthless lawyers and the public unwittingly pays, then I think we should be told!

In one bound, the Home Office was free from any further responsibility and the item would be taken forward to the next Authority meeting on the 13th March 1998. We had ridden out the resignation demands but I wondered what other unpleasantness we would encounter. As the meeting progressed, Leon Gibson, the wily Clerk, smugly told us that he was 'a servant of the whole Authority,' and he 'trusted' that he had 'served the Authority with integrity.' I reached for the water jug to curb my disdain for this man, and nearly choked when he obsequiously stated: 'I have attempted to be entirely honest with the matters, and I think the records of committee meetings and correspondence will show that.' None of us would know that he was on borrowed time as our Clerk and Monitoring Officer.

Michael Argent notched up another sparkling victory when, in a shrewd move, the Authority disbanded the Complaints sub-committee on which Dennis and I served, and widened membership to embrace the entire Authority. It handed power back to the 'Cronies' and effectively neutralised Dennis and myself. Widening the Complaints Committee had been suggested by a magistrate member and without a majority; the Labour Group lost the vote. I had always believed that magistrate members also risked compromising themselves. They sat in judgement over a defendant who was being prosecuted by an officer in the force. The JP served on the force's Authority, and could sit again in judgement on that same defendant if that person lodged a complaint against a senior officer. I felt this was an incestuous arrangement, and if the JP was also a freemason – the Brotherhood being known to frequent police ranks – the conflict of interest was without parallel! My Labour colleagues held the same view, but yet again we were out of step with the majority. I should have taken the enlargement of the complaints committee as a compliment to my strength of purpose and knowledge, and confirmed by Brother Charles Ley, JP, who 'felt unable to control Dennis and myself.'

Weeks after Leon Gibson, the Clerk, had skilfully attempted to undermine 'our' report, the *Daily Post*, of the 2nd April 1998 announced that the District Auditor's report 'had stunned the people of Anglesey over the behaviour of its chief executive.' Several highly critical allegations of impropriety were reported against Leon Gibson, none other than North Wales Authority's Clerk and Monitoring officer, including juicy by-lines: 'Report rocks council' and 'Council undecided on question of sackings'. 'Scandal' was emblazoned in two-inch high letters on the *Post's* front page and amongst various allegations, Leon was also accused of accepting a 'junket' to Paris for a rugby match. Days later, the *Post's* coverage further astounded me. I learnt that our Clerk was still under investigation by the North Wales Police Fraud Squad! None of this had ever been reported at any committee meeting. Was this the reason why the Clerk had never advised that any complaint made against senior officers, however serious and persistently made, should be investigated? Surely not? 'Why was the Authority not told?' We demanded answers at the next Authority meeting, particularly as the Chief Constable had put his entire faith in the integrity of the Clerk when savaging us at that appalling 30th January meeting. The reply was that it was not relevant to our general deliberations! We learnt later that Mr Gibson quietly resigned from the committee, leaving it bereft of the legally required Monitoring Office. The Authority then entered a period of fudged and dubious appointments to the role of Clerk and Monitoring Officer, which gave me little confidence that the administration of Authority business was yet under control!

From the long list of people seeking our help, Keith Davies stands out as an indefensible example of poor management and even when exposed, there followed a shabby attempt to defend inexcusable behaviour by senior officers. He was a former Detective Constable who had started civil action against his force seven years previously as his former bosses, for reasons unknown, downgraded his excellent yearly staff appraisals and returned him to uniform, always regarded as demotion. Keith then discovered that a recent, very complimentary appraisal report had been materially altered. His federation supported his legal action against the force for Malfeasance in Public Office and Malicious Falsehood, but the case had become bogged down and, returning from Canada where he had started a new career, he tracked me down and asked for help. Dennis and I met him at County Hall and we knew immediately from his story and supporting documents that his case was strong and delay was the only weapon left with which to defend his force!

Even Dennis Parry, hardened by years serving on the Police Authority, blanched when Keith explained that the named officer he believed responsible for Malfeasance in Public Office and Malicious Falsehood not only had been promoted, but was in charge of Special Branch and the department responsible for standards of ethics and honesty throughout the force.

Keith alleged that the police lawyer dealing with the case, Jenny Trigger, sent his team a document vital to his case which should not have been disclosed. The police were forced to admit that a relevant paper 'had gone missing from headquarters.' Keith believed that the judge hearing the case was losing patience with senior officers and the extraordinary delay and was 'minded to call the Chief Constable to court to explain why vital evidence had vanished.' Although Michael Argent had not led the force when Keith's appraisals had been 'doctored', he became responsible for defending his force and if Keith was right, Michael Argent risked being summonsed to explain himself to the judge.

I have never understood why an incoming Chief does not demand an audit of outstanding civil actions against the force. It would present an opportunity to review progress and, if necessary, cut costs by seeking settlements. It would be cheaper in the end because any lawyer, instructed by police, as was the case with Kevin Fletcher, is able to run the legal fees meter for years without challenge of scrutiny. The public picks up the tab for this legal gravy train where costs are rarely disclosed, and the cost to the public purse is colossal! Michael Argent's jaw dropped when Dennis and I casually requested a written report on the Davies case at the following Complaints Committee. He responded by briefing the Committee verbally; a method of reporting much favoured when the item is embarrassing or very sensitive, and with nothing written down, it's almost impossible to prove what was said. When pressed to determine the court date when Argent would be called before the judge, the full Authority received a further verbal briefing seeking our views on how the case should be settled.

The case was important and any costly settlement demanded a written paper to supplement the verbal briefing. A six-page document was duly presented and the Complaints Committee was obliged to read it, with the Clerk and the senior officers watching closely and waiting for us to finish. Far too quickly, the Chair was calling us to order and the report was whisked away by the officials. No opportunity was offered for us to keep a copy or refer to it whilst we asked questions! Various options had been listed and despite our limited knowledge of the Davies grievance, but far better than the knowledge of most other members, Dennis and I began to probe further. Information was scant and the Authority was ordered to make a decision. Dennis and I secretly knew that Michael Argent was now two weeks away with his appointment with the presiding judge, and that this appearance would be harmful to the force's moral image.

I also felt some sympathy for him and I made the suggestion that we should settle and make an apology to the officer, using the avoidance of further cost as the excuse. My suggestion was eagerly grasped, and, coming from me, had been entirely unexpected. The committee unanimously supported the settlement route but balked at issuing an apology to the defamed ex-officer! How sad that the 'Cronies' were unwilling to admit to any wrongdoing. I could not withdraw my suggestion to settle the case but felt aggrieved that members were so mean-minded as to refuse a rightful apology.

On the 8th May 1998, at the High Court in Mold, the two counts of Malfeasance and Malicious Falsehood against the Chief Constable of the North Wales Police were discontinued. Although a confidentiality agreement was imposed, by mistake the Chair informed the press and we learnt that the episode had allegedly cost £170,000. Cheap at the price, I thought. It had dragged on for eight years. When discovering that the force insurers had refused to pay any of the costs,

I was rightfully angry and this refusal now lent weight to a worrying rumour that had been circulating from a reliable source for months. The insurers had sent in their assessors to find out what their client the police had been up to and, allegedly, did not like what they had discovered. What was required to nullify the insurance claim and pass the costs over to the public? Missing files from HQ and a judge apparently demanding explanations from the Chief maybe?

I felt we had all been duped. Although I had to speed read, I recalled nothing in the six-page document that indicated that the taxpayer would pick up the entire bill. Had I known that, I would have demanded that the case should go to court, as I will not support impropriety. Although Dennis and I attempted to formally establish why the insurers had refused to pay, once again, the Chief Constable's club closed ranks and we were sidelined. When asked, the Clerk did send us a copy purporting to be the one presented to us and then snatched back. My concentration and previous speed-reading course must have failed me on that occasion. The copy sent to me clearly stated the full cost would be met by the public. How strange that we were not allowed to keep our reports at the time. Stranger still that this important topic had not been dealt with under normal committee paper rules, whereby Authority members must be served their committee papers under legally scheduled deadlines. Dennis and I had to press for a written report. Why was this document subject to special treatment? No one was telling, not even Bryan Grew the insurance company representative, who by sheer coincidence became my election agent when I stood as an Assembly member. Keith never received his apology, but neither did the taxpayer who footed the entire bill!

Although I enjoyed the challenge and buzz of serving on seventeen committees, including the Community Council and Police Authority as a county councillor, my mind was focusing on the looming elections for the Welsh Assembly, now a year away. I wanted closure on the dysfunctional and shabby conduct of the North Wales Police Authority, and had been bitterly disappointed with what I had seen first hand. I was deeply committed to Labour's pledge to 'gender balance' in the new Assembly, and felt I had something to offer. I knew it would be very hard work; the travel alone was a daunting prospect. Encouraged by people I trusted, I decided to throw my hat into the ring and submit myself for election as the AM for Delyn.

Campaigning capers with mission accomplished!

'Democracy substitutes election by the incompetent many for appointment by the corrupt few.'
George Bernard Shaw 1903

As 1998 rolled on, I made great strides towards being elected as an Assembly member whilst Michael Argent failed at his third bid to escape from his current command into another force. His attempt to return to Merseyside, where we had both served as Assistant Chief Constables, was dealt a killer blow when 'Campaign for Justice' sent a red-hot newsletter to all Merseyside Authority members. If revenge was the motive, it succeeded. As a well-placed friend on the selection panel reported, 'He [Argent] did not have the qualities necessary to do the job.' Doubtless, wide coverage of our 'secret report' to the Home Secretary and uproar at public Police Authority meetings (that required the visit of the local Her Majesty's Inspector of Constabulary (HMI) to quell the unrest), was not the sort of thing that another Authority would welcome. Michael was firmly stuck with North Wales, or, more to the point, the force was stuck with him.

My written application to be a Labour candidate was just one from 6,000 hopefuls who lined up in March to start the race to appoint the first 60 Assembly Members. I was amazed that Tom Middlehurst, my mentor, failed the paper sift, and doubly pleased when his appeal succeeded. On the 28th June, a hot Sunday better suited to getting out the garden loungers, I drove to Yale College in Wrexham to be interviewed by senior Labour Party worthies. The smiles were friendly and the questions both civil and uncontroversial. When asked would I always obey the Labour whip, I wobbled a bit. I could not swear that in no circumstance would I not be whipped but I told them that if there was a problem, I was confident I would be allowed to put my point of view. 'Life is all compromise,' I added, and the interview moved on to how I would handle tough media attention. I was on very familiar territory and entered into the spirit of things when one of the interviewers moved into the role of nasty journalist. Using humour, I refused to be bullied. I left the interview feeling that although I had not capitulated, they seemed to like me.

I read the panel correctly. The successful result arrived in July. I was given the thumbs-up and had to ride out considerable coolness from some failed candidates. Tom and I agreed that if his appeal succeeded, I would accept Delyn, although we both lived in the Alyn and Deeside constituency. Much to the amusement of the political watchers, Delyn would be battled for by women candidates. With David Costa's wife Cath Sherrington (her campaign name) as a rival, I thought that my luck had run out. David, a senior party apparatchik, was the regional head based in Llandudno, and Cath, a highly experienced campaigner, knew all about telephone canvassing and other essential skills needed to get out the vote. I felt that with my total lack of canvassing experience I would be 'dead in the water,' but I pressed on.

The selection procedure became chaotic with huge problems over 'twinning' certain constituencies to achieve the promised balance of men and women candidates. Some branches consistently refused to endorse the 'twinning' processes. Everything slowed down whilst the Party struggled to impose its will on unruly, chauvinistic 'Old Labour'. Val Feld was fighting for her Swansea seat against a backcloth of brutal tactics. She endured razor blades and other ghastly items enclosed in her mail. I had met Val Feld many years previously through my discrimination action. She was the Equal Opportunities Commissioner in Cardiff, so she too knew much about entrenched attitudes and dirty tricks. She won through, achieved her constituency nomination, and took her rightful seat on the Assembly. I gave November and December 1998 over to campaigning. My usual robust health gave way to feeling ill and a persistent cough that three courses of antibiotics refused to shift.

Chest, sinuses, x-rays and blood tests were all clear, so I abandoned self-pity and got on with the job, spending many evenings telling Branches in Alyn and Deeside and Delyn how wonderful I was. As Branches frequently met on the same night, it meant juggling to make one presentation, then hurtling cross-country to another party venue for more of the same.

Greenfield Branch gave me a very rough ride, and challenged everything I said. Peter York, the Branch secretary who had written inviting me to attend, was gentler, but he probed me too. The North-South divide was a big issue. I was pressed hard over how I would stand up to the South Wales Tafia to ensure North Wales got its cut of the cake. I must have said the right thing, as I got that important Branch nomination, guaranteeing me some votes when push came to shove at the vital final Hustings meeting. Cath and I kept falling over each other, trailing around Delyn in search of votes, but we were both well disposed to each other, knowing there could only be one winner. Neither of us could have guessed the result.

The dice stopped rolling for me when 'we hopefuls' were called before the Mold Branch to set out our respective stalls. Bryan Grew, the Branch secretary and Delyn MP David Hanson's election agent, left the Council Chamber to brief us. He explained that members selected order of appearance, and the time allowed to make our pitch. Mold, the largest and most influential branch in Delyn, was a key one to capture. I was particularly nervous, and my diary written shortly after the ordeal recalled that I was not amongst friends, as I picked up an aura of cool indifference when I entered the Council Chamber. I was completely thrown when the time allocated to present my case was suddenly halved before I had even settled. Then a card was pushed towards me and I was told to answer the three questions in whatever order I chose.

Diary states: 'Cath is given the questions whilst I am presenting first. Bryan Grew, David Hanson's agent, is there. All the rules change.' The five to ten-minute presentation changed to five and I had to read questions in front of the audience, including Carol

Hughes (Carol also pressing to submit herself as an Assembly candidate). Diary continues, 'Everyone looked very "po-faced" apart from Chris Bithell. Was he savouring my discomfort? It was clear that – name written in – favours Cath. I learnt later that night I had lost by one, as had Tom to Tudor Williams.' When I had confirmation that Cath had indeed been given the questions whilst I was making my presentation, I asked someone in charge before I left the Town Hall why I had not been given the same treatment? I knew better than to press the matter when an airy wave of a hand dismissed my question.

The promise of a set time for my 'spiel' was subsequently, and unexpectedly, reduced again on the 20th November. I should have learnt by then to be more flexible with a five and a ten-minute speech ready up my sleeve. Diary notes: 'Labour Club: Connah's Quay was the shortlisting and another disaster; again, the five to ten minutes expected suddenly changed to five. I've worked hard on my speech length but abandoned it, knowing it was too long for the time allowed. Waffled for four minutes, was told I had another minute, and started again. I was first again with Cath and Karen Sinclair following me in.' I left once I had done my bit, and the phone call later that evening told me that Cath, Karen Sinclair and I were all shortlisted. Tom now had one rival to beat; I had two.

More bad news arrived a week before the final Hustings meeting when Linda Lee, a fellow Flintshire councillor initially really helpful with my campaign, unexpectedly withdrew her support, leaving me to do my own campaigning. I was upset at being dumped at short notice and a 'bust up' followed. It made my campaign more difficult as she had promised to do the all-important 'phone round' to secure votes on the night. With less than a week to go, I spent an evening doggedly on the phone, contacting most of my fellow councillors, and as many constituents as I had the time and energy to reach. I spoke to Linda apologising for my outburst, and was shocked when I was told 'If you can't take the pressure, you shouldn't go for the Welsh Assembly.' I bit my tongue hard. I thought my capacity to stand pressure was rather good, but I accepted her criticism and we patched up our differences. She and Meirion Matthews called round a day or so before the final meeting to hear and time my speech, and gave it the thumbs-up – to my relief.

All too soon, the 15th December dawned, a meaningful date for another reason besides the Hustings event. Informed that the selection process would be well over by early December, I had paid a deposit on a holiday abroad. I was shocked to learn that the day of my Costa Rican jaunt mysteriously clashed with the important Hustings meeting. The choice was bleak: not take the holiday or lose the chance of standing in the Welsh Assembly election, as I had no chance without appearing before Party members to state my claim. I collected Tom in my taxi en route for the event and saw that he was also nervous. We had just pulled away from his house when he found himself without his glasses. He said he could manage but I insisted he really should have them. He charged back into the house and soon we were off again to Connah's Quay club.

Diary notes: 'I drew the last straw – literally – and was last on. I wore a red jersey skirt and white over jacket. Wandered round to local supermarket for cold water, the jug provided being hot. Put in heel guards as gold shoes were slipping off.' I had taken my book, *No Way up the Greasy Pole* and pretended to read avidly as, one by one, the candidates left for the main hall for their date with fate. The 'hopefuls' became more and more agitated and Cath Sherrington persisted in reminding the dwindling audience of her exceptional 'phone canvassing talents'. I kept quiet about my feeble attempt to embrace this skill after Linda Lee withdrew her services. With reckless modesty, my faithful diary recorded: 'I slayed 'em. Long walk to five steps to stage. Would knee give way?'

Despite working assiduously on my speech, timekeeper Bryan Grew, squatting near me on the platform, rang the bell before I had finished. Refusing to miss delivering the punch line, I ploughed on. 'Never again will North Wales be the poor relation, I will be a powerful voice…' The bell was dinging wildly. Ignoring everything, I finished my presentation and staggered down those five steps to thunderous applause. The count started immediately. Soon rumour spread that I had won the postal votes and the hall was buzzing that I had 'walked' the contest. All I had to do was what I did: turn up on the night and the prize was mine. I'm not sure the Mold Branch would have concurred, but the people had spoken! I had been selected with a handsome majority of 198 votes, followed by Cath Sherrington with far less, and Karen Sinclair, who trailed with a brave ten. I had been worried that Karen and Cath chose to contest Delyn as well as their local constituencies, but more attempts the better I suppose was the safe option. I embraced the losers in genuine sympathy, as I had learnt all about the stress of winning and losing.

Having obtained more votes than Tom, I was entitled to choose which seat I would contest in a National election. Looking anxious, Tom piped up that he would prefer 'A and D' (Alyn and Deeside). Living in the constituency gave certain advantages over a candidate who does not, which all became clearer as events developed. Both MPs were watching hawkishly as I politely said that I would be very honoured to stand in Delyn. I could not wantonly rob Tom of his home constituency when he had introduced me to politics. That was the noble part of my conscience speaking. The other reason was because I knew that I could never work comfortably with Barry Jones, the Alyn and Deeside MP. The chemistry had once been good and he had asked the previous Government some tough questions fed to him by Robin Makin, my esteemed lawyer friend. Robin had won my phone-tapping case against a Tory Home Secretary and my former Chief Constable, the now elevated Sir James Sharples, in 1997. With no redress available in the UK, Robin took the 'Bugging Affair' to the court of Human Rights and won a handsome victory. The Regulation of Investigatory Powers Act entered our statute books and stands today to protect others from similar abuse of powers.

MP Barry Jones, Robin and I had once taken tea convivially together in a local Ewloe hotel to discuss the phone-tapping case, and he seemed well disposed towards me. When I became a councillor, the relationship changed dramatically. A definite coolness descended and I lacked the courage to ask him what was wrong. I was not the only woman councillor who suddenly realised that I was no longer on his 'Christmas card list'.

The deal done and knowing I would contest Delyn for Labour, I went to the bar and bought a large round for all my supporters. Bryan Grew accepted a half of beer and in comparison with my euphoria, looked somehow crestfallen. Strong supporters of Cath looked equally bemused and I did not blame them. I was an English woman with no Welsh, holding a Party card on which the ink was still wet having lived in the area just four years, and I had won the golden chance of going all the way to the Assembly. I made conciliatory noises and bought more beer for friend and foe alike.

The next day the phone never stopped ringing to offer congratulations and support. Having lost the Costa Rican holiday, I found a last minute place on a Kenyan safari, and the next day was on a plane bound for Mombasa. On Christmas Eve in a lovely Safari hotel, as I listened to an African choir, someone stole my prized binoculars from my bag within inches of me. Although police were called, I never saw them again. Watching birds without binoculars was almost as stressful as running an election campaign with fickle friends. Christmas Day was spent viewing wild beasts and handing out wrapped sweets to local children. I felt sad as I watched poorly clothed kids grab these tiny treats. Such pleasure obtained by these destitute children from the distribution of a bag of boiled sweets made the loss of my mega-expensive binoculars suddenly totally irrelevant.

After the holiday David Hanson, Delyn's MP, attended a little bash I arranged in a local pub to thank local journalists for their support thus far. The *Chester Chronicle* and the Flintshire Leader's goodwill were vital, as even I knew that the 'oxygen of publicity' was a necessary ingredient to get elected. Delyn was not always a Labour stronghold, and David had won it only by a lengthy and dogged assault on a Tory majority. He had now held the seat for some years and he was confident I would win for Labour. I listened carefully when he solemnly announced that although I was the prospective candidate, it was my campaign, and I must make the entire running. Members of the Fourth Estate turned up in good numbers, scoffed 'sarnies' and drank deeply, but I happily picked up the tab. The all important local news hounds had come, and I felt that my campaign was starting well.

I instinctively declined the Party's election campaign manifesto and poster printing service. Cardiff seemed too remote if a late change was necessary to my 'shop window'. I preferred to support a recommended local printing company in Wrexham who made me welcome and gave me a tour of the building. Things were very hi-tech, far removed from setting letters by hand. My choice of manifesto provider turned out to be a wise decision. Foolishly, my manifesto portrait was taken wearing blue! I did not possess much red and despite blue being the main Opposition colour it suited me better. The photographer used his best beautifying lens and the result was flattering. I would not run away from the poster when it hit the streets and was hung in supporters' windows.

I'd already defined my goals and policies, and soon a smart manifesto of striking red and yellow took shape. Both MPs willingly posed with me for manifesto material, and a trip to Mold Market captured me sporting a large rosette talking to one of the party faithful against a backdrop of laden stalls, wearing red this time. I felt comfortable that my manifesto and poster, despite the blue clothing, would be delivered on time and on budget. They were!

When collecting the printer's handywork, the number of boxes loaded into my car appalled me. I could not believe I could ever offload this entire stock of political bumph onto a possibly indifferent public. The 3,000 calling cards stacked in boxes felt like overkill too. I meant to win and if a forest of trees had to be sacrificed to state my brilliance and suitability to be an AM, then so be it! No great effort was incurred in gathering my campaign team together, as helpers were sparse indeed. David Hanson's agent, Bryan Grew was the obvious choice to be mine, but I felt uneasy with him for reasons I could not explain. I dared not rock boats by seeking someone else. He knew the ropes, held the party membership data, and knew who would turn out to shove my gaudy leaflets through doors. David was always encouraging and kept telling me that I would 'walk it'. Bryan accepted the agent job and remembering David's words, that I made the running in 'my' campaign, I knew that although I had made the right decision, I could not afford to sit back and rely on others.

I felt more comfortable with other members of my campaign team: Viv Williams, a long time party supporter, and Peter York, the assertive Greenfield Branch Secretary. The three of us formed the main core of 'Team Delyn'. Both turned out to be real gems. Every day, Viv arrived at David Hanson's pad, the Transport and General Workers' Union (TGWU) office in Flint, and stayed for a greater part of each day operating the phone and keeping the diary. All this was willingly done and unpaid. Peter volunteered to drive the van and be with me everyday, and worked tirelessly introducing me to Delyn people and doing much work on the 'knocker'. I was astounded that almost perfect strangers were prepared to give up free time to get me elected.

On the 11th January 1999, an unwelcome interruption from campaign preparation came in the form of a phone call from North Wales Police Head of Legal Services, Jenny Trigger. She asked to meet me on an employment relations matter. She told me that as a member of the Police Authority, I was her employer; thus I had no choice but to agree to a meeting. Frankly, I was amazed! She was not my friend and we Labour councillors believed that she did little to help us obtain fair treatment for the many complainants who had sought our advice. She never gave an inch, particularly over the case of a young man accused of rape that led to Dafydd Wigley's involvement in his case.

The fact that she sought me out, rang my home number and wished to visit my house for advice totally confounded me. I began to 'flap' when she asked to bring her husband, knowing he was a local judge. The house was thoroughly cleaned, with the lounge tidied and the dogs consigned to quarters. Drinks were discretely laid out – best glasses polished – as I assumed that one of them, if not me, might want a libation whilst discussing the problem.

The couple arrived promptly at 6.47pm. The judge wore a gold V-neck sweater and Mrs Trigger wore jeans and a chequered jacket. I was pleased I had not selected my best frock for the occasion. We stuck to coffee, water and cashew nuts, and as the evening progressed, the nut bowl took a hammering. Her story was simple. In readiness for the January Authority meeting, she had sent the quarterly report required by Authority members, giving details of all civil actions settled by the force to the senior officers, including the Chief Constable as usual. Believing it was cleared for distribution, she had dispatched it with committee papers to meet the required agenda timescale. However, inexplicably, the report had not been 'sanitised' by the Top Team before being distributed.

Although she did not say as much, I assumed that it contained a wealth of juicy information about costs and reasons why the police chose to settle rather than defend their actions in court; areas the Chief would have preferred to keep to himself! Two cases read badly for police procedures and begged closer scrutiny from nosy members. Mrs Trigger had suddenly become vulnerable. Case 93 stated that 'Documents undermining the police case had come to light and a rapid settlement was reached in the best possible terms to the force.' Case 95 looked even worse: 'A pre-trial conference raised doubts over the police case.' Not only did the evidence of two officers conflict, a vital videotape forming part of the evidence could not be found! Hmmm! By mistake, the Head of Legal Services had unwittingly handed sensitive information to Labour councillors, who could be expected to pounce, ensuring that the Chief Constable would have to answer some very hard questions.

Early into my term as a member of the Police Authority, I had asked for regular detailed reports about civil actions against the force, which resulted in the inclusion of a written report for every meeting. With a steady escalation of the burden of settlements, it was sensible to demand such information, and the reports invariably gave the Authority good reason to become alarmed with every passing month. Our duty was to provide effective and efficient policing and we were entitled to regular updates and explanations. I was surprised when Mrs Trigger admitted that 'her' reports, in essence Police Authority reports, prepared for us at our request, were always sent to senior officers and went for their clearance before circulation. I had no idea that our reports were subject to senior officer interference and the red pencil treatment before we were ever allowed to see them. The real issue behind the Trigger visit lay in an official internal memo to Head of Legal Services from John Cooke, the Assistant Chief Constable in charge of Complaints and Discipline. When she produced it I knew that it spelt the end of her career with the force. John Cooke was not her line manager and had no right to make those discriminatory demands.

She described an angry John Cooke on a mobile phone exchange on her way back from a training course. He was furious with her, and then the bombshell memo had floored her with its bluntness. When she reported to the Chief Constable to discuss the memo, his demeanour was cool and non-committal. He told her that he was waiting for a report. She felt it would be damning. The John Cooke memo seemed to give a good case for breach of contract against the force, and a 'technical' constructive dismissal for good measure. The memo took her to task for putting items into the public domain that the bosses believed to be inappropriate and 'open to misinterpretation'. She was aware that a draft should be submitted for examination and approval before onward transmission to the Clerk. Because she had ignored this instruction, the patience of the Chiefs was exhausted.

John Cooke regretted that he must now 'drastically change the way in which civil actions are managed.' It would have been nice if John Cooke had sought the consent of his Police Authority before embarking upon this dramatic change of job description! She was an employee of the Authority, although in the ludicrously conflicting role as legal adviser to the Chief. Dennis Parry and I had frequently railed against this anomaly, but our complaints were dismissed. It appeared that Michael Argent had allowed the memo to be released without considering the harm it could do to Mrs Trigger and the force. The memo explained that 'The Chiefs had discussed this situation and concluded that it was no longer acceptable.' The final indignity was to be told that a Superintendent would take over much of her work and confirmed that she was no longer responsible for civil actions. She was to be relieved of a large chunk of her caseload, and her pride had been severely jolted, when she learnt that her deputy had effectively taken over her job.

I read the 8th January 1999 memo carefully. I could not believe senior officers had been so stupid as to show bias and indiscretion. I concluded that the Head of Legal Services was being pushed out of her job. I said, 'Why have you come to see me?' Judge husband replied for her, 'You have the experience of dealing with rogue cops'. He described how he perceived the force was being run. Michael Argent was weak and the real boss was the longest serving senior officer, the Deputy Chief Constable, John Tecwyn Owen. That fitted, as he had applied for the top job when the vacancy occurred, but the Home Office rules disbarred officers from achieving all senior promotions without previously working in another force. The Authority had approached the Home Office pleading for a rule change to permit John Tecwyn's promotion, which was refused. 'Have you told anyone you were coming to see me?' I enquired. 'Oh yes', she replied innocently, 'I've told the Clerk.' My heart sank, knowing this snippet would be passed quickly to the chief officers. It would be seen as an unforgivable act of disloyalty by a person who had already lost their trust.

The cashew nuts were replenished again as we considered her options. I knew there was only one, but did not want to sound cynical. Option one: soldier on and accept the humiliation of loss of face and staff. Option two: fight back by producing evidence that she had weapons that could hurt them, causing them to re-appraise her worth to the force. As she had been a creature of the Chief Constable for so long and wore 'two hats', I presumed that she could say and show much about the unhealthy way some matters had been dealt with. She told me primly that she had no damaging material; she did not work that way, so that sneaky option foundered. 'That leaves a third', I told her as gently as possible. 'Consider going sick and obtaining legal advice if you really want to start a civil action or complain about John Cooke's behaviour.' I told her I believed that her career with the North Wales Police could not continue, as 'they' would never trust her again.

We discussed tactics a little longer before they left. She promised to think about what I had said and would consider sending me the relevant documents. I rang Rex Makin, my lawyer, to warn him that I advised her to seek his advice, his being the only firm I could ever recommend. I knew how the senior officers' mindsets would work when they learned that she had visited me, the most 'troublesome' member of the Authority. She had served them faithfully for years, working with Leon Gibson to keep a lid on most complaints. Now she was no longer trusted. I just knew that having dared to seek my advice, her career was all but finished. In 2002, with just seven months of the first term of the Welsh Assembly to run, my bleak prophecy came true.

I really wanted to move on from battling with the police. I only had a couple more meetings to endure before a new political life beckoned. I decided not to stand again as a county councillor and had put all my eggs into the Welsh Assembly basket, soon to be free from frustrations created by my Authority membership. The Police Authority was due to meet on the 15th January. Trigger's unique 'unsanitised' civil action report was on the agenda. Dennis Parry and I discussed the Trigger meeting. We believed that most of the Authority was not aware of the John Cooke memo or that she was consulting the best lawyer in the north-west, and if a civil action was started against her employers, namely us – the Police Authority – she must surely win. The costs could be substantial and the fallout great. Trying to head off, if not close down such an inflammatory situation of an ACC sending the most senior legal force lawyer a damaging memo, Dennis Parry and I met Norman Land, a former Clerk to the Authority. He had retired but was dragged back into service when Leon Gibson was forced to retire, after being exposed by a critical District Auditor's report and a hard-hitting TV documentary. Norman was a decent, honourable, chapel-going man who always behaved with integrity during the few months he was the Authority's temporary Clerk.

The meeting at County Hall was open and frank. We made our plea to be allowed to tell colleagues what a hole the force's finest was digging. When the meeting ended, Dennis and I understood that we would report, albeit belatedly, to our colleagues that we faced an embarrassing situation concerning our legal adviser. Norman had known nothing of Mrs Trigger's changed job description and accepted that the situation was grave.

The Legal Department and Authority would struggle to perform efficiently unless the matter was resolved. Norman agreed to call an extraordinary meeting coinciding with the scheduled meeting. Also we should circulate a letter informing colleagues of the 'bombshell' memo and the potential trouble ahead. With little time to spare, Dennis and I summarised the facts, which were faxed to the Clerk for transmission to other members. We duly arrived at Police HQ on the 15th believing we could speak to the item. We had briefed Malcolm King and his Wrexham Labour colleague of this new development.

We soon discovered that, yet again, it wouldn't be a normal meeting. Far from being allowed to give colleagues the slightest clue of the dismissal memo and possible legal action against senior officers, we were muzzled. Charles Ley, the Chair, just would not bring us in, batting us away every time we raised our hands. In desperation, I said, 'Chair, you know that we have something of great importance to impart to the Authority that concerns one of our employees.'"Yes, yes, Cllr Halford you will be heard', and then he ignored me again. I was beside myself with rage as only on the 12th January I had rung him giving a factual account of the Trigger affair as I knew it. He seemed relaxed about the whole thing.

When Mr Ley ignored our pleas to speak and then offered the Chief Constable the opportunity of making a statement, Dennis and I were ballistic. The Chief was part of the problem and the complaint. It was wrong for him to be allowed to offer the Authority his version of events before we could address the committee. Norman Land looked embarrassed. Little wonder he had reneged on the agreement reached with him in County Hall. Yet again, the Chief Constable was being allowed unfettered freedom to give his point of view whilst Dennis and I were muzzled. As Michael Argent rose to begin his speech, I gathered my papers, angrily pushed back my chair and marched from the meeting. To my amazement, my three colleagues joined me. We stood outside in a shocked huddle, realising that we were witnessing yet another 'stitch up'. The *Daily Post* duly filed the headline, 'Walk out after muzzle storm'. I was reported as saying that, 'We called for a report to bring certain grave facts to the notice of our colleagues on the Authority, but we have been denied the opportunity to make any statement whatsoever.' The paper also suggested that we were 'on collision course with the Police Authority'.

Before storming out, the usually ponderous and courteous Malcolm King pulled no punches, accusing officers of 'acting illegally by denying the media copies of the complaints report that had been given to members.' He savaged them again. 'This body is not interested in any of the normal procedures that apply to public bodies and it is an absolute disgrace.' He was right. Chairman Ley had succeeded in keeping the memo and the plight of the Head of Legal Services from the members and the press. Sadly, our once ethical Clerk had failed us too. Having staged the march-out, we were milling around the foyer of HQ. Norman Land, the Clerk, slunk by us, looking sheepish and avoiding eye contact. His behaviour had been inexplicable. 'Norman', I hissed, 'you are a disgrace.' He turned white and scuttled off. Within minutes the building was buzzing with the rumour that he had quit. The four of us left HQ dispiritedly and I dismissed the morning as just one less horrible meeting to attend. Norman's resignation letter arrived a few days later. The forced press release blamed his resignation squarely on me. My remark, blunt and deserved, may have been a factor, but I think it went deeper than that. He probably recognised that he was a pawn in the plot to ensure John Cooke's blunder remained secret. Being a decent man he wanted no more Authority antics. I had just provided him with the excuse for him to resign. The Authority began its search for yet another Clerk. I turned my thoughts to my political agenda.

The original leadership contest between Ron and Rhodri was to be decided in Newport. As candidates ourselves, sporting our special badges, Tom Middlehurst and I travelled there with other Flintshire councillors. I was too naive to know that the winner was important to Tom, as favours could follow a win. The crowd was enormous and milled around impatiently waiting for the result. I finally understood how much this contest meant to Welsh Labour. With an eye to future publicity as my own political career began to ascend, and hoping to be caught on camera in the media frenzy once the leader was known, I had chosen my seat with care before the hall filled up. It was humming with activity and TV crews were prowling, ready to roll and catch an interview with the victor. Ron won, and luckily I had chosen rather well. Ron went straight to an attractive lady accompanied by a bushy-haired teenager who were sitting in front of me. I assumed that they were Ron's wife and daughter and they all held each other in a family embrace after the result was announced. The verdict was popular and the applause continued for a while. I was watching Welsh history unfold. Only my left knee made it into the TV footage that rolled later that night, but at least I was there.

I was there too for the Rhodri-Alun hustings head-to-head in Connah's Quay Labour Club, after Ron had been forced to withdraw. Ron Davies's Clapham Common 'moment of madness' had given Rhodri a second shot at heading the new Assembly.

Alun Michael and Rhodri Morgan's battle to become the first Prime Minister of Wales required constituency support and the Flintshire contest was scheduled for the 5th February. I nearly blew my own chance of selection, and certainly lost any credibility with the man finally elected as First Minister, by breaking loose from party protocol to pose a probing question to Alun.

MP Barry Jones's crystal ball must have been working well that night when he chaired the meeting. It was a tightly controlled event; all questions had to be short and to the point. Barry then announced that he would take just three final questions before closing the meeting. My upraised hand had been studiously ignored all evening but God loves a 'tryer'. One of the three questioners had already been rejected. I continued to flap my arm, and butted in to suggest that I could provide the substitute question. Barry had no choice but to call me. I had drafted and re-drafted my question, knowing that Barry would cut me off if it was too long. I was polite but pointedly asked Alun 'if he would give more support to potential Assembly colleagues than he had to Labour members of the North Wales Police Authority?' The Chairman looked murderous as I quickly listed the problems we had encountered. Alun knew exactly where I was coming from, as did much of the audience, as policing was an issue. Alun had already faced down the threats to close North Wales police stations unless our Chief Constable was given more funds.

The dispute had been well reported and caused public concern. A woman in front on me was nodding vigorously as I charged through my question. I assumed she liked my point, as probing as it was. Alun gave no hint of animosity and gave a polished political answer. The meeting ended and I waited for my colleagues' reprisals. Little was said to me after the event but the body language indicated that I had 'fouled up'. The unstated message was that it was not good form to ask tough questions of a party colleague, especially with an election aspirant. Had I been challenged, I would have replied that it was not good form for a minister to duck responsibility when asked for help with a wayward Police Authority. Even ignoring my part in that report to the Home Secretary, it had been signed by three long-serving Labour councillors, including an experienced Authority member and former leader of Delyn – the constituency Labour had selected me to win.

As junior Home Office minister, Alun had denied us help and we had been thrown to the wolves. Dennis and I had been castigated for our efforts and bore the humiliation created by the front page of the *Federation Force* newspaper. The hurtful caption screamed, 'We believe you have done tremendous harm!' Dennis and I didn't deserve being held up for ridicule. We had worked diligently as councillors for the good of the people we were elected to represent. As a Police Authority member, I had assiduously burnt the midnight oil attempting to help complainants and then write that detailed report.

The article, written to support the chief officers, ended with another swipe at us when it was claimed that '70% of staff had responded to an in-house survey and were dissatisfied with the service provided by local councillors.' Being a canny politician, Alun could have checked the facts, even with the local HMI, and discovered that the Labour Group was under fire and found some way to support us. Alun's Pontius Pilate performance was cowardly, and delivered an insult we did not deserve.

My election campaign got under way on a wet and windy day in April 1999. The press focused particularly on Delyn, as my police background apparently made me an interesting candidate. They were also intrigued that Delyn was the only constituency in Wales where all the main contenders were women. My rivals were the Tory candidate but Liberal Democrat, Eleanor Burnham and Plaid Cymru Meg Elis who campaigned hard for their parties. Eleanor and Meg's chances of election were thin, but Plaid Cymru's Janet Ryder was a strong contender in the campaign trail in Delyn. She was top of Plaid's party list, with the goal of capturing a North Wales regional seat. Although from Wrexham as a 'list candidate', not a 'first past the post' runner (as I was), she was free to roam all over North Wales.

I was miffed that all my rivals were free to take on causes and cherry pick the best events, while I was confined to campaigning in and on Delyn issues.

Despite this drawback, I got on well with all my rivals. It was foolish to do otherwise as the Assembly leadership was seeking a consensual form of politics, far removed from Westminster's 'Ya Boo' antics. Embarking on scoring points from each other seemed ungracious and counter-productive. Our campaigns became rather a circus as we all accepted invitations to address this and that, or go to whatever event, and none of us wanted to miss the chance of extolling our virtues. I certainly fought to get myself in the papers as much as possible by accepting any invitation that came my way.

Opportunity to grab the headlines came in good measure when the two Labour heavyweights in the Assembly contest invited themselves to my patch. When Alun Michael rolled into Flintshire on his exceedingly large, black, hi-tech 'battle bus', I, with other Party members, welcomed him warmly. We were impressed how it could be manoeuvred up our narrow Delyn roads. Tinted windows hid a wealth of technology plus waggy-tailed, fresh-faced party apparatchiks – PAs in every sense of the word! Before Alun commandeered this magnificent vehicle, we were amused to learn that it had been used by numerous stars trekking the country, including Madonna and her famous basque. No wonder the windows were so heavily tinted!

All animosity forgotten, I helped rescue Alun from a deeply committed Labour supporter, who pounced the moment he stepped from his bus and pushed the diminutive Alun against a convenient letterbox. Angry party members towered over Alun and I thought blows would be struck, but many hands stepped forward to calm an ugly situation. The community had waited too long for a new school; feelings were running high in Greenfield over this issue and Alun took the flak. I soothed my warrior friend by telling him that as soon as Alun and I were elected, we would work together and his school would be built.

Excitement over, Peter York and I had to lead the 'battle bus' to the local community hospital for a bit of glad-handing and a precious photo-call. Anxious that we should not get lost, we managed to beat it to the right hospital before the great vehicle swept in. I was prowling around outside the hospital, ready to make introductions as courtesy demanded. As the grand tour commenced, Alun firmly told me to stay with him. I followed meekly as if on a leash. As he was chatting close by and his party seemed to have halted, I plonked myself onto a patient's bed for a natter. Suddenly, I became the focus of press attention and cameras popped profusely. It seemed that the photographers felt this was a more interesting study than Alun processing through a ward. I scrambled from the bed, waved a cheery goodbye and went in hot pursuit of my would-be leader. I had no idea I had presented such a good photo opportunity and wanted to do nothing to remove Alun from the focus of attention.

The cameras popped again when I sat in a new, hi-tech blood pressure machine just acquired by the hospital. There was much jolly banter when my blood pressure shot almost off the scale. It was taken again and it spiralled upwards. We all giggled and I joked about the stress of campaigning. Unaware that I had a blood pressure problem, I was so concerned and broke canvassing to gallop to my doctor for a second opinion. Blood pressure registered very normal. Either the hi-tech machine had a glitch, or Alun's presence had set my pressure rocketing.

Alun and Rhodri were not the only VIPs who took the long road north to canvass with me. Days before Alun arrived, Ron Davies surprised me when he phoned to ask if I wished him to campaign with me. I was startled because his fall from grace was so new. Was he a liability or an asset? I mused. I thanked him and said 'yes'. The Wednesday Mold Market Day was by far the best chance of getting a large number of people together, and we met in heavy rain in front of a stall festooned with ladies' underwear. Ron was great: bouncing up to strangers, shaking their hands and skilfully introducing me as the person that deserved their vote. He preened when the press gathered round and relished being followed by a *Guardian* reporter, who had been sent specially to cover the event. Whilst I bought a tape of 'Mae Hen Wlad fy Nhadi' in a Welsh bookshop, he waited outside. A crowd gathered around to wish him well. No recriminations over Clapham Common in sleepy Mold, it seemed. The visit had gone very smoothly despite almost monsoon rain, and soon he departed without even accepting my offer of lunch.

I was very flattered when I played back my answerphone late one evening and heard Rhodri Morgan's voice. He left contact numbers and wanted an opportunity to campaign with me too. I knew that I had been too open about my support for Rhodri a few days previously when I took a call from Peter Hain, who was heading Alun Michael's campaign. Overawed that the Welsh Secretary should ring me at home seeking my support for Alun, I naively blurted out that Rhodri would get my vote and began to justify my choice. Somehow, we must have been cut off as the phone suddenly went dead.

Rhodri's busy leadership contest schedule against Alun brought him to Delyn on a Sunday. He demanded a good crowd so he could make contact with the largest number of people in the shortest possible time. A tall order as Mold, Holywell and Flint were all graveyard quiet on Sundays, and I began to panic that I could not meet his demand. Suddenly, inspiration struck and I remembered the 'Fun Ship' market at Greenfield, and the old cruise liner I could see from the other side of the Dee when I resided in England. The venue was a success; we walked about shaking hands and having little chats with enthusiastic shoppers. It was all going very well when an aide took a call and, suddenly, Greenfield market lost its appeal. In the battle for votes, the chance of a lunchtime television programme at very short notice was not to be missed. Rhodri tore off to his studio appointment and I got home in time to watch the programme. Despite being ditched, I knew that my choice of candidate was not misplaced.

Election Day, 6th May, was fast approaching. I was most relieved that I'd chosen to have my campaign material printed locally, as it was delivered in good time. Tom was desperate to get his manifesto and posters from Cardiff, and he was forced to start his campaign with nothing to push through letterboxes. Every day was spent on the trail of votes, with Peter York taking up a greater part of co-ordinating the street offensive, whilst Viv Williams kept the office going. I soon learnt a mantra to be broadcast over the bus's loud speakers and it was all great fun. I thought I had been particularly witty by inventing the slogan, 'Forget the rest, vote for the best.' Lists of helpers were put together and I rapidly learnt about the geography of my chosen constituency: mostly rural interspersed with small market towns, luxury mansions and ageing housing estates.

I had good local support from party members, but the Cardiff candidate helpline continued to ignore my messages for balloons and pens – freebies that always went down well. Didn't they want me to win? I was new at all this 'on the stump' lark and could have expected some reply. By the 24th April, having left a third message for balloons, stickers, and useful thingies to hand out to voters, I left a sarcastic message saying I would not bother them again. Suddenly, balloons and stickers appeared as if by magic. A rather apologetic official told me that they had been diverted from another constituency seen as a 'key' marginal and all effort was going into getting the candidate elected. 'I want to be elected too', I muttered petulantly.

I had assumed we would all receive the same level of support from the centre, particularly as my campaigning experience was woefully inadequate. I soon realised that this 'key' marginal constituency seat that had a surfeit of balloons was being fought by Party official David Costa's wife, Cath Sherrington. Money, outside help and much-prized balloons, were flowing freely further up the coast. Having heard amazing stories from Viv Williams about David Costa's heavy reliance on unpaid party members to do the leg work whilst he conducted events from behind his desk, I was happy that he was not part of my campaign team, even though he controlled the balloons. Everyone was working too hard and we were getting jumpy.

Bryan Grew, my agent, put in his first appearance in my campaign on the 4th May, two days before polling day. I had even made a generous contribution to upgrade his computerised party records and we could have made use of the data. As Viv and I had not seen him since the 17th April, I felt flattered that he assumed we were capable of running a successful campaign. Did I imagine that he would look a little surprised when he saw how organised we were and how well we were managing my campaign? I was doing no more than recalling MP David Hanson's advice that it was 'my campaign to go out and win'.

As a full time insurance assessor, Brian would have to have eaten into his holiday had he helped me throughout the campaign. I only discovered what he did when the conversation turned casually to the financial settlement awarded to ex-Detective Constable Keith Davies in May 1998. By amazing coincidence, Bryan assessed his company's liability to pay part or all the police costs. Having a drink in his local one evening, he vaguely broached the subject and I gave what knowledge I had. I desperately wanted to know why his firm had rejected to pay anything towards the hefty settlement. Of course, I knew the answer, but did not have the courage to ask him outright. I finished my drink, said goodbye and the Davies affair was never mentioned by either of us again.

Election Day finally arrived. I voted for Tom by 9.35am and felt frustrated I could not vote for myself. The campaign bus began its patrol for the last time and I was on the microphone, beseeching the voter to get out and do just that. David Hanson took over the driving for the last few hours, but it was impossible to get round every polling station. It is considered too late to use the mike after 7.30pm. I ended the day at Holywell Polling Station, and then went home. Because there were so many candidates and the count is further complicated by 'list' and 'first past the post' candidates, no counting started until the following day.

I took two of my oldest friends with me to the count at Deeside Leisure Centre: June Jeffreys and Scrabble, my elderly Border terrier, a part of my life since 1985. Decked out with a large Labour rosette, she trotted contentedly at the end of a lead and seemed to revel at being the centre of so much photographic attention. Tom was circling the tables and we stopped to chat. 'That's a good wheeze,' he said rather wistfully. Scrabble was still pottering around wearing her rosette when the result was finally announced, much later than the Returning Officer had promised. Shortly after 12.50pm, I learned that with 10,672 votes and 32% of the poll, I'd won Delyn. Tom took Alyn and Deeside, the largest Labour Constituency in Wales with 9,772 votes on a 44% turn out. Flintshire had voted by 47% against a Welsh Assembly during the referendum, the highest 'no vote' throughout Wales. Thus we were both pleased with our results, particularly when it was rumoured that all the Assembly campaign material had been dumped in the Labour club never to see the light of day.

Alun Michael scraped into the Assembly though the list system and although he remained MP for Penarth, he also became the AM for Mid Wales. It was a formality that he won the Group's backing to lead the first minority Government. His long working hours are seen in some quarters as over zealous, but he wasted no time forming his Government when the Assembly doors opened for business. With Scrabble, Quince and old Fudge (my beloved Schnauzer) plus Puffin my cat, I drove to Cardiff on the 10th May 1999, ready to be sworn in as the first Assembly Member for Delyn on the 12th May, a momentous day in the history of Wales. Full powers would only be transferred to the Assembly from the Welsh Office on the 1st July, but we had been sworn in, allocated our seats in the Chamber and were up and staggering if not running. For the second time, Rhodri lost his goal to lead the Assembly and bowed graciously to Alun as the First Secretary of Wales.

Shaky beginnings: Ron and Alun and the Opposition!

'But without the trust of the people, no Government can stand.'
Confucius 479 BC

Throwing caution to the wind, I had decided to buy property in Cardiff even before winning the Labour candidacy. I got lucky when a sale fell through on a property being built on Cardiff Bay, and stepped in to buy it. Taking out a large mortgage caused some sleepless nights, but I reckoned I could always sell it if unelected. I'd realised I could not leave my menagerie at home, nor could they go with me to a hotel, so the options were few. If elected, I would need a roof over my head from day one in Cardiff. It overlooked the Bay and I could see the tantalisingly close proposed site of the new Assembly building across the mud flats. The controversial barrage was not finished. I did not then know that when closed, water would fill the Bay and that special mud bank habitat around the barrage was doomed, requiring the birds to be provided with other feeding grounds.

I would have to wait until July 2000 before one of the many Auditor General reports into this multimillion pound Cardiff Bay project informed us that the removal of the birds to an alternative site had spiralled alarmingly. Originally estimated at £5.7 million, the true cost levelled out at £10.4 million. Spending beyond original budgets became a regular feature of scrutiny for the Audit Committee, and it became clear that no project would ever stay within budget and building time scales.

On the morning of Wednesday the 12th May, Alun Michael began to announce his Cabinet, a procedure that was to continue for most of the day. Tom Middlehurst was the only North Wales Assembly member to scoop a Cabinet post, much to the chagrin of John Marek from Wrexham, who rightly complained that it was 'not healthy for the Labour Party. By rights, North Wales should have two Cabinet positions and I feel that having one is wrong.' Whatever the rights and wrongs of the North-South numbers game, Tom's held the only portfolio which was wide and disjointed. It embraced 16+ training and education, culture and sport and lifelong learning. If not sufficiently challenging, Tom also took responsibility for Welsh language policy, a controversial national issue that was closely watched in brief, particularly as 50% of the new Assembly members spoke Welsh fluently. English-born Tom was not one of them, but he handled the mutterings against him well. Having to get to early Monday morning meetings from North Wales must have been a weekly nightmare. As the Assembly progressed, all the original portfolios proved to be far too unwieldy and over-ambitious. Time would show that portfolios changed and new ministerial decisions were imposed as if tied to the ebb of the tide. Not easy to monitor performance, however, if jobs and titles constantly changed!

Tom was not the only interesting choice in Alun's first Cabinet. 24 out of the 60 Assembly members were women, thus moving Wales into second place in the world for its percentage of women in a parliament, a statistic clearly not lost on Alun. With a minority of 28 overall, he needed friends around him and despite pre-election leadership promises, the day ended without Ron Davies being called to the fifth floor, the First Secretary's domain. Disappointment registered on his face when captured on the front pages of all Welsh newspapers, quoted as saying that he thought Alun would have kept his promise to include him. Rhodri Morgan was the only other MP to get the magic touch on the shoulder, joining the nine strong Cabinet team as Economic Development Minister.

The Labour Group office, situated on the third floor of the make-do office block that doubled as a temporary Assembly building, was headed by Mike Penn and some very toffee-nosed young women whose job was to offer 'special advice'. We were told the offices were allocated only temporarily whilst Alun formed his Government. Throughout the day, people vanished from various offices then the 'toffee-nosed brigade' would sweep in to remove personal effects to the fifth floor.

I found myself sharing a lunch table with Lord Elis-Thomas and Ron. The two seemed close and Ron approved of Lord Elis or 'Lord El,' as was the shortened form. It was soon announced that he would be Presiding Officer. That was identical to Speaker of the House of Commons, attracting a much larger salary and the usual perks of high Government office. As Alun's friend, Jane Davidson, a former youth teacher, shot up the wall bars of career enhancement by accepting the burdensome task of deputy Presiding Officer, also with a higher salary and a very well appointed office. I did not envy her job, but when I visited her to seek help with ever-tedious expense claim problems, the pictures loaned from the National Gallery of Wales were breathtaking.

I knew so few Labour colleagues before we all met for the triumphant photo-call of all 28 Labour members, and then the fifteen women AMs clustered round the Welsh Labour Party Secretary, soon to be ennobled, Anita Gale. I knew and liked Rosemary Butler who gave me an occasional call during the campaign to bolster my spirits. I knew she had considerable experience representing Caerleon for over two decades. She was given the pre-16 education portfolio. I had some knowledge of Blaenau Gwent's Peter Law, when his photograph had appeared in the *Police Review* magazine when demanding greater police accountability. Amazed to find someone of mutual thinking, I had dropped him a letter offering my support. Now face to face, the chemistry was immediately good. I was delighted for him, when late in the day he received the call from 'on high' while we were in the Milling Area, the big meeting place right outside the Plenary Chamber. He shot off, to descend later, his grin broad.

His portfolio was massive, probably one of the biggest, with responsibilities for transport, local Government, planning, housing and waste management. Knowing little else but policing (and that was not devolved) and being a county councillor, I plumped for his committee and got it. He was a delightful man and I liked the way he operated. His sense of humour and amusing style of delivering speeches in the Chamber soon made him a firm media favourite.

Finally the awards to faithful Alun supporters were complete. His most challenging decision was reserved for the agriculture portfolio given to vegetarian, Christine Gwyther. She had been a county council planning official having no immediate connection with the farming fraternity, a fact eagerly pounced upon by disbelieving farmers. Giving her no chance, the rural community soon began a campaign against a woman and a vegetarian. Their cause was fanned by the 'beef on the bone' ban response of Westminster to the Creutzfeld Jakob Disease (CJD) scare. T-bone steaks were off the menu officially which affected farmers' livelihoods. Christine showed herself to be a spirited and effective minister in the Chamber and seemed unconcerned by the constant carping in the papers about her eating habits. Soon, calls for her resignation began to rumble round farming journals. The movers and shakers in the rural community were just not prepared to have a woman in charge of agriculture, especially as the usual photo-calls of a minister drooling over a leg of prime Welsh lamb or chomping a beef steak in Wales were off limits now. Patting a live cow or holding a lamb was the closest Christine could come to embracing meat.

Alun's more sensible choice was giving Edwina Hart control of the Welsh budget. From a banking background, she was a formidable lady who took no prisoners and proved a feisty, 'no nonsense' performer in the Chamber. I also approved of Alun's choice of Jane Hutt as Health and Social Services supremo because of her good track record in public posts. She had headed Chwarae Teg, and seeing her in action in earlier discrimination presentations held in North Wales, she had a nice disposition and was approachable.

My office looked over waste ground and did not inspire me, so I asked for one overlooking Cardiff Bay. The offices had been roughly and temporarily assigned according to party strength. So Plaid Cymru, the next largest majority party, had one side of the building with the attractive bay views. Their leader had a smart office, but nothing matched the First Secretary's palatial pad on the fifth floor surrounded by offices holding protective minions and 'gofers.' The 'third floor toffee noses' did not enthusiastically receive my request, but knowing that I would remain a backbencher, I was determined to get a decent office for the next four years. I found to my cost that I was given the one used temporarily by the two Janes, Davidson and Hutt. My greed for a south facing office soon rebounded on me as not only was it hot, I kept getting calls from people who thought it was still Jane's. As numerous moans to the switchboard failed to remedy the problem, I was still apologising for not being Jane Hutt, even two years later.

Ron took over my first office, and seemed happy with his view of the waste ground, soon to be converted into the controversial and costly Wales Millennium Centre. We chatted when we bumped into each other, and at the first Labour Group meeting, I admired his intellect and outstanding political brain. He shone very brightly in contrast with several other AMs. As the Assembly progressed and gained momentum in its decision-making processes, I was frequently amazed that he could see political elephant traps miles ahead of Alun and Rhodri. I thought it ironic that judgement on his personal life was suspect, but he never faltered when dealing with complex political and administrative decisions. As the Assembly progressed, I learnt that his ability to withstand pressure and hassle, resulting from some of his personal shortcomings that would have completely pole-axed lesser mortals, was awesome. Perhaps that's why I liked him. He was a real survivor.

My new Labour chums were mostly friendly and seemed very impressed with that long-ago discrimination action. We were invited to a talk by Jon Shortridge, the senior civil servant who had shouldered responsibility for getting our show on the road. Mr Shortridge was a tall, good looking, smoothly confident man who bore his responsibility as head of the Welsh Civil Service with easy grace. He explained our powers and how the civil servants had tried to put themselves in our shoes in planning for our needs. Mostly, the anticipation had been good. The temporary debating chamber, where all plenary debates would occur, was nothing like the Westminster model. Each seat was allocated a number and a personal user profile embedded in our touch screen monitors that popped up in front of us. We could receive and send emails, and the whip and ministers' statements also appeared at the appointed time. We could even keep up with events in the media as the information was updated daily. We could send messages to each other and even to the Presiding Officer, seeking his indulgence to speak. Apart from the occasional glitch, this part of the computer technology worked well. Sadly, with so much emphasis on hi-tech computer systems, paperless offices and emails for communication, the system was slow, prone to crashing and, taking everything into consideration, the AMs were not well served by the chosen provider.

Although our offices were equipped with PCs it took much longer to deliver the fax and printers that were vital tools for our jobs. The initial IT teething troubles were bad enough, but problems and complaints about the IT communications dogged the entire first term of the Welsh Assembly. Trainers were available to show us how to send an email and the like, but the communication process was stressfully slow, particularly in constituency offices removed from Cardiff, where phone lines were not fast enough to make the system smooth. The concept of a paperless office wobbled when members realised that it was our individual responsibility to print the necessary committee papers but getting them was the first hurdle to clear. The Committee secretariat produced papers in emails on the intranet service in dribs and drabs. Just when I thought I'd printed all the papers needed for the next Committee, more would arrive with little time to read them. Sometimes, I would print a document only to learn that it had been diverted to another printer in some other office. The technical helpline did a roaring trade as we logged the faults and waited impatiently for a technician to get us up and running again. Committee papers were delivered late or on the margins of the four days specified in the embryonic Assembly rules. I burnt much midnight oil on the eve of Committees, frantically reading great 'wodges' of paper and getting to grips with important issues. After a time, with no improvement in sight, I began to think it was a ploy to ensure we came to Committee less-informed and thus unable to challenge the officials' papers.

It took seven weeks to have a PC installed in my Delyn constituency. I kept badgering the IT helpline for an installation date and they seemed genuinely surprised I was asking for the tools to do my job. No constituency PC, then no emails, and therefore my staff had no means of finding out what was going on or being able to access necessary papers. Eventually my personnel profile was built into a PC duly delivered to Delyn some 170 miles away from Cardiff. That really exposed the failings in the 'paperless' system. The slow phone lines meant that logging on and off each morning could take forever. Printing out papers was a nightmare and my record was over two hours to print off just part of a committee agenda. As the printer was a combined fax machine, even that means of communication was out of action during a print run.

The technical 'bods' instructed my staff to remain online throughout the working day. The first phone bill BT sent to Delyn was well over £2,000. We were horrified, as at that rate, the office allowances would run out in weeks. The Fees Office was obliged to hastily think again when we were instructed to send phone bills to them for payment. No deduction would be made from members' office allowances after all. Then the Fees Office failed to settle the phone bill and my Delyn office got cut off for a while. All very embarrassing, but it allowed us to build a good rapport with Wayne Cowley, the civil servant who headed the Fees Office. It must have been an unenviable job to pay our expenses claims and to keep a tally of our various pots of money for living costs, staff salaries and the like, although, unlike Westminster, nothing was authorised without a receipt. The entire process of making official claims was a complete nightmare in those early days and everything seemed a matter of trial and error. This procedure had just not been thought out properly. Policy on what was deemed a reasonable claim seemed to be made on the hoof. We had to print the claims forms ourselves from the intranet system. They were not designed for our purposes and had to be tweaked to make the form fit the claim. Life was becoming really stressful, as everything seemed to be bounced for the smallest reason. Wayne was always patient and helpful, but his seniors showed little understanding of the stress it caused by putting more and more hurdles in our way before the account was settled. One of Wayne's bosses, a senior woman civil servant, acted as if she had lost the key to the coffers, or it was a personal affront, that I should wish to draw on my living allowances. Had I stayed in a hotel and presented a bill excluding drinks, it may have got paid without hassle. Having set up my place from scratch, no one seemed to know if I could claim for the bed, carpets, and kitchen table. I brought as much as possible from home, but living in two properties could never be easy. I wrote a couple of long and detailed letters asking why the Fees Office would not honour this or that receipt even when accompanied by a photocopy of the cheque, and her reply was always unhelpful.

In frustration I asked the senior accounting officer Jon Shortridge for a meeting. He was the ultimate head of civilian staff and with my patience exhausted, I had no time to constantly battle to get my phone and other utilities paid on my Cardiff pad. One morning, Jon Shortridge came to my office with his chief accounting and sat attentively whilst I showered him with documents and copies of cheques and invoices rejected by the Fees Office for footling reasons. I rattled off my grievances against the unhelpful lady Clerk waving our exchange of letters at him. Finally, I said that I just did not know how to determine what I could claim and how I could get my expenditure accepted. He looked grave but he had taken all my grumblings on board and studiously promised to look into my complaints. I felt rather a fool when he'd left my office as I could not have gone higher and he had patiently and courteously listened to my litany of complaints. Suddenly, things eased and the logjam began to move. I was sneakily pleased when 'unhelpful Clerk' moved to another post. Life was getting very busy as the work of the Assembly took off in earnest. The horrors of driving back and forth on inadequate roads, lugging a cat and three dogs in the back of a car and all the problems of running two houses were now being faced head on.

When the Labour Group met for the first time, the elected members were attended by the third floor support staff with Mike Penn as the party secretary, taking his seat next to the Group chair, Ann Jones. Apart from Tom Middlehurst, Ann was the only North Wales Member holding some position of influence. These Group meetings acted as the nub of Labour political activity in the Assembly and provided a forum where both ministers and back benchers could exchange views, plan strategy and develop Government policy. Members reported events and concerns in their own constituencies and allowed the ruling party a valuable insight into Labour affairs across Wales. It was the sounding board for the Cabinet and we worked collectively to undermine the Opposition, who were attempting the same against us by mounting hostile debates and tabling unhelpful motions for plenary debate.

Under Alun's stewardship, the South Wales 'Tafia' fared much better in his influential allocation of non-Cabinet jobs. Lorraine Barrett, Alun's former political secretary in his south Cardiff and Penarth constituency, became Chief Whip. She now shared her constituency seat with Alun, and was ideally suited to fight for her constituents knowing their problems from her previous job. Several of us were sitting round a table in the 'Members' Tea Room' in the very first days of Assembly life and congratulating ourselves for our achievements, as the competition had been tough. The 6,000 original applicants had been whittled down to 151 people with a chance of getting a seat. Selection had been a long, bitter process, rendered more cumbersome by the man and woman constituency selection 'twinning' process. The male/female equality battle for constituencies went to the wire, with a legal challenge thrown down in some constituencies which increased the muddle. Labour had rightly determined to ensure proper representation of women, but the change had been won at a cost to Party cohesion. The battle for equality had been hard fought, but Labour was right to bring more women into politics, and this was the main reason I stood as candidate. My constituency was content with me and I was thankfully spared this infighting, which formed an unwelcome backcloth to an already stressful election process. Devolution had been rejected in the first referendum and the vote in the second in 1997 could not have been closer. When the result was announced on TV, Welsh Secretary Ron Davies grinned broadly as he turned to his permanent secretary and murmured in Welsh '*Iawn baby*.'

Around that table, in the Members' Tea Room, Lorraine was one of the triumphant winners of the selection process. Having worked for Alun as his secretary, her loyalty to him was boundless. She seemed to live and breathe politics and was beside herself with joy. Exuberantly, she gushed, 'What's a valleys girl doing here in a place like this?' Her achievement was well deserved and surely the nub of devolution? Power had moved from a Westminster-centric Welsh Office with a Secretary of State for Wales, unable to sing the Welsh National Anthem, rightfully back to the people of Wales. I did not consider on this joyful occasion that possibly those handed the baton of Government in Wales might not be up to the task. I did not foresee that some of the power and privileges previously invested in the Welsh Office might be hijacked by some now empowered to govern. And far from closing the North-South divide as suggested, they seemed intent on securing as much Bloc Grant as possible for their own constituencies, mostly located in South Wales. We all agreed round that table that we were truly blessed, and then dispersed to struggle with the latest computer glitch.

It took a little while and some deferred meetings before the Labour Group could appoint the prestigious chairs of the various committees. Political balance was a statutory requirement and so the spoils just could not be divided between the majority Labour

Assembly members. Rumour abounded that appointment to chairs was delayed because Ron, the architect of devolution, was waiting in the wings demanding a position. To have crashed out of the Westminster Cabinet as Welsh Secretary, to become a mere backbencher when he had brought devolution into being, was too cruel. On the 13th May Ron accepted the post of Economic Development Committee (EDC) chair and yet again a comeback commenced.

Now everything Ron was involved in seemed to grab the glare of the media. His chairmanship of the EDC was no exception. All the committee work of the fledgling Assembly took place under the glare of the internal TV camera, but the public seats seemed fuller when Ron breezed in to start punctually. That brutal exchange between Alun Michael and Chairman Ron was widely observed by press and public alike. These men were very angry with each other and their spat must have been a gift from the Gods. It certainly spiced up normally dull committee work. Winding himself up to the task, Ron attacked the civil service for producing vague papers. The whole atmosphere was described as 'sour' by committee watchers.

Between Ron and Alun trading verbal blows, Val Feld AM, who represented Swansea, was concerned with the continual spending on Cardiff Bay. Little did she know that spending thus far was the merest drop in the ocean, and the people of Wales through the Welsh Assembly were locked into a financial agreement that would greatly increase Cardiff's infrastructure and wealth. Taxpayers of Wales, impoverished valley people and those better off would be handed the bill for Cardiff's improvements for years to come. Some cynics would say that Cardiff ratepayers had never had it so good!

Building a barrage turning the Bay into a freshwater lake had been controversial for years. Legislation had been passed by Westminster years before, with most Welsh MPs voting against the project. The Barrage Act included a winding up procedure once the barrage had been built. This ambitious scheme required funding to include ongoing development of most of Cardiff Bay waterfront area. Property values increased, as did the cost of finishing the barrage. The Assembly was destined to take over the unfinished work and to fund all the many projects and land and water quality improvements. Regardless of how Welsh MPs had voted, members with Cardiff constituencies, particularly those bordering the controversial Bay project, could expect financial advantages to the area they served.

Even before our campaigns began, on the 1st April 1999 (just over five weeks before the Assembly began trading), a 'memoranda of understanding' was signed with the City and County of Cardiff Council. It was agreed that the Cardiff Bay Development Corporation (CBDC) would sell the valuable Ferry Road land to the County. The Office of the Secretary of State for Wales, in legal speak 'the Department', was one signatory. Alun Michael became The Secretary of State for Wales, following Ron Davies's demise. 'The Department' also agreed with the Mayor of Cardiff, Cllr Russell Goodway, to create the unique 'Cardiff Harbour Authority' to manage the inland lake and to accept many of the assets from winding down the CBDC. All this winding-up, moving of assets, and deciding who would maintain the inland water quality, had to be resolved as the CBDC was to be completed by the 31st March 2000, albeit still almost a year away.

None of this was on my radar in those early days. Only when the Auditor General's detailed reports into the machinations surrounding the Bay and the wind-up process began to appear frequently on the agenda, did the significance of this Labour pact, and its meaning to Cardiff, dawn on me. The Bay saga prompted not less than three detailed reports. If the Auditor General devoted so much time to this subject, surely something was not right? The chair of Audit was Plaid Cymru's Janet Davies and she would have been able to give the Auditor General a steer into subjects worthy of thorough audit. The committee could also draw up its wish list of important topics, but whoever decided on the Auditor General's work schedules, the digging continued into the Bay, the Barrage and the wind up of the CBDC. Some of the Auditor General's findings were indeed worrying, casting long shadows over ministerial conflict of interest and value for money issues.

The Welsh Assembly donned its collective party frock to spend most of the 26th May 1999 celebrating our official opening by the Queen, accompanied by Prince Charles and his father. We had a splendid lunch in the cavernous interior of the National Museum and Gallery of Wales. Whilst waiting for the dignitaries to arrive, we wandered around the magnificent impressionist art collection. There were so many wonderful paintings. I forgave the sisters who had bequeathed this wonderful collection to the nation for not including Sisley's 'Les Toits Rouges.' Another feast of entertainment was laid on for the afternoon but I was desperate to rescue my dogs, as they had been locked in the Penarth house for hours. There was a small enclosed yard, but as yet no dog flap. Puffin the cat managed well with a litter tray, but the confined dogs played seriously on my conscience.

My long-suffering animals accompanied me to the concert, the highlight of an already memorable day. Set in the open against the backdrop of Cardiff Bay, the cast was star studded. Shirley Bassey and Tom Jones belted out one melody each. No encores were allowed however much the audience showed its appreciation. Two vast covered stages had been set up. As one performer finished, another took over on the adjoining stage. Two comperes kept things flowing and we were all enthralled. The bowl in front of the twin stages thronged with promenaders, all drinking in the fact that at last Wales was governing itself. The evening was warm. As darkness fell, the spotlights lit up the auditorium and we were dazzled also by the magnificence of the celebration.

The Queen's party stole in quietly during an act, raising a cheer from a bubbling crowd. Finally, the sky was ablaze with a thousand fireworks cascading down into the Bay, lighting up the Pierhead Building and Penarth across the water. I winced as the show developed into noise as well as colour. My poor dogs! How would they cope with cannon fire? I squeezed through the crowd and dashed to my car parked on waste ground nearby. I worried that the noise would have scared them into a funk. All was well as I opened the car; they were sleeping, oblivious to the firework display crashing over them. The two older dogs were quite deaf, but they were pleased to see this elusive woman who was changing their lives so dramatically.

I drove back to Penarth with a sky still glowing over the arena and watched the final fireworks fall into darkness from the other side of the Bay. My neighbours were out in full force, leaning on the railings with glasses and bottles in hand, watching the remains of the spectacle I'd just left. Willingly I accepted a glass of wine and spent a little time enjoying the street party before walking the dogs round the block. Then, contemplating my wonderful day, I felt it was a fitting climax to a small but proud Wales coming of age. It was exhilarating to be part of that team to go down in history as the first Government of Wales. With confidence high that this administration would avoid the mistakes that had forfeited public confidence in politicians, I walked the dogs, stroked the cat and went to bed.

Just one month after his appointment to the chair of EDC, on the 13th June the *News of the World* published shots of Ron in woodland looking shifty. Yet again, a tabloid had shone a spotlight on his reputation and integrity. Ron made an immediate denial and countered the allegation by complaining that whilst bird watching, he had been confronted by a stranger who, after making suggestive remarks, had been told to go away. The denial stated that 'Any suggestion of lewd behaviour is denied.' I wondered why he had no binoculars – a vital part of any bird watcher's equipment. He followed up with a formal statement to the eager media, that 'having discussed the matter with his wife, in order to put a stop to the intolerable stream of lurid and inaccurate stories, I am left with no alternative but to confirm that I am and have been for some time, bisexual.' When filmed with a male in woodlands, to deny impropriety and being required to admit to being bisexual seemed contradictory. Had Ron lost the plot?

Alun said nothing about the Ron Davies saga during the Labour Group meeting on the 15th June, which followed soon after his 'I'm bisexual' statement. The atmosphere was tense and the vultures were obviously circling ready to feast on his political corpse. After the Labour Group broke up, I found myself holding clandestine chats with Lee Waters, Ron's researcher, providing feedback on the Group's mood. I was trying to play the role of 'honest broker' to find a way of turning negatives into positives. We discussed the situation and I blurted out, 'It just seems he can't stop taking risks, he just seems to want the excitement of living dangerously!' Lee looked mournful but nodded his agreement and left me to return to his master's side. The rest of the week's business groaned on and I was grateful when I could pack the freezer bag with remnants of my Cardiff fridge, heave my animals and laundry into the car and drive back non-stop to North Wales. I could not get my mind off Ron, pondering whether he could survive this latest damaging incident.

On Sunday the 20th June, just a week later after 'bird watching' in woodland, without the seeming need for optical assistance, Ron made a further statement indicating that he was undergoing therapy. Driving down to Cardiff on the Monday morning and with only a few miles to go on the A470, the radio announced that the treatment was to counter his compulsion to place himself in high-risk situations. I whooped with pleasure, recognising my suggestion to Lee just a few days previously and it seemed to have been relayed by a faithful researcher. As I continued to drive I mulled over Ron's predicament. His statement would cause the Labour Group more difficulty when it met, in a few days time, on the 22nd June. How could we kick out a colleague who was actively seeking help for his problem? Ron was further weakened when the Wales Labour Party felt he should resign. He doggedly refused to budge. *Wales on Sunday* reported that the Group was unhappy with Ron's combative handling of the first Economic Development Committee. If he had challenged the officials for producing vague committee papers, shouldn't he take some blame having been their boss at the Welsh

Office? Ron must have begun to loathe Sundays when, for the third time in succession, his future grabbed the *News of the World* headlines. The heavyweight elder parliamentarian, Sir Ray Powell of Ogmore fired a withering salvo: 'It's time to go Ron,' insisting Ron was mentally unfit for office. He would have had the low-down on Group indecisiveness from his daughter, Janice Gregory, who had won the constituency as an AM.

The *Welsh Mirror* would have done little to raise Alun's morale by making a plea for Alun to give the Welsh Assembly some good old Welsh passion. 'Proceedings are described as dull as dishwater.' Compared with Ron's exciting, high-risk existence, Alun was not a charismatic, loveable politician. The smooth running of his empire in Wales was not helped by the influential Cabinet Minister and Chancellor Duchy of Lancaster, Dr Jack Cunningham's decision that Westminster departments should refuse to co-operate with members of the Assembly and the Scottish Parliament in a bid to prevent 'turf wars' between MPs and the devolved administrations. Denied the right to oversee the police and crime matters in Wales, the Assembly had few sexy areas of responsibility on which to cut its teeth, apart from horror stories about the ailing NHS and horrible housing in Wales. Alun could not be blamed for what was devolved; his archrival, Ron, should stand up and be counted for the carve-up of powers between Westminster and Cardiff.

Come Tuesday morning, as soon as I was back in the Assembly, the Labour Group meeting was told that Ron would be making a statement to us about the latest revelation. Ron had lost a great deal of weight since his resignation as Welsh Secretary and was always immaculately turned out. He had shaved his hair, giving him a lean and more youthful look than when apologising for the Clapham Common affair the previous October: no red eyes or the word 'sorry' sketched on his hand as we all sat in Conference Room C awaiting his delivery. He found it 'all profoundly embarrassing' and offered assurances for the future. He'd lived under intense tabloid scrutiny: friends and family were harassed, his past dug over, then the *News of the World* tried to invent something. He had walked in woods near his home for 40 years and nothing like that had happened before. This time he was approached by two people, now known to be journalists, both with track records for such set-ups. No sexual act took place. The police had never received any complaint against him, and he was bisexual. He had decided to sort out the compulsive disorder for some time and wished he had faced up to it earlier. He had only recently realised his desire to expose himself to 'risk'. I gulped; these words raced across my mind, as I recalled my conversation the previous week with Ron's researcher. Ron's description of the devil within him was much more eloquent than ever I could capture in my notes. My pen flew across the pad jotting down the gist of this brave personal statement. I had never lost the habit of taking notes, my compelling desire to record everything taking place at meetings. I'd learnt to write fast as an assessor on a Home Office three-day Extended Interview Panel, where good recall of candidates' performance was required.

Ron composedly told us he had been advised that the condition made no impact on his work, but he needed support. A journalist heard about his treatment, so he broke the story himself. He intended to draw a line under the story and offered his apologies. He said that he had 'much support and should he lose his job, trade unions would fight and people would not get help.' To the best of his knowledge there were no further shocks. He asked the Group to accept his personality disorder; he was getting help within the NHS, and wanted people to still have confidence in him. He would not bow to tabloid pressure. He felt that others would be in the firing line. He concluded that he had put his political record on the line and felt a line was now under the matter. He wanted to get on with his life, his constituency and the Welsh Assembly.

The Group was wary and undecided on how to deal with this masterful ploy. Ron had resigned and apologised after the Clapham Common situation without actually admitting anything. This time he still was not admitting anything nor was he saying sorry. More importantly, he certainly was not going to resign. Chairperson Ann Jones side-stepped taking a vote. Most members stayed silent and just waited for reactions from each other. Those came from several AMs who felt strongly about Ron's behaviour. 'For' Ron were: Brian Gibbons, a medical doctor, John Griffiths, a gentle, unassuming man, and Christine. My note does not specify which of the two 'Christines' was in this Group, but I think Christine Gwyther supported him. She had problems herself over the vegetarian issue, and probably Ron, who had once held a similar portfolio, had shown her sympathy. Several members spoke against him. Edwina Hart, Finance Secretary, said bluntly that 'enough was enough'. Alun Pugh, the ambitious North Wales AM also demanded that Ron should stand down, but he would say that, wouldn't he? Huw Lewis, AM for Merthyr Tydfil, believed that the media would never stop pursuing him, therefore it was 'exit left' time. I said nothing. I thought we could not lose his talents at such an early stage into the Assembly. The meeting ended without reaching a decision on Ron's future. With one bound, it seemed that Ron lived to fight another day. That day came sooner than Ron could have imagined after his bravura Group performance.

The Sunday papers' suggestion that Ron would quit after one last tour-de-force performance as chair of EDC came true. Just seven days after our indecisive Group meeting Ron made a short statement at lunchtime on the 30th June. He 'deeply regretted the embarrassment that the events of the last few weeks have caused.' He would remain an active member of the committee but relinquish the chair at the next meeting. Alun Michael had assured him that this decision would not prejudice his future in the Assembly. Events dictated that Alun himself was on borrowed time so Ron could never call in that interesting and highly suspicious assurance.

Assembly life gathered pace as June gave way to July and we trundled and groped our way towards the first summer recess. The North Wales Regional Committee sat for the first time on Friday the 2nd July 1999. West Wales met too but it was those held in

North Wales that would always be well-attended, lively affairs. Under the chairmanship of Welsh speaking AM Gareth Jones, Plaid Cymru member for Conwy, our regional wagon rolled under the brooding presence of Conwy Castle. Assembly security staff and police, along with Assembly officials, had travelled north to provide their services to the committee. The audio technicians set up their equipment across the hall. A microphone and translation earphones were placed beside the name label of all the North Wales AMs. Tea and coffee was free and there was a buzz of excitement as Gareth took the Chair to call the meeting to order for the first time. As we started discussing how to proceed and what should feature on subsequent agendas, I realised that no translation facilities had been offered to the audience. As Gareth spoke mostly in Welsh and we could keep up with the headsets, I wondered how non-Welsh speakers would feel to be excluded from much of the debate. I nodded to an official who came over to me. I asked if there were any spare head sets and if there were, could they be offered to the gallery. Soon a few sets were being passed around amongst the public to nods of approval.

Knowing how politicians love to hear their own voices, I wondered how we could give the public their chance to address us with their opinions and concerns. I saw little point in AMs who have every right to speak in Cardiff doing the same thing throughout regional meetings – a recipe for disaster in the long term. Based on my knowledge of the police consultative forum model, I suggested to the Chair that a system could be devised for a member of the public wanting to speak to fill in a little form giving us notice. I knew the process worked well in police community consultative groups and the value of a two-way dialogue was clearly recognised. My colleagues accepted the idea and the Chair said it would be minuted. Having completed the business of this first regional committee, members congratulated each other and we moved en masse outside for a group photograph. When I got home, I faxed a note warning Alun that Welsh language zealots might attempt to make capital from the unequal treatment of committee members and the public, as headsets were not offered to those who wanted them. He replied quickly, thanking me for my interest and I felt rather smug that I may have headed off trouble. My smugness grew when some eight weeks later, the next Regional Committee of North Wales began an 'open mike' system that proved such an enduring winner.

On Tuesday the 6th July 1999, before the plenary session formally opened at 2.00pm, we were addressed by Philip Lader, the US Ambassador, and the first visiting dignitary to our National Assembly. His speech was rather good, paying us many compliments and wishing us well in our endeavours. The press and radio did not wish us well, soon picking up the controversial issue of increasing our allowances by £3,000. The news headlines for that day all started with 'National Assembly members set to vote themselves a large pay increase in allowances.' True, but unfairly slanted, as our goal was to pay our staff a decent wage, impossible on the original figure. I had taken on Peter York to run the Delyn office and at first we thought he could do all that was required. That proved wishful thinking as the correspondence mounted, the phone clanged and the computer kept crashing. I had struggled alone whilst in Cardiff trying to keep up with everything demanded of me, but I soon threw in the towel and tracked down a researcher to take over committee paper collation, table questions and draft my speeches. Unfairly, the media outcry was vociferous and protracted; the North Wales papers had a field day fanning our discomfort. The Assembly really had few friends in the north and the problem was compounded by coverage given to Barry Jones MP. He seemed rarely out of the headlines, overtly and frequently sniping at this Labour driven new Assembly.

Barry was a devoted Member of Parliament with many years to his credit, but I winced when I saw he was preparing to lead a farming delegation to Westminster to resolve their grievances, inferring that Cardiff was useless. Farming policy was devolved to the Assembly but as turkeys do not vote for Christmas, the legislators did not write into the Act that MPs no longer had a role in devolved issues, nor was it decreed that we should receive the same remuneration. None of our allowances matched those of the MPs with whom we shared constituencies, but not the same workload. English MPs were still answerable to their electorate for everything, and did not have the luxury of picking and choosing what they would take up as began to happen in Wales. MPs earned more, regularly voted themselves generous pension increases and accepted hefty allowances allowing them to employ more staff to run their constituency offices.

The difference in having expense claims accepted was also huge. MPs appeared to face none of the restraints imposed on us. Several of the AMs' researchers, having worked previously for MPs, had first hand knowledge of how the expenses regime operated at the other end of the M4. Claims were apparently accepted without any proof that the expense had been incurred. As a county councillor, I heard frequent mutterings that Barry Jones did not have his own formal constituency office for constituents to visit. It was accepted that he could be contacted at the House of Commons, or at his home address if really necessary. David Hanson, now 'my' MP as we shared Delyn, had his office in union offices in Flint. It was a handy place to call for a bit of photocopying and catch up with the gossip. Barry had one of the largest Labour majorities in Wales and had fought ferociously to retain the workforce for two of the largest manufacturing industries in Wales – British Steel and the Airbus factory at Hawarden. He held regular surgeries, knew everyone and sent out all sorts of reports from Westminster to interested constituents. Despite all this, not having a local office rankled, as ringing his home could be a risky move, which I found out later to my cost.

The vote to increase our allowances went through and I immediately set about finding a clerk/typist to help Peter with the burgeoning workload. Jon Shortridge and Sir John Bourn, the Auditor General for Wales, gave new Audit Committee Members their first briefing on the 8th July 1999. Mr Shortridge, head of the Welsh Civil Service and principle accounting officer, had full responsibility for the £8 billion (rising to £14 billion by 2006) that

Westminster gave Wales to spend. In 1999, to allow ministers chance
to discern what was going on, the budget was fixed for two years.
Sir John Bourn was much older than Shortridge. Sir John was tall and
thin with a fine head of hair, but silvery-grey. His suit and tie looked
top drawer and he spoke with a quiet authoritative voice.
He listened whilst Jon Shortridge warned about public dislike of
gravy trains, chauffeur driven cars and expensive frolics to Ireland
and abroad. Such matters could end up before Audit Committee.
I wanted to know about confidentiality clauses, still smarting from
Police Authority practices. Sadly, high spending agencies, namely the
police and Police Authorities, were off-limits to the Wales Audit
Office, as powers were not devolved.

I was sceptical that these two very successful 'establishment'
mandarins would really welcome unearthing financial improbity,
certainly when the 'Old Boy network' thrived in Cardiff. Val Feld's
public denouncements of the 'all male' nature of the Cardiff and
County Club threw up spectres of freemasonry and hidden agendas,
particularly as women's membership applications always failed.
My confidence was blunted by the antics of the police and its North
Wales Authority and I had grown cynical. I could not stop myself
blurting out, 'Whose side are you on?' to the urbane Sir John.
Without hesitation he replied, 'I'm your man. My loyalty is to you.'
That instant response was definitely noted in my diary.

Meanwhile, the Welsh farming fraternity kept Chris Gwyther in
their sights and held a special meeting in Aberystwyth on the 8th July
to decide whether to endorse her appointment. Their arrogance left
me breathless. Since when had a bunch of heavily subsidised rural
yobs decided they could endorse ministerial appointments? Two
days later, the Farmers' Union of Wales seemed to think better of
their new Agriculture Minister because they found themselves on
the back foot when they were accused of performing a U-turn.
It seemed they wanted to call a truce. Christine Gwyther's earlier
support for Ron was well placed, as he had been a leading light in the
agriculture committee in Westminster. He told the Group startling

facts about subsidised farming. Ron knew how little farming contributed to domestic output, and how exporting produce cost more than was returned in sales. That sector was a drain on the entire Welsh economy and we got nothing close to value for the money dished out to the farming community.

Our dilemma was acute; did this new administration cut back on what many of the Group understood to be obscene subsidies thereby deeply offending all the farmers of Wales? Two Group members hated subsidies and could not end them soon enough. They railed against the well-heeled farmer hogging so much public money, whilst forgetting the plight of small-scale hill farmers who eked out a living in desperate circumstances and needed help to survive. As Delyn is a farming area, I was more cautious remembering my day with the sheep and dairy farmers. If the mutton trade had collapsed and sheep were losing their teeth, I didn't want to see the countryside littered with starving sheep and rotting carcasses. I thought such sights would do little for the hard-hit tourist industry. Having kicked animal welfare around, the agenda moved on to discussing tactics for the next plenary session.

At the same time as Christine got used to fighting on more than one front, the Ron Davies saga continued unabated. His bravura performance chairing the first EDC meeting might have made riveting viewing, but it upset Alun's supporters in the Labour Group. There was no consensus to enforce his resignation as he had done so much to create the institution that paid our wages and gave us the right to decide policy in Wales. His high profile and political experience could not be discarded without measured thought. I viewed the *News of the World* coverage as unfortunate, but no shock horror facts about lewd behaviour were uncovered. It was suggestion and innuendo as far as I was concerned.

The battle raged quietly in the Group. 'He's been at it for years and everyone's known about it', was one frustrated female AM's opinion: 'He brokered devolution; we can't kick its author into the long grass.' Pressure began to grow that Ron 'must stand down'. Ron duly kept his promise and on the 14th July stood down as chair of the EDC. Still, the media would not give up on Ron. Readers of the *Western Mail* were treated to journalist Martin Shipton's view on Ron's declining fortunes and ITV Wales's 'Waterfront Sunday' news programme repeated the onslaught. Despite his political world collapsing around him, Ron's capacity to remain focused and get on with his public life as if nothing had happened, was awesome. Val Feld, AM for Swansea East, took over the chair of the EDC.

My office was next to Val's and we gossiped frequently. She viewed me as a star for taking discrimination issues forward and throwing a torch on the murky recesses of police attitudes to women in their ranks. I saw her as a pioneering woman and her previous organisation had masterminded my victory, sticking by me through thick and thin. Soon she confided to me that Ron was giving her a very rough ride at every EDC meeting. She told me that she hoped a change of committee clerk might ease matters. She was concerned that Ron's disruptiveness made EDC business difficult to progress, and there was an urgent need to improve the Welsh economy. I had taken no interest in that committee as I would have either been beavering away on my subject committee or preparing for something else. I just knew that Rhodri Morgan was the Economic Development Minister and would have been present at every session, but Val did not mention him. Whether or not he was supportive or played any part in shielding her from Ron's tantrums was not explained. I listened and sympathised but could do no more.

Apart from Val, I had another friend in Rosemary Butler, AM for Newport West, who put my name forward as Chair of the Voluntary Services Committee in Group one day. Several people seemed to think it a good idea. Flattered, I let my name go forward, lost by a small margin, and thought little of it. I had never come to Cardiff to start on the first rung of yet another 'greasy pole of promotion'. I was a bit concerned that when so many colleagues thought me worthy of the post, it became an inexplicable humiliating defeat. I'd had enough of rejection for new jobs and promised myself never to volunteer again. Buried amongst all the other breaking news in the *Western Mail*, page sixteen threw up the snippet that the Bute Avenue project contract would soon be signed. Even if I'd read it, it would have meant nothing to me, and I recall no discussions in Group or in plenary about the Private Finance Initiative (PFI) scheme that would be part of Cardiff's enhancement at taxpayers' expense under the Cardiff Bay winding-up process. I hardly knew that a Bute Avenue even existed, let alone that all taxpayers in Wales would soon be locked into a 25-year scheme costing over £5 million a year. This avenue was part of a grand scheme allowing developers to turn the area into one of the most prestigious in Wales.

As one of the signatories to the memorandum of agreement, the First Minister was doubtless joyful that the plan to regenerate Cardiff was going so well. Plans to regenerate the rest of poor Wales were not progressing at all well, as a vociferous Opposition continued to remind Alun Michael at every opportunity. Slowly the campaign mounted, unable to deliver these desperately needed 'Objective One' funds in time to begin to make them work for the valleys and West Wales. The transformation of Ireland was an unequivocal success, becoming one of the most dynamic economies in Europe. Why wasn't Wales making up for years of neglect by pushing the Treasury into releasing the money that would in turn open up the Euro coffers? Plaid, the Liberal Democrats, and the farming supporting Welsh Conservatives, had found a most useful tool to beat the minority Government hard and often. Alun faced two censure motions while Christine had three; neither appeared to lose much sleep over these Opposition antics.

In the fag end of the first session, the 20th July to be precise, plenary became lively when the Welsh Conservatives savaged the planned new Assembly building. They despised the need for an Assembly in the first place and certainly loathed the thought of a purpose built debating chamber with an even deeper passion. Instead, they wanted the money diverted to construct a children's hospital for Cardiff. Sitting just behind the Tories I could see their method of operation clearly. I felt their strategy was pure electioneering, trying to make capital from the unpopularity of the Assembly. I always felt a new democratic institution deserved its own building, assuming it would act as a powerful statement for devolution. Although I supported a new Assembly building, the design was both futuristic and spectacular, with its glass walls and odd roof appendages. I was uneasy as it was built on a plinth and apparently had no crèche facilities.

These vital items had been promised months earlier when I attended a Labour women's rally in Cardiff. I wondered how wheelchair users could actually access this building, grandly set up to overlook the Bay. So when Alun had invited its architect to talk us through the design, I asked for clarification on disability issues and crèche facilities. Under pressure, the designer conceded that he would look at the design again. Mine was not the only voice of concern, as several women knew we had called for reassurances about access and child care facilities in that Cardiff conference. We were surprised that the lobbying had fallen on deaf ears. Even I knew that disability legislation would soon be implemented and the International Year of the Disabled was close. I could not understand why the designers and commissioning authority had failed to grasp this perceived weakness in Richard Rogers's design. As of 2006, some seven years later, the Assembly, unlike the Scottish Parliament, still has no crèche facilities.

The delay imposed by AMs who wanted their new building to live up to its promised inclusiveness added considerably to the cost. We had not been informed not only that there was no formal contract between architects and the Assembly officials, but that any design change would immediately enhance the architect's fees. Of course, there was worse to come when the Auditor General put this project on his 'little list'. The mind-blowing incompetence his reports threw up filled me with despair. Not blessed with the gift of hindsight, I had blithely accused the Tories of time wasting and trivialising an important project during that plenary debate. I felt

I was supporting a Government determined to press it through despite its flawed design. I was committed to the new chamber and had proudly photographed the proposed site close to Crickhowell House, during an early 'recce' to Cardiff. As I learnt more of the facts of how officials and ministers got it wrong again, I felt guilty that I had berated the Tories for putting a children's hospital before our brave new building project.

Apart from the ceremonial 'cutting the sod' by the Presiding Officer who managed to pull the right levers on the JCB with its gaping shovel without decapitating an appreciative audience, nothing much else happened to the Lord Richard dream child for the following four years. I took one of my dogs, Scrabble, on her lead to witness this historic event and an air of celebration rippled through the crowd. The contractors started brightly and dug a large hole. Then everything stopped completely. I tell a lie. A large and substantial fence sprang up one day, presumably to shield the hole from prying eyes and to curtail Opposition questions on lack of progress. It cost £30,000 and no one on the fifth floor occupied by Welsh Assembly Government seemed to notice that the hole was clearly visible from the communal canteen and all the windows overlooking the site.

On the evening of the 20th July, I had to get to Penarth to feed the animals and then out to a Group meal. Rosemary Butler took me under her wing and raised the abortive Voluntary Services Chair vote. 'They should have sorted it out,' she muttered, as if she too was unhappy with the back-stage manoeuvring. Alun Michael arrived late when most of us had found seats and were tucking in to good pub food. We had to sit together and were both frantically burying the hatchet. When relaxed, he is good fun and we swapped stories *sotto voce.* I said that although he'll never top my Christmas card list, I felt he was doing a good job. A few more yarns were swapped before I baled out, as the party was moving up a gear. My enormous Local Government Committee was the next day and having not read a paper, I needed time for the effort. Early the next day I knocked off the rest of the vast bulk of the committee papers and took part in a positive meeting concentrating mostly on housing issues. Peter Law solemnly announced that news on the North-South road improvement front was bad, there being no subsidies. I winced as I'd really hoped the Assembly would open up roads and get rid once and for all of this destructive 'South gets all – North gets nothing' debate, that has so long dogged Welsh politics. Had I known how close the Bute Avenue PFI contract was to signing, I would have been much more vocal and questioning about how the money for roads is divided. In my salad days as a first term backbencher, I could have challenged much more in the interest of equality of treatment. I was not on the inside track and it was not easy to find out what was going on.

Tabling questions either for oral or written reply from Cabinet ministers was the mechanism for the purpose, but Table Office had quaint ways of rejecting all sorts of probing questions with inexplicable logic. My researcher and I got better and began to use wider ruses like, 'What discussions has the First Minister had with the Home Secretary on police matters relating to Mostyn Dock?' That would mask the real question in the 'supplementary' if lucky enough to be drawn within the first seven or so questions. I was not alone in being constantly frustrated by Table Office, who would throw out a perfectly reasonable question on the flimsiest excuse. We would then have to start a dance of the seven veils until it was acceptable by Table Office staff. At first, questions about policing were completely forbidden, as it was not a devolved power.

When Alun Michael announced in plenary that the Home Office and the Assembly had worked out a protocol making the Assembly responsible for crime prevention, the door was thrown wide open for asking a range of policing questions. There was much needed questioning, particularly as South Wales Police constantly received bad publicity for one seeming miscarriage of justice after another, to give but one example. Although Table Office kept an even tighter rein on police topics, the cat and mouse game over what would or would not be accepted, continued unabated. Giving the Assembly responsibility for crime prevention was the only practical solution as Local Authorities had formed crime prevention partnerships with their local constabulary some time previously. As the Assembly funded Local Authorities and extended some control over them, for the Assembly to play no part at all, even in peripheral issues, was not sustainable.

My last day in Cardiff before the long summer recess was hectic. It started with a Housing and Tenants Forum that brought together eleven movers and shakers in that very impoverished area in Wales. Through our committee work we would learn that Wales had some of the worst housing in Europe, and the Wales Office had made no attempt at a housing audit to determine what must be done. Housing improvement was one of my manifesto pledges. So many ills dog those living in sub-standard buildings of inadequate housing. Wales has one of the highest incidences of heart disease, drug misuse is out of control and teenage pregnancies are the highest in Europe. Wet, crowded housing in areas of high unemployment presented huge challenges. The housing forum people were very enthusiastic to be so high on the Local Government Committee agenda, and clearly had confidence in its chair, Sue Essex. Serving a Cardiff constituency, she was known to most of them and was sufficiently relaxed to talk about the 'cold hand of the civil service' holding back progress!

I had to dash away straight after committee, having accepted an invitation to take part in some lunchtime programme. I knew only it involved TV channel S4C, and at least a car would collect me. I was anxious to get back to Penarth and pack up the house for the long summer absence. Thus I was cross when shown a sofa and told I'd be collected. At last I was shown into the Chairperson's office. Over sandwiches, truly excellent I accept, I was lobbied for greater access to her channel by easing planning regulations. I listened politely as I munched and was impressed that a woman held such an influential position in Wales. My first plenary question to Alun Michael asked how many women headed the numerous Quangos in Wales. He happily reported that he was responsible for appointing the one female Quango boss there was, and more would be in the pipeline. Having decided to leave one magnificent sandwich on the plate not to appear a total pig, I promised Elan Closs-Stephens I would naturally do whatever I could. The company car soon whisked me back to Penarth where I hastily emptied the fridge and closed down the property for the duration of the summer. I loaded the animals and turned the car towards the Brecon Beacons with a joyful heart – I was free from Cardiff until September.

Lavatory conversations and Trigger down the pan.

'There is no mistake; there has been no mistake; and there shall be no mistake.'
Duke of Wellington 1889

By the 20th September, summer recess gave way to the long autumn term and constituency work would once again be compressed between Friday, the weekends and Monday.

Claims by the National Teaching Union that Local Authorities were diverting Assembly money for education to other priority budget heads, put the Government on the back foot. As my postbag filled with complaints from headteachers and governors that money for schools seemed very scarce since the Assembly arrived, they had my sympathy. 'Who the hell had the money: Local Authority or Assembly?' remained an unresolved mystery during the Assembly's first four years. Alun Michael denied there was a problem and blamed the councils. No one in the Assembly would produce any proof of specific monies going to Local Authorities. Edwina refused to use hypothecation – the ring fencing of funds for a particular purpose. Meantime, Delyn schools emptied buckets from under leaking roofs, and teachers toiled to keep buildings open in compliance with Health and Safety rules.

Dragons Led by Poodles by Paul Flynn MP hit the bookshops and deftly stirred the murky waters of the damaging leadership contest that cost the Assembly its Labour majority. How else did Labour lose the Rhondda Valley heartland, or Helen Mary Jones win Llanelli by a whisker for Plaid Cymru? In Group the leadership fiasco was taboo, because Alun was Tony Blair's choice and Rhodri Morgan quietly accepted the job of Minister for Economic Development.

It was soon clear that much of the Labour Government's energy was spent heading off threats of 'no confidence' votes mounted on two fronts. The Opposition was furious at Alun Michael's perceived inability to obtain Objective One – money needing match funding from the Treasury, and to remedy the escalating crisis in the farming industry, made him a target. Probably Rhodri would have fared no better as leader, but the enduring picture of Alun being 'parachuted' into the Assembly could not be denied. Alun's refusal to bow to persistent demands to sack Christine Gwyther also left him vulnerable. On 15th September, she survived a Conservative motion of 'no confidence'. Both Plaid Cymru, under Dafydd Wigley's charismatic leadership and the Welsh Tories – with their abrasive leader, Rod Richards – seemed determined to bring her down.

One issue that infuriated the Group and the Opposition related to the Home Office's arrogant behaviour in deciding to house 5,000 asylum seekers in Wales, mostly in Cardiff Gaol, thus causing public outrage. The Assembly cabinet had not been consulted before the prisoners were dumped in Cardiff. In plenary, Edwina Hart vigorously condemned the action and spoke eloquently against her Labour confrères at the other end of the M4, but apart from giving this hot topic an airing, we were but an impotent 'talking shop'. Prison policy was not devolved; thus the Assembly had no powers to overrule the Home Office who could fill our Gaols with whoever they pleased!

In October, Ron bluntly stated that the Welsh Assembly must get a grip on its funding of economic and social regeneration in Wales. His view was re-enforced by 'senior Welsh Assembly officials', who declared Wales might 'lose Objective One money if not spent within two years.' Ron was always listened to, even now as only a member of the prestigious Economic Development Committee. His high status gave him a platform to attack Alun who was now struggling to keep his own job. Probably aware of the fast approaching anniversary of his own *annus horribilis*, Ron was reminding political watchers that he still exerted force in Welsh politics.

On the 18th October 1999, after completing the non-stop evening trip to Cardiff in three hours 40 minutes, enhanced by wonderful sunshine, I unloaded the car and dashed to a Group meeting. Labour's policy and plans for plenary voting were formulated at these meetings and they should have been a useful bonding session for members. Attendance was always mixed: members living closest to Cardiff were inevitably missing, yet North Wales were usually present. Some south based AMs seldom bothered to attend the ever-increasing number of receptions hosted within the Assembly, however compelling the cause. My greatest embarrassment was when I and three other AMs attended a hi-tech Navy presentation, with a double podium presentation with all the trimmings. Reception sponsors soon learnt to advertise by email in the hope someone would accept.

Later that day I learnt that an extra Group would be held after office hours as items were stacking up for consideration. John Marek was missing again and people were beginning to mutter about his poor attendance. As he was still an MP, I presumed that he was giving his Parliamentary commitments a higher priority, but he lost the nomination to be our Assembly Commonwealth representative. That evening's priority was a weighty one: to draw up the draft manifesto, our political 'wish list' that would become our Party's written promises and policies for the next election. I thought the unrealistic promise of freedom from crime could return to haunt us and I chose a more practical goal of introducing high-speed phone connections across Wales. The snail's pace of connecting to Cardiff by computer irked me and, I presumed, small businesses too. Having contributed to Welsh Government policy, my fourteen plus hour day ended with dog walking. Scrabble, my old Border terrier, looked fragile and declined her supper.

The Labour Group turned out in force the next day and plotted to kill yet another 'no confidence' vote in Christine Gwyther. We clapped loudly when she entered the Group room, a TV camera trailing her. The Opposition lost by 27 to 30 votes and we cheered again. She handled these regular assaults on her competence well, giving as good as she got. The Assembly's Table Office had drawn my

Assembly question, allowing me to ask the question of Alun on the floor of the Chamber followed by a supplementary question of my choice. These could be wide ranging and catch out an ill-prepared Minister. Sue Essex accosted me later and giggled. 'Alun froze', she said, 'waiting for your supplementary. I wish I could have such an impact on people,' she laughed.

Alun himself survived another 'no confidence motion' on the 2nd November. Contemptuous of their attempts to unseat the First Secretary for Wales, Edwina Hart glided to the podium and announced that £8 billion was being released for increased spending on services in Wales. The Opposition greeted this 'good news' story with glum faces. Not the outcome they had been looking for!

Rod Richards's career wobbled again when his trial for allegedly assaulting a young woman was confirmed. Sitting next to him in plenary, Rod quizzed me about the Crown Prosecution Service. I warned him to trust no one, admit nothing and get the best brief he could afford. He nodded sagely, then, following his usual routine, stayed just a few minutes before quietly leaving the chamber. I remembered back to when we were both guests on a BBC TV political chat show with Jamie Owen after the Assembly opened. Rod's performance was as accomplished and eloquent as mine was faltering and inept. After the show Rod enjoyed a close encounter with a bottle of red wine, but it did nothing to ease his combative attitude to folk around him. I did not linger. It was a wild night and more flooding was forecast, so I left him to the wine. I arrived home dry in every sense of the word. Rod was an able politician, with an ability to ask clever and probing questions capable of upsetting his opponents. He seemed as smart as Ron Davies. The similarities between the men were fascinating. Although they stood on either side of a deep political divide, both had progressed well up their own political greasy poles. Both had mastered the black arts of politics. Both were survivors, apparently with a streak of arrogance and ruthlessness seemingly so essential to real political success. It was ironic that despite such talents, both men were destined to crash dramatically.

The first Welsh Assembly Audit Committee got under way on the 21st September. The Auditor General's role was important as he audited all the accounts the Assembly controlled, exploring the acquisition, use and disposal of assets and other resources by public bodies and Quangos in Wales. Whether the public was getting value for money was the real concern of the Auditor General and the committee. Edwina Hart attended the first meeting – although not a committee member – stating that she regarded the work of the committee as a key part of the Assembly's operation, and hoping we would be tough where necessary. After she left, Sir John gave us estimates of the work his staff could undertake for different sums of money. The Opposition preferred the highest figure. I hedged – not because I did not welcome a 'Rolls Royce' service, but I worried that Edwina's budget had to accommodate so much and wondered if the Auditor General should cut his cloth accordingly.

The passage of time showed that opting for 'Rolls Royce' scrutiny was the best option, as there was so much to occupy his staff for years to come. A review of the wind up of the Cardiff Bay Barrage development immediately caught my eye, as did 'An Examination of the Bute Avenue Private Finance Initiative Project'. Did the Auditor know of the arrangements allegedly agreed behind closed doors between the Lord Mayor and the then First Secretary? Sir John's scrutiny list included the Environment Agency, the Higher Education sector, the handling of clinical negligence, and the preservation and conservation of old buildings on our behalf through Cadw (a Government body from the Welsh word 'to keep', with the mission to protext, conserve and promote appreciation of the built heritage of Wales). Clinical negligence costs were frightening. The total forecast for 1997-1998 exceeded £144 million. We rapidly concluded that although some control would be introduced in April, this drain on the public purse warranted a high priority.

The Audit committee unanimously agreed to review the Assembly's accommodation arrangements. After months of teasing delay, Ron Davies, Secretary of State for Wales, had blithely announced that Cardiff Bay was his chosen venue, a choice welcomed with derision in some quarters. Swansea was particularly aggrieved, as were Local Authorities who had accepted the invitation to submit schemes for a site outside Cardiff, at no small cost to taxpayers. Ugly rumours abounded that the choice of Cardiff was inevitable, making Local Authorities' bids a costly sham. It would be shown that such rumours had merit, and bidding authorities were right to consider that they had been hoodwinked. One that felt aggrieved was my own Flintshire Council, although realistically, a North Wales venue had not a snowball's chance in hell of being accepted by the establishment.

Assembly Audit Committee powers were weak compared with the draconian powers of Parliamentary Select Committees sitting at the other end of the motorway. Westminster committees could summon ministers and officials and interrogate to learn the truth. Although we had power to summon officers, our wings had been severely clipped by officials responsible for agreeing Assembly powers. Interrogating ministers was off-limits; the task of speaking on behalf of ministers falling to the Permanent Secretary, who became a regular witness before us. Further, only current senior Quango personnel would give evidence even if they were not in post when things went wrong. Never calling 'wrong-doers' to account seemed wrong where they escaped unscathed to possibly higher positions! I was so annoyed that I raised my concerns in Group. When MP Rhodri Morgan had chaired the Public Administration Select Committee, (a prestigious fact finding committee in Westminster), although he offered explanations as to why Westminster did things differently, frankly, they never made sense to me. Shortcomings aside, the Audit Committee remained the Assembly's most powerful scrutiny tool. Was the exclusion of Assembly powers to interrogate ministers an oversight, or a deliberate ploy? Cynics would say that the architect of devolution, Ron Davies, with his brilliant political instinct and ability to foresee pitfalls, would have known the dangers of exposing ministers to Audit Committee interrogation, and that his own decisions as Welsh Secretary would soon come under our microscope. Had the Audit Committee been allowed to take his evidence, particularly after leaving office, about areas of concern, such things as the new debating chamber or why the 'bonfire of the Quangos' fizzled out would have been truly fascinating. Although the Auditor General's reports were agreed with the Quango or agency bosses before coming before the committee (thus removing any potential dispute before we became involved), we were rightly allowed to go 'off message' and not stick to Sir John's recommended questions.

On the 14th October 1999, before the public gallery, press and internal TV cameras, we dipped into the mysterious world of protecting and conserving the built heritage in Wales by Cadw. Did Chirk Castle in North Wales give value on its maintenance grants? Karen Sinclair sidled into my office, pleading to maintain the status quo for this castle in her constituency. Chirk Castle guardians gave a spirited performance, blamed the high costs on the tons of lead on the roof needing constant maintenance, and disagreed that the grant should be cut. As the Chirk Castle officers had put up a feisty performance, I promised to visit them when time allowed. Because Audit reports were detailed and probing, we developed trust in the Auditor General's staff and invariably accepted his recommendations, backing his findings without quibbling, but only after giving witnesses a probing examination. Cadw struggled to explain why the Church of the Holy Spirit, in Ewloe, was not a listed building. I later found out it was because when their inspectors called they could not get in and had not realised its status! My ears pricked up. It was close to home and I had attended a Civic Sunday service in the church when I had been a councillor months earlier.

Sir John's team compared Wales with England over progress in preserving ancient monuments. They were not impressed with Cadw's performance. On the contrary – having failed to complete a 'buildings at risk' register, some 250 buildings were vulnerable.

Cadw was firmly called to account and I viewed this 'Spanish Inquisition' approach as a good omen for the Assembly's commitment to openness and transparency. Cadw's little glitches paled into insignificance as we got into our stride, and the Auditor General really began to roll out some hard hitting and challenging reports. Not only would he review in great detail the 'Winding-up of Cardiff Bay Barrage' and the 'Accommodation Arrangements for the Welsh Assembly', another – 'the disposal of 'the Mid Wales Hospital' – would prove to be very strange indeed.

A Mrs Shelia Bailey, purchaser of part of the hospital estate, had urgently faxed the Secretary of State for Wales, who allowed her to make a late bid that proved successful. Her fax to Alun Michael had allegedly sealed the deal that seemingly scooped up a very generous bargain from a valuable publicly owned asset. Much later, we were to learn more when the Auditor General's report came to the Audit Committee on the 24th October 2002. I was already aware that Martin Shipton's frank revelations in the *Western Mail* seemed extraordinary.

Even though I was well used to years of assimilating police documents and preparing complex complaints against police files, I found Audit Committee papers hard work. Alun Michael once remarked to me, 'Like me, you must be used to 'slabs of paperwork'. We agreed on something! Much of the paper preparation problem was attributed to the dreadfully slow printers in my constituency, and other office duties virtually ceased when the printer ground out each page. The practical solution was to print them when back in Cardiff the night before the committee sat. Thus, I burnt much midnight oil familiarising myself with the contents, but at our inaugural meeting Edwina had commended us to be tough and thorough; I doggedly followed her advice throughout my four years on that challenging committee.

On the 21st October I hosted my first reception for a band of Christians who had walked from St. Winefride's Well in Delyn to Cardiff to raise awareness about poverty. Refreshments had been organised in the Members' dining room, and I prayed that the reception would be well attended by AMs. Jim Hynes and his wife Freda, big fundraisers from Delyn, were deeply committed to eradicating injustice and poverty. Happily, several AMs arrived, including Jenny Randerson, a Cardiff Lib Dem AM. A Wrexham delegate pleaded for help to set up breakfast clubs to stop children falling asleep at their desks. 'Just a slice of toast in school would make all the difference,' was the plea. I ushered the last of the stragglers out by 7.00pm and headed to the Penarth pad, pleased with the outcome. Some years later, I was happy to see the Labour Assembly commit itself to provide free healthy school breakfasts across Wales.

I regretted not having made the effort to travel to Ewloe that night because the following day, against a backcloth of torrential rain, black sky and menacing clouds with roads awash, I plodded over the Brecon Beacons muttering prayers for safe deliverance. Great swathes of water were thrown up by passing lorries buffeting my 4x4, and smashed against the windscreen leaving me momentarily blinded as, even at full speed, the wipers could not cope. After four hours of frightening driving I was just grateful to reach Flintshire. With nerves taut from the stressful journey, I rang Peter who cheerfully asked what he should get me from the canteen. 'No time for such luxury!' I snapped. I had to get to a two o'clock meeting in Mold and needed to unload the animals. A leisurely lunch had now become a rare indulgence. Puffin had travelled badly. She had been sick, so some of the luggage had to be cleaned up, and thus more precious time was lost. I charged into Mold Town Hall only to learn that, through a mix-up, I had arrived an hour early! Who made the mistake? No-one was saying. I thought that all the arrangements had been properly agreed with Cllr Bithell, who had also thrown his hat into the ring for Assembly selection. I had sensed a change in attitude towards me after my selection and now felt uneasy with him. Being a very dutiful elected councillor, he wrote regularly to my office with a variety of issues and continued to press for results. I could not complain. He was only doing his job and as I had won the right to represent Mold, I too should perform well. Chris Bithell and I had agreed over the unfairness of proportional representation at the Delyn Constituency meeting one evening. I mentioned Ron Davies's belief that without proportional representation the Assembly would never have materialised. This fact was digested, and the meeting moved on to give full scrutiny to my detailed newsletter of Assembly events, and what I had done to earn their vote.

Walking the dogs in Ewloe on Friday the 29th October, I was flattened by a bouncy dog. I had to hobble home and was unable to drive; this meant I could not get to the Assembly the following week. This was for the best as Scrabble, my rescued Border terrier, had to be put down as she was fading fast. She was taken to Brynford Pets Cemetery to be reunited with her departed sisters. Scrabble had never been any trouble and had tolerated much in the years she had been with me. She had been trundled out to parade before press cameras during my equality battle and endured hours in the Welsh Assembly car park. I was pleased she had died at home. A few months later, Puffin, my beloved cat, was not so lucky and I brought her ashes back with me from Cardiff.

Meanwhile, the Trigger saga was still bubbling. The North Wales Police Head of Legal Services, and legal adviser to the Police Authority, Jenny Trigger, was suspended from duty on the 16th November 1999 by some of the members, who had met previously as a formal Grievance Panel to adjudicate on her complaint against senior officers. Under the chairmanship of John Anderson JP, her claim had been dismissed, leaving the way open for her suspension. Presuming that sufficient evidence existed to justify suspension, why then, on the 30th November, was it necessary for Acting Clerk, Diana Few, to commission one D. Abraham (a public sector employment consultant) to examine Mrs Trigger's performance of her legal duties for the force? To me, the events were out of sequence! Diana Few's flexibility, and seeming willingness to fit into whatever role the fast changing events within the Police Authority required, showed a remarkable diligence to duty. Having had numerous conversations with Andrew Wilford, one of the 'Campaign for Justice' leaders, who had frequent dealings with Mrs Few in his quest for justice from the force, felt she was on their side and wanted to blow the whistle.

She candidly admitted to me in a phone conversation that she loathed Jenny Trigger. Diana Few obliquely indicated that Mrs Trigger had at times been less than helpful towards 'Campaign for Justice's' many complaints. Diana had agreed to meet with me and Andrew Wilford a few days before Christmas in 1998 and a venue was agreed. Andrew was jubilant with this development and was pleased to find someone was listening to them at last. 'Whistle-blowing' Diana would have been a real bonus for the campaigners. The meeting never materialised and in further conversation, she admitted that a job she had applied for did not materialise. Career move scuppered, her only option was to stay put. Andrew was disappointed by this setback. Her withdrawal did not surprise me. She was taking a huge risk and if things went wrong, her career with the force or in Local Government would have been severely threatened.

After Norman Land resigned on the 17th January 1999, despite holding lower or no legal qualifications, her elevation to Acting Clerk gave Diana Few superiority over Mrs Trigger, enabling the Police Authority to continue working towards Mrs Trigger's suspension behind her back. Events would show that Diana Few's appointment would be a major factor in scuppering Mrs Trigger's career too. On the 6th May, Few sent Trigger a terse letter informing the top force lawyer that, acting on advice, Few, as Acting Clerk to the Authority, 'was causing an investigation to be carried out because of the Chief Constable's concerns, all contained in a report dated 15th March'. As Polling Day was the 6th May, I had no knowledge of Few's damaging letter, and even if I had known, I had more on my mind than the travails of Mrs Trigger.

Piecing events together later, it became clear how fast senior officers moved from defence to attack, heading off potential trouble from John Cooke's amazing memo. With masterful ease, the force had grabbed the initiative. Trigger's adversaries were not only the Chief Constable, but it seemed that even her employers – the Police Authority – were against her.

With me out of the way, apart from her Union, Mrs Trigger had no friends at court to challenge the forces marshalled against her. She should have heeded my warning that she would now be *persona non grata,* and maybe it was foolish to have refused whatever financial compensation had been offered to her.

Diana Few's elevation to Acting Clerk would have surely required instructions from the Authority Chairman, possibly the more cerebral Vice Chair, (the same who eventually dismissed Mrs Trigger's grievance against the Chief Constable) and other members, to arrange the 'Emergency panel' devised to deal with the crisis caused by former Clerk Norman Land's rapid departure. The truth of Diana's amazing promotion was found in the statement of the Deputy Chief Constable, John T. Owen to Mr Abraham. Mrs Trigger confided in the DCC that I had rung and believed that the Authority was acting unlawfully because they did not have a Clerk and did not have a Monitoring Officer.

'What did you tell her?' asked the DCC.

'I'll have to tell her [Halford] she's right', she said.

'That's silly', he replied, 'If you are saying that we are acting improperly then we need to correct that, rather than simply tell Alison Halford we're doing it wrong.'

'So, why don't we arrange with the Chairman for Mrs Few to be Acting Clerk and for you to be Monitoring Officer?'

And so it was arranged, followed by a God almighty row between Mrs Trigger and Mrs Few. Understandable, as the Acting Clerkship had already been promised to Jenny Trigger. I was shocked when reading John Tecwyn Owen's opinion of me.

Replying to Mr Abraham's question about the alternatives open to Jenny Trigger having received the damning memo, the DCC affirmed, 'I thought it was the most crazy thing to have done...

Councillor Halford had made it abundantly clear from her first arrival on this Police Authority that she was out to wreak as much harm as she possibly could on the police service at chief officer level…but she certainly had her own agenda as far as chief officers were concerned.' His view of me was completely wrong. Having escaped from a bruising encounter with the Merseyside Police Authority, I had moved on and wanted only to be a good servant to the public and the Authority. That I had 'caused nothing but havoc' was not my doing. So, keen to ensure I was not a threat, an administrative plan had been devised that proved to be unfair, unjust and in fact ethically unworkable. John had admitted that Jenny Trigger was serving two masters, a point the Labour member of the Authority had made repeatedly. The chief officer's fear of me had produced a dog's dinner of an administrative system. Mrs Few's appointment had suited the 'chiefs' and the Authority apparatchiks as well. They had ensured that, with the compliant and inexperienced Mrs Few at the Police Authority helm, her trusted hands would do their bidding and the chiefs would once more call all the shots.

The David Abraham report continued to provide revealing material on several counts. Mr Abraham suggested seven alleged disciplinary offences against the Force Head of Legal Services, ranging from 'general incompetence over the way she handled civil claims that led to a breakdown of trust with senior officers' to 'allocating work to her husband's chambers that undermined confidence in her integrity'! Her much maligned integrity was further challenged when another allegation suggested 'that she had appointed a friend on a temporary basis without recourse to the appropriate procedures.' When I read Mr Abraham's report I learnt that I was not an interviewee, despite mentioning me in his thirteen-page discipline synopsis. Jenny Trigger's visit to my home formed the basis of the second charge, the first accusing her of the 'way she handled civil claims on behalf of the police force in the period up to early 1999, which was unreasonable and led to a breakdown of trust and confidence between her and senior officers.' Mrs Trigger and

I had locked horns at most Authority meetings and, invariably, I hit a brick wall every time I tried to obtain even a minimal level of justice against North Wales Police.

Jenny Trigger was part of the system that, in my opinion, was geared to ensure senior officers never faced a disciplinary enquiry. Consulting me was seen as treachery and consumed much of Mr Abraham's discipline investigation. Mrs Trigger was quoted as assessing me as a 'lone voice, doing what all of us would hope Police Authority members would do' and that my questioning of issues was 'incisive and direct'. She felt that Ms Halford's character was being 'blackened' and added that the DCC had made disparaging remarks about her (which had discomfited her and her husband) during a chief officer's dinner. I began to understand how Jenny Trigger must have agonised over the decision to seek my help. She recognised the 'Chiefs' loathed me, but knew I had the knowledge and integrity to do my best to help her. Maybe she should have realised the extent of the damage she had done to her career by consulting me!

The Abraham's dossier mentioned several fee notes from both Mrs Trigger's husband, and Gareth Thomas, by now an MP, who shared legal Chambers. Mrs Trigger, rejected the claim that she had 'encouraged her staff' to deal with these Chambers, as Judge Trigger was a notable authority on licensing matters and the force needed good advice. Jenny Trigger also believed that she had done nothing wrong in temporarily appointing the wife of Mr Thomas to undertake conveyancing work in the force Legal Services department and gave several reasons to justify the appointment. Mrs Trigger also admitted that she had been under pressure, as seventeen complaints had been received against the chief officers in 1997. Leon Gibson, the Clerk, 'was disintegrating as he had his own problems with a criminal investigation into the affairs of Anglesey Council, and a report had been sent to the Home Secretary making wide ranging allegations against the chief officers'. When Mr Abraham returned yet again to question Mrs Trigger about 'the considerable time spent with Alison Halford', she praised my performances as I asked pointed and searching questions at numerous Police Authority meetings. It worried her that I was not liked by the chief officers 'and as result she [Halford], was the butt of derogatory remarks by these officers on many occasions'.

Unaware of the unravelling Trigger saga, the 1999 autumn term wore on and I settled to the task of being a good AM by accepting as many invitations as possible. One took me to MP Barry Jones's 'patch' at the Broughton wings factory on the 29th October. Each enormous wing was flown to Toulouse by a bizarre looking plane and everyone was proud of this major employer's achievements. Having escorted us round the workshops, Barry ducked the buffet lunch I tucked in to with Peter York, who had accompanied me. It seemed he had something on his mind. Back in Delyn, he confessed that, having met Barry in the toilet before lunch, he had been shocked that the MP had indicated that I had some mental problem, but that he and Peter could work well together. Peter was upset by this test of his loyalty. Barry's attempt to drive a wedge between my office manager and me was disingenuous. Neither of us wanted an altercation with a highly respected MP, but I just could not ignore it. We kicked the problem around and finally agreed to send a courteous letter asking Barry to confirm Peter's perception of their conversation or clarify his position. A suitably drafted letter went to the House of Commons. Receiving no reply, a firmer letter was dispatched, repeating the need for clarification. It came by way of a phone call to the Delyn office informing Peter that 'a very angry Barry was on the verge of instructing lawyers'. Peter was more shocked by this abrasive response than by the original conversation.

David Hanson and I met on the 11th November 1999, Remembrance Day. Fortunately, David seemed to have no problem with me. It was not David's fault, but at Civic Services, I became miffed that the clergy offered prayers for the MP but never for the AM. As I always shared the front pew with David and even read a lesson, I could hardly be missed! I felt the representative of the new Government of

Wales needed divine intercession as much as the MP. So, I wrote to the local bishop and raised my concerns. Would he 'consider asking his clergy to add the AMs to the prayer list?' The bishop responded positively and promised to remedy the problem.

On the 3rd December, I attended the opening of another wing of Plas Bellin, the 'Save the Family' charity's home, headed by the energetic fundraising founder, Edna Speed. A senior patron, the Duchess of Westminster, was joined by an impressive array of local dignitaries including Barry Jones. Again, I was amused to find him right at the front and well positioned for prowling photographers. Within feet of each other, he ignored me completely. To add insult to injury, his staff had not followed the usual courtesy of informing the incumbent that the neighbouring MP would be officially on 'my patch'.

Seeing great chasms opening before me, but entitled to defend Peter who had received no acknowledgement from Barry on the 'loo' affair, and disappointed yet again at being cut dead so publicly, I wrote a third time to Barry on the 7th December 1999. 'Why', I asked, had he 'ignored me at Plas Bellin?' and also, 'could I have the name of his lawyer so that I could put mine in touch with his?' I felt uncomfortable with my blunt communication but I just felt I must flag up my concerns that Barry's behaviour was hurtful; it seemed he wanted to both isolate and belittle me in public. This latest letter gave Barry the chance of remedying the situation if Peter had misunderstood their toilet conversation. I was saying, 'Get your tanks off my lawn or you will have to engage mine'. As no response ever came, I put Barry's behaviour behind me and moved on.

On the 2nd December I unwittingly gave the Welsh tabloids an early Christmas present by way of welcome relief from the boring grind normally associated with reporting Welsh Assembly politics. During plenary, having hassled the Presiding Officer by using my touch screen to email him, asking him to let me have 'an intervention', he suddenly and unexpectedly called me to speak. In panic I staggered to my feet, and with no clear idea what I was going to say, began to waffle. In my confusion, I called the Opposition, 'little people'. David Davies, the only 'first past the post' Welsh Conservative shot to his feet. Being, 6 foot 3 inches tall, he objected strenuously to being described as 'little people'. His seat was directly in front and one row removed from my chair. Articulate and combative, he rarely missed the chance to make points of order. I rather liked him and thought he had a great future in politics. Not wanting to lose face, I found myself babbling about admiring David and announced that I thought, 'He has one of the nicest bottoms in the Assembly!' David sat down hurriedly and the place erupted with laughter. The Presiding Officer looked hysterical but made no challenge for improper behaviour and I sank back in my chair, mortified by the wayward comment.

I cheered up when Ann Jones emailed me, saying she thought my remark was brilliant. Mark, my then researcher, was appalled, muttering about the dangers of discriminatory remarks when I returned to our office. Fearing trouble, I hastily emailed David hoping I had not offended him. I signed myself 'Granny Halford'; that was just about right as the age difference between us was considerable. Back came a reply by return: 'Dear Granny Halford, no offence taken.' He 'always enjoyed [my] contributions which were always unpredictable, and this occasion was no exception.' I giggled and felt this would end the matter! Not a bit of it. The tabloids had a field-day; we both made several front pages the next day. 'Bum rap for Alison', shrieked one and 'Just when you thought politicians in the Assembly were dull, grey and boring – finally, the Assembly gets some character,' shouted another. The *Welsh Mirror* went into orbit placing Glyn Davies's (another Welsh Conservative) mug shot next to mine with the captions, 'She says Tory member has a nice bottom', and 'He gets caught driving without his trousers'. Police had in fact stopped a trouser-free Glyn Davies whilst driving a trailer load of sheep. He explained that he was wearing only wellies, pants and jacket because he'd fallen in a huge pile of manure and did not want to soil his posh car. The press could not get enough mileage from the 'no trousers' and David Davies's 'bottom', pronouncing them to be the best stories to come from the Assembly for some time.

Although I declined to be interviewed, David basked in the media attention coming up with witty little gems like, 'He was able to turn the other cheek'. Glyn's smelly trousers feat didn't stop him writing to me: 'I hope you will not consider me unduly 'cheeky' in raising a rather delicate matter with you on the Conservative Group Whip's "little bottom". I will set aside any disappointment that I may feel about your sizeist predilections (since I am personally built of much sturdier proportions).' He continued, 'My concern is solely from an Equal Opportunities perspective. What would the Assembly have said if any male AMs had commented, favourable or otherwise, on the size of your bottom?' Lost for an answer, I copied Barry Jones and ducked replying to this amusing epistle. Steel making in Wales faced meltdown as Euro-funding was on a knife-edge, but the tabloids preferred to focus on the Presiding Officer's Armani suits and his passion for Armagnac, Glyn's underpants and David Davies's 'nicest bottom'! To cap it all, David and I were presented with a silver shield, our prize from the *Western Mail* for the quote of the year.

Christmas was fast approaching, but the pace of work never faltered. On the 8th December I was drawn to speak in an Assembly debate on the Queen's Speech, settling on the Freedom of Information bill. I was very annoyed by the Home Office's refusal to provide facts on gender statistics, data about grievance procedures against forces, their cost and outcome, as well as important details allowing insights into how police forces managed personnel issues. Why should the Home Office Permanent Secretary, John Gieve, (the same who would later achieve ministerial condemnation in 2006 when John Reid stated that the Home Office was 'not fit for purpose', and later still in 2007 would be mauled again for incompetence by MPs investigating the run on the Northern Rock saga) continue to prevaricate if there was nothing to hide? Why had the Government pledged, when elected in 1997, to introduce a Freedom of Information Act – the White paper 'Your Right to

Know' had been widely welcomed, but little changed. My speech suggested that when responsibility for drafting the Bill was handed to the Home Office, brave promises were suddenly forgotten and, that, in its present form, it contained nothing to break the shackles of the pervasive culture of secrecy in British Governance. Even with a few bland concessions, the bill fell far short of the promises in the originating White Paper. I had already drunk at the fountain of Establishment hypocrisy when I won my phone-tapping case against the Government and my odious former Chief Officer, Jim Sharples, in the court of Human Rights in 1997.

In theory, a warrant signed by a Home Office Minster is needed, but this was pie in the sky; chief officers were busily bugging phones without the Home Office consent. As a new ACC, I naively signed the proffered form and meekly accepted that my rank could give the authorisation that allowed Special Branch and senior detectives to bug and eavesdrop under the guise of 'doing their job'! I'd voted Labour in protest against a Tory Government hell bent on secrecy and obfuscation, but now elected, New Labour's commitment to 'open every corner of the bureaucratic process, was suddenly forgotten.'

On the 20th October, Welsh devolution received a slap in the face when we learnt that the Welsh Grand Committee, chaired by Barry Jones, would continue to sit. This U-turn took the Assembly by surprise as once the 60 AMs had taken charge of an £8 billion budget, that forum became redundant and its retention betrayed Westminster's reluctance to cede its powers. A farce that occurred the previous day in the Assembly helped neither us in Cardiff nor the Labour Government in Westminster, because when Christine Gwyther lost the Opposition 'no confidence' vote, the weakness of our powers became evident as the Assembly had no means of removing her. Grinning broadly, Christine offered her opponents the proverbial two fingers and remained in post.

Not forgetting his youth worker roots and willing to be creative, Alun confirmed his commitment to the Youth of Wales in his plenary statement on the 7th December. He launched 'Young Voices/Llais Ifanc' in which he envisaged a virtual youth assembly, allowing young people all over Wales to give their views daily on issues via the internet. By setting up links between schools, colleges and young people's forums, the eventual goal was to give young people the chance to communicate directly with himself and the Cabinet. Wayne David, ousted from a safe Labour seat in the Rhondda was tasked with setting up 'Young Voices'. He became the Wales Youth Agency supremo with the goal of the Assembly hosting an event in July 2000. With Christmas in the air, the Opposition could not criticise this scheme as it provided a sound means of involving young people in the despised world of politics.

Not to be outdone, the Foreign Office announced it would play host to any school applying to visit that Department. Schools in my area were naturally enthusiastic, but who would pay for pupils and supervising teachers to accompany them? With school budgets always on a knife-edge, I felt that this wealthy department should dip into its reserves to fund their most worthy idea to widen knowledge of their work. Foreign Office Minister, Baroness Scotland, former top QC and rare black member of Government, flatly refused to accept my point. The Minister's reply to my plea for help with travel costs was a blunt 'No'. I resisted the temptation to query details of the yearly Foreign Office travel budget to determine if funds could be diverted for school pupils' visits. MPs can fund constituency visits to the House of Commons, but AMs had no such perks. North Wales schools that were unable to afford the journey were denied a visit.

My journey back north after Assembly business was as frustrating as ever, and I had to resist many temptations to overtake slow moving traffic as safe passing places were scant indeed. There was no respite from driving the next day either, as the Regional Committee was in Caernarfon on the 10th December and I always made an effort to attend, believing these sessions were some of the most important in which the Assembly was involved. I cheered up when the 'open mike session', allowing the public some say, was included as a regular

Regional Committee feature and was obviously greatly appreciated. Then back again to Cardiff for a 'three line whipped' Group meeting on the 14th December. That finished, and lunch off the menu, I dashed to our second Audit pre-Committee briefing. These briefings proved invaluable, allowing queries to be ironed-out and to ensure we worked as a team when witnesses came before us. The Committee was scheduled for the 16th December, the last day of the autumn term.

I had not planned to be 'Madam Nasty' but it soon became clear that some Committee members just lacked the will, guile or confidence to engage professionals with a series of probing, 'on the spot' questions, required to elicit facts and not be fobbed off by meandering replies. I'd spent too much time in my former profession, either in the CID or force recruitment and promotion boards, to be overawed by high-powered waffle. This was the one Assembly committee with the power to scrutinise officials and their mistakes; I would do my bit for the public who paid me. Welsh Conservative Alun Cairns shared my desire for accountability and although frequently abrasive, he too had the intelligence and poise to push witnesses hard. He proudly wore an ostentatious silver '$£$' brooch on his lapel, his banker trademark, and was always well prepared; he took no prisoners either.

Despite his small stature, I found him an attractive man with his black glistening hair, distinctive check shirts and elegant cuff links protruding from well-cut suits. Despite our different age, size and political ethos, we liked each other and formed an unwritten alliance to prise out the truth. We soon received feedback that we were the 'ones to watch out for'.

Before our 'Further Education Funding' meeting on the 16th December, we had one more plenary to endure. At this stage in the term, I was flagging badly as the autumn session was always the longest and most arduous; not helped as nights closed in, and journeys made more irksome because they were done in darkness. The final task was to take evidence from the witnesses in the cosy but costly world of 'Further Education in Wales'. Professor Andrews received scant festive goodwill as we pressed hard for answers. The Further Education Funding head, Professor Andrews, adopted a seemingly unshakeable complacency until I began to press him. Clearly he observed his Quango's performance through rose tinted specs. He perceived the 'few little glitches' unearthed by the review as not really much to worry about in the general order of things. Sir John, the Auditor General, did not share the Prof's cosy perceptions. His report indicated that vast sums of public money thrown at certain colleges was just not acceptable and things must change. Later my diary noted, 'The complacency of both men is quite incredible! (Jon Shortridge and Prof. Andrews)' and 'managed to get a mild sweat off the professor.' Not the most eloquent of diary entries, but true, as he and I had locked horns during the session. He seemed prevaricating and dismissive over a crucial issue and was not used to being challenged. The Auditor General had reported that the administration needed improvement and, thus, I won the bout and felt justified in pressing him hard. There seemed little point in accepting that the Audit Committee would play a significant role by keeping tabs on official wastage of 'our' money, and the Auditor General's work had to be paid for and not call allegedly failing Quango 'Chiefs' to account. Taking the task of saving taxpayers' money very seriously, I would continue to be tough even if eminent Quango supremos were 'roughed up a little'.

Back in Delyn, the run-up to Christmas was filled with surgeries, office duties and offering sympathy to my staff because the Assembly computers and printers still performed badly. Someone had definitely been bounced into equipment that was not 'fit for purpose'. The 20th December was Millennium Tree Planting Day at County Hall. Barry Jones was first on the ceremonial spade and ignored me again. I assumed shovelling soil required keen concentration. Of course, I should have understood his extreme fury at my challenging letters. I disliked the scrabble for publicity, dreaming up stunts to obtain a mention in the local press and the torrid press releases on any subject likely to catch the editor's eye. Hypocritically, as an AM, I unashamedly courted the camera with the real pros like Barry, accepting that people who paid my wages wanted proof that I was working for them. I worked for them almost up to Christmas Day. Knocking off the 22-mile round trip from home to Delyn office was 'easy-peasy' compared with the stressful and debilitating trips to the capital and back. My contempt for our wretched IT system moved up a gear when I returned to Delyn after the Christmas break, only to find that dreaded computer refused to allow me to log on. More precious time and money lost waiting for the engineer to arrive. The excuse of 'user error' had worn very thin.

I found time to observe a gorgeously full moon, which on the 23rd December was the closest to Earth since 1932. My heaven and moon watching came to an abrupt end when heavy rain suddenly burst from a cloudless sky. I attended Midnight Mass at Pantasaph, the Capuchin Friary on my 'patch'. I wanted to thank God for his help during my first months and to remind him that I needed such assistance for three more years. The Christmas recess ended on the 17th January, and, re-invigorated, I threw myself back into work in Cardiff. On the 20th January 2000 Jane Hutt received a delegation from Delyn, who demanded answers from the Health Minister over a 27 year delay to build a hospital for Holywell. The delegation, including Cllr Karin Davies and Alun Williams, the Town Mayor, brusquely demanded action. Under pressure, Jane promised early help whilst the official frowned deeply and shuffled his papers. The Group were delighted with the meeting and we rapidly cobbled together a press release before they dashed off to catch the train to Flint. I guessed that Jane had overstretched herself and her ministerial promise might not materialise, but, facing such joy from my visitors, I kept my fears to myself. The following week I basked in the praise heaped on me, courtesy of the *Chester Chronicle* over the Minister's promise. At the meeting, I guessed Jane's official would not have been so forthright with early promises to build the new hospital but kept quiet, so as not to dampen the happy perceptions my mates took back to Holywell. I was right. As I write this in September 2006, the first brick of the hospital – promised faithfully on ministerial oath – still has not been laid.

Waving the party goodbye, I galloped to a lunchtime meeting to review the latest plans for the new Welsh Assembly debating chamber. Despite the escalating cost, this project would certainly be built once 'little defects' like the statutory duty to provide disability access were rightly resolved. How wheelchair users would climb the steps of the plinth was still a mystery and, even with so many women AMs, the promised crèche was still not guaranteed!

On the 2nd February before plenary, whilst staring at the 'mock-up' model of the Assembly building situated in the Milling Area, I noticed Roy Hattersley in earnest conversation with Ron Davies. We had met in Manchester at a Literary Lunch with various literary luminaries, all keen to flog books we had written. Before the meal we each had to describe our masterpiece, and hope that punters purchased it. It was a sufficient ordeal competing with Roy Hattersley's witty urbanity as I described the contents of the book, but I suffered further as I lurked behind my huge pile of *No way up the Greasy Pole*, praying someone would buy one. I did a brisk trade and cheerfully waved Roy farewell after my table was depleted. Rudely, I barged up to Roy who rose and smiled as I blurted out our tenuous connection. 'I remember it well', he replied gallantly, 'and also that your pile was reducing faster than mine!' I simpered with delight and beetled into to plenary, leaving my researcher impressed with the company I kept.

Alun Michael faced another rocky ride from the Opposition over his handling of Objective One funding at a plenary on the 8th February. Plaid Cymru leader Dafydd Wigley tabled another 'no confidence' vote. Ron, who had not helped the Party's jittery mood by calling for increased powers for the Assembly, was critical of how Labour was coping with governing Wales. The Group had issued a statement on the 25th January confirming our unswerving support for Alun. To move the spotlight from Alun, a major policy paper,

'A Better Wales', setting out an action plan for Wales, was launched. It proved insufficient to quieten the barking of the Opposition dogs. Desperate to hang on to power, rumours abounded that Alun had tried to woo Mike German, the Lib Dem leader, into coalition. The cooling wine in Alun's penthouse office was waiting to be uncorked if Mike made a pact. The bottle remained untouched. Mike German allegedly failed to show up, thus leaving Alun not only to his drink alone, but to pray to Chancellor Gordon Brown to save him by announcing Westminster matched funding. Gordon, refusing to submit to perceived blackmail, refused to deliver. Westminster turned its collective back on the Prime Minister's hapless choice of First Secretary in a newly devolved Wales. The countdown to vital 9th February Plenary began.

I gatecrashed the 12.45pm meeting of the Group Executive Committee as I recognised a power struggle when I saw one, and was curious to watch events unfold. My appearance did nothing to soothe the tense and nervous mood of the committee members, who were desperate to resolve the looming crisis: namely that Alun could lose the no confidence vote. With a 'worst case scenario' in mind, the Executive planned to hold another meeting at 7.00pm, ready to brief the media on the Group's views. Christine Chapman confessed to being shocked by the 'vicious briefings within the Group of member against member.' This was news to me as I was not an Executive member, but her remarks indicated that the Labour Group was in turmoil. The meeting ended and the only clear decisions reached were to exclude the political special advisers who usually sat at the back, and to hold a secret ballot on Alun's future at the 4.30pm Group meeting after the plenary result was known. 'To hold the line should things go wrong for Alun,' was the Executive's message! As Val Feld explained later that afternoon, 'Politics is dirty and 'old Labour' fights in a particularly dirty way', confirming that Rhodri supporters were locked into a battle to the death with Alun's team. How naive I was to think that only the Opposition wanted to oust our First Secretary.

Grim faced, Alun arrived in the Milling area with Lorraine Barrett beside him at 2.17pm, and had to plough through the media scrum as he strode to reach the opaque glass doors. Peter Law, standing at the podium, was ploughing doggedly through oral questions, and at 2.19pm the Presiding Officer terminated his ordeal. Once Alun sat down, the circus performance started in earnest, with all three Opposition leaders taking turns at the podium to savage Alun. Nick Bourne (having assumed the Welsh Conservative leadership from Rod 'Rottweiler' Richards in August 1999) and Mike German were eloquent, and, in his opening remarks, Mike seemed to support Alun. Had that wine been drunk after all and a partnership sealed? Suddenly, Mike started reciting Alun's lack of achievements as the Lib Dems began throwing him to the wolves. This was all so unfair. The late night emails I had occasionally received from Alun indicated he was a hard worker and astute. It was not Alun's fault that he had been unable to conjure up the matched funding needed to release the European Objective One money. The rules had been tightened after the Irish had made such carefree and spectacular headway with European funding! The three leaders' brutal remarks took my breath away. Why would any sane person want a career in politics?

Alun took the podium at 2.57pm, and soon an edge came into his voice as he battled to control his emotions. 'Phone a friend', yelled Rod Richards, raising guffaws of laughter from the Tory ranks. Suddenly, Alun had an envelope in his hand. He threw it angrily across the Presiding Officer's desk where it lay untouched. His voice breaking, Alun announced that he was resigning for the good of the party. He carried on for what seemed two more minutes, and then utter confusion broke out. Lorraine Barrett looked white and was standing and shouting. Alun Pugh was jumping around in his back row seat babbling and shouting too. Sitting next to me, even the normally quiet Chris Chapman was making her opinion heard. Ignoring the rumpus, the Presiding Officer called us to vote on the censure motion and the warning lights on our consoles flashed urgently. Pause too long, the vote would close and one of the three buttons – 'for', 'against' or 'abstain' – wouldn't activate. Without hesitation, I thumped the middle button – 'abstain'. What else should I do – the man had just resigned. Whatever the result surely the vote was null and void? Our collective voting flashed on the overhead monitors: 31 for the motion, 27 against. I was the only abstention, and a 'no confidence' vote was carried. I walked out of the chamber leaving the stunned Labour Group wondering what had hit them. The media ruckus was at full frenzy in the Milling Area. Eleanor Goodman of Channel Four News pounced on me, asking why I'd abstained. A microphone was thrust in my face. 'Are you happy with the result?' My researcher, hovering close to my elbow, turned very red when I told Eleanor that I would not be supporting Alun again. Uncompromising and disloyal I know, but we must move on and Alun was now damaged goods.

I wandered up into Group Office on the third floor, not territory I often visited. Ann Jones and Jane Davidson were in close discussion with the Party apparatchiks. Ann was vigorously declaring her intention to table a motion censuring the Presiding Officer. Thinking this a silly idea born in the heat of the moment, I casually suggested that the decision should be made by the Labour Group. I could not see that 'Lord El' had erred in calling a vote. The Group, including Lorraine Barrett, had been caught out by the resignation but the Presiding Officer still had to bring the debate to a close. With Ann Jones in the chair looking tearful, the Group was back in Conference Room C at 4.30pm. Lorraine was beside herself with rage, the rest looked sullen and confused. When it became clear we were expected to declare for or against Alun in Paul Murphy's presence I felt uneasy. He was the Secretary of State for Wales, with huge political sway and had I been politically ambitious, I certainly would not have wanted to declare my position in front of Paul. I just wanted people to be able speak freely without being inhibited. I asked Ann whether Group should determine if Paul should stay. Wearily she told me to shut up, and John Marek next to me whispered that I should accept her advice. Apart from suggesting that Alun needed some water as he struggled to keep back tears, I said no more during the 90 minutes it took to decide very little.

Alun's supporters were angry and accusatory; Huw Lewis accused us all of stabbing Alun in the back! Val Feld protested mildly at his unfair comment. As the meeting broke up, John Marek and I were unclear as to whether Alun's resignation still stood or not! The Members' Tea Room beckoned and, entering it, the tense mood of Committee Room C suddenly lightened. Sue Essex, Carwyn Jones, Jane Davidson, Brian Gibbons and John Griffiths were all chattering, looking pleased. Carwyn suggested cracking open champagne and, to my delight, Jane Davidson asked me to join the revellers for a meal. The penny dropped – Alun was not coming back as leader and Rhodri supporters had started celebrating. Had that angry and inconclusive meeting, chaired by a tearful Ann Jones, not achieved what I now assumed Alun wanted? Was his public resignation captured on TV just a sham? Had he hoped that the Labour Group would save face and rally behind him even if he lost the confidence vote? If anyone had asked Alun to stand again in that chaotic, tension-charged meeting, I suspect Alun would have grabbed the offer, knowing the Opposition could not re-group against him yet again for a while. Rhodri Morgan quietly assumed the mantle of 'leader in waiting' officially later that evening. Alun's cronies resigned en masse and a new chapter in Welsh politics began.

Most of the newspapers focused on my abstention. *The Times* gave my decision far more space than it deserved. I felt that a round robin email to my Group colleagues would give me a chance to clear the air. My message to Group at 3.20pm on the 10th February explained that I'd abstained because it seemed only logical, having tried to raise a Point of Order with the Presiding Officer seeking clarification. Lorraine replied by email at 3.57pm. 'We all realised why you abstained, and the Presiding Officer was out of order for not adjourning proceedings to allow everyone to decide what to do.' Having since watched the video of events, she thought the Presiding

Officer was out of his depth. During several critical interviews that day, she'd informed me that she had faxed him suggesting that he needed to decide where his loyalties lay: impartial Presiding Officer, or a vote carrying Plaid Cymru Member. 'He won't like it, but I don't care, it's helping me get through the day,' she admitted candidly. Despite his ordeal, Alun found time at 7.49pm to email me his thanks for making my position clear. 'It was absolutely obvious what you were asking for through your attempted Point of Order and it deserved an answer. As I recall, you said very loudly 'In this case it doesn't make sense so I'll have to abstain'. The rest of us voted against because it was the default guidance, but also because a motion which doesn't make sense, should be opposed, but I certainly don't think your motives were in any doubt whatsoever. I have had a couple of calls on this point and said as much.' I could only admire his cool-headed ability to take in such detail of what was going on around him in that maelstrom of noise and confusion. I couldn't fathom his logic. If he'd lost the vote, why not throw down his resignation letter then, rather than before the vote? Had he gambled that by causing such confusion, the Presiding Officer would not proceed to a vote? He would have been spared the agony of losing and, back in the Group, he could be re-elected, making it difficult for the Opposition to run the ploy again. Had his master plan to survive backfired badly?

The Bay, the Barrage and burgeoning Budgets.

'I am disgraced, impeached and baffled here, Pierced to the soul with slander's venom spear.'
Shakespeare: Richard II act i. 1

My move into the Assembly meant that I was now a small part of the Government, a fact not lost on Robin Makin, my lawyer, who was pressing me to meet the new Home Secretary, Jack Straw. Robin is a dedicated, liberal lawyer who excelled with high profile cases and had won my phone-tapping case for me. He had a long legal agenda created by these complex cases, and needed the weight of the Home Secretary to resolve several issues. As both Robin and I had failed miserably to be granted this meeting, I reluctantly asked MP for Alyn and Deeside Barry Jones for help. Barry arranged it without quibble and fortunately the appointment was scheduled for the 10th February 2000 and narrowly missed Plaid Cymru's 'no confidence' vote in first Minister Alun Michael, which I would have been obliged to attend. Robin was concerned that I had never been awarded the Queen's Police Medal, despite my outstanding career as the first woman to reach the top as an Assistant Chief Constable, and wanted to redress the injustice!

The story begins in 1990 when I was forced to start my discrimination action against the then Home Secretary Kenneth Baker in 1990. Jim Sharples, the Chief Constable of Merseyside, announced that 'it would be vigorously defended.' And how! I discovered the defence was truly vigorous! Delay was the first tactic, followed up by brutal and unethical behaviour with nothing spared to discredit me or to do whatever was necessary to ensure that I lost my equality battle. Official police files were doctored, agenda sheets removed or tampered with: the objective being to diminish my case. If that was not enough, my phones were tapped (I believe both home and office), courtesy of the force's Special Branch, presided over by non other than by the Chief Constable James Sharples. Perversion of the course of justice is a criminal offence, and I was not surprised when the Home Office threw in the towel and sought an urgent settlement only when I had finished giving my evidence and it was my detractors' turn to reply. I concluded that the risk of allowing Jim Sharples, and other senior officers, to give evidence against me was too great. Their defence was based mostly on a tissue of lies, leaving David Henshaw (the Merseyside Police Authority Clerk/Chief Executive of Knowsley) to inform the public of my latest demeanours with regular monotony – courtesy of the local evening news programme. I happily gave my evidence for 24 days, but, of course, I was speaking the truth, a concept not well understood by my detractors. Some three years later the Home Secretary of the day, Michael Howard, awarded my phone-tapping detractor a knighthood: the reward to Jim Sharples for services to discrimination. Robin believed that his knighthood should be rescinded, but as his officials refused, this was another item on his agenda with Jack Straw.

The advantage of listening into private calls to my lawyer and to the Equal Opportunities Commission would have been enormous. Once the case was settled, Edwin Glasgow, a Treasury Barrister who acted for the Home Office, hinted that I should continue with my wish to take my 'bugging' complaint to the European Court of Human Rights. The Home Office admitted the strong possibility that my office in police HQ had been tapped, but were less willing to admit my home phone had been intercepted too. In June 1997, the Strasbourg judges found for me and had harsh words to say about Jim Sharples's contemptible behaviour.

On the day of the fateful meeting with Jack Straw, Robin bustled into the House of Commons' main foyer, plonked himself on my bench and we started shuffling wads of papers into bundles in preparation for the great event. We had barely finished when the imposing figure of Barry strode across the flag-stoned floor.

He looked through me as if I was not there, but greeted Robin with much warmth and bonhomie. Under orders from Robin to 'do nothing to antagonise Barry,' I meekly fell into step several feet behind the two men. Arriving outside the office, I realised that I could offer Jack Straw first hand information on the shock resignation of Alun Michael, Wales's First Secretary. As we waited, I regaled Jack's PA with the previous day's drama. Alistair Campbell and Margaret Beckett, the then Leader of the House of Commons, drifted by, deep in conversation. Alistair Campbell had a hard, almost mean looking face and even from this fleeting encounter, I assessed him as a man who took no prisoners. Barry stiffened immediately and his body language indicated he was no friend of Tony Blair's highly controversial spin doctor.

Margaret Beckett and I were both ex-pupils of the convent of Notre Dame in Norwich. She had become Head Girl some years after I left. Our school experiences were totally contrasting; I was always in hot water for minor demeanours such as eating lollipops in the street, or spraying water at teachers from a joke flower on my lapel. To have achieved the accolade of Head Girl, Margaret's behaviour must have been faultless. The nuns and lay teaching staff liked me and realised I had some potential, despite my many escapades. They would have been so proud of me had they envisaged that I would welcome Margaret Beckett to my Welsh Assembly constituency when she visited Mostyn Dock months later.

With Jack's PA hanging on every word of Alun's demise, I stopped in full flow as Jack Straw – jacketless and in braces – bounced out of his office and invited us in. I hung back, waiting to be told where to sit. Barry positioned himself next to Jack who took the chair at the head of the table. Jack opened with my discrimination case and announced that if Labour had been in power, the Home Office would not have defended the phone-tapping action. He felt that Sharples had behaved outrageously, but that was all water under the bridge. I meekly mentioned that I had done nothing wrong. I was not touting for one, but I also said I had never been awarded the Queen's Police Medal, the medal invariably awarded to senior officers in normal circumstances. I explained that I was commenting on the merits and weaknesses of the reward system. He nodded but did not reply. I was surprised that the chemistry between us was good. He called me Alison; his eye contact was sustained and he seemed genuinely friendly, a situation far removed from Barry's warning that the Home Secretary did not like me. Robin launched into his agenda, and was not fazed even when the Minister forcefully attempted to challenge Robin's various arguments. A mini-battle developed with both lawyers refusing to give way. Barry sat ramrod straight, rocking in his seat listening intently and banging his fist on the table every time Jack Straw scored a point. The banging and swaying increased as both men vigorously argued their case. I found Barry's gyrations most off-putting, and was amazed that the protagonists could keep their minds on the argument faced with this distraction. From the back row an official called time, and we were just shaking hands when I asked about the paucity of police gender balance statistics. Jack Straw looked surprised but I barged on by complaining they were being withheld by a senior official, despite numerous attempts to obtain them. I said that unless the true cost of sexual harassment, discriminations, civil actions and the ensuing medical retirements were exposed, forces would never learn to improve personnel management issues. Barry preened when I mentioned that he had asked for data in the House on my behalf years earlier, only to be told that the cost of producing them would be 'excessive'. And this is from a Government that spends £758 million on the Millennium Dome! As the Home Office called regularly for detailed statistics from Force Personnel Departments, and as Her Majesty's Inspectors of Constabulary inspected each force annually, such figures should have been routinely available. 'Have a look into it Steve,' said Jack Straw to his official, and the door closed behind us.

As things had gone so well, I had refrained from mentioning that valuable Equal Opportunities Commission case papers, collected over the years, had been sent to Bramshill – the Police Staff College – to start a Gender Balance Data Base, (all the information I had been assiduously pursuing for months with the Home Office without success), but Bramshill had inexplicably managed to somehow lose the lot! Barry strode back the way we had come, then hesitated as if coming to some decision. Barry's manner towards me had been affable in the Home Secretary's lair, but cooled when we left. Suddenly, he turned to Robin and offered tea. He stalked into a room stuffed full of chintz chairs and low tables, with waiters in formal uniform weaving about holding trays of cakes and teapots. We waited for service, and rather than risk antagonising Barry again, I mooched to the window and gazed at the London Eye across the river. Barry offered us cake to accompany the tea.

Amidst chattering and bustling, Robin did his best to make small talk to Barry. Suddenly, the MP sat bolt upright and, recorded later, hissed at me furiously that, 'His wife was going to skin me alive because I had made her angry, but he was not angry and I had seen nothing yet.' His voice rose and I thought he would have a seizure as his pent-up fury erupted. 'He was going to skin me too and I had not seen him angry – yet'. Faced with this unexpected outburst in such a public place, my police training kicked in. This was not the time to retaliate. This was the time to get things under control and try to get things back to normal. People began to turn round in our direction. I muttered quietly that there was no need to raise his voice, and I was sorry if I had offended him.

Robin continued munching on his cake ignoring the drama enacted over the teacups. Barry demanded that I write a letter apologising to his wife, and suddenly he was back in control as if nothing untoward had happened. I was shaken when I realised that somehow I had badly upset Janet and that Barry had just defended her. Back in his stride, Barry courteously introduced me to a Lord who had meandered up to speak to him. I offered to pay for tea but Barry waved this away. We followed him briskly out to the main entrance where he bowed and vanished, leaving me in mild shock.

Robin was still elated with the meeting with the Home Secretary and I apologised to him for Barry's outburst. Still unfazed, he thought it important that Barry had got his rage out of his system. 'I've spent a lot of time with mad people,' he confessed. Of course he was referring to his client, Ian Brady, judged criminally insane, whom Robin had visited regularly in his high security mental hospital. 'You must write that letter to Janet', he said earnestly, 'do it soon and get the right note.' I promised I would and I left to travel back to Cardiff.

On the train, I reflected on what I had done to offend Janet Jones, a tall, rather remote woman with whom I had minimal contact. Our closest encounter had been at a Branch meeting when Barry was up for re-selection. I had offered her something to drink as I was heading for the bar. She had declined coolly. Apart from the tearoom interlude it had been a good day, and we had achieved the goal of meeting the Home Secretary. Barry had brought that about and we were grateful. Returning to Delyn at the weekend, I wrote a humble letter of apology for my perceived discourtesy towards Janet! I hoped that it would draw a line under my poor relationship with Barry.

Unable to get back to North Wales for the North Wales Regional Committee the following day, I bounced into Crickhowell House and found Mark, my researcher, beavering away on an article for *The Independent* newspaper, who wanted an inside view of the Alun Michael resignation fiasco. I added a few tweaks and finished by admitting I would be retiring from Assembly life after the first four years. In my naivety, I thought I had already explained this to my party colleagues. When the article was published, the revelation shook my Delyn colleagues who saw it as some sort of betrayal of their vote for me. I had not seen it that way, and I had to work hard to persuade colleagues that I was not being disloyal, nor would I stop working hard for them until my term ended. On the contrary, setting myself a timescale ensured I was still young and fit enough to give them my best shot and I was determined that when I did hang up my political boots, I would be a very hard act to follow.

Experienced with heading up important departments in police forces, I enjoyed introducing systems and procedures that were effective and efficient. I saw the new Assembly as a fresh piece of paper upon which to lay down a template offering a fair, balanced and ethical set of rules, that would ensure this important institution got off on the right footing and would succeed. Knowing that I was immune from Party politics or petty loyalties, I thought I could make a genuine contribution as to how the Assembly would conduct itself as it developed. I just recognised that the first four years would be really the only time that proper rules of engagement could be fashioned.

Despite encountering snow on the Brecon Beacons, I made good time on the journey to Cardiff the following Monday, which happened to be Valentine's Day. It was an opportune time for the Party to express love for a new leader. It was going to be a memorable week with the new leader walking onto the Assembly stage but on Monday Rhodri Morgan still had hurdles to clear, ending with a packed meeting in Transport House (Welsh Labour HQ), where anyone who was anyone squeezed into the conference room to vote. He came through the selection by AMs and the Welsh Labour Party with flying colours. Looking relaxed and confident, Rhodri started well by pledging his support for Tony Blair, a shrewd political gesture to bury the hatchet over Tony's gaffe in denying Rhodri his rightful throne. The press also reported that the new First Secretary had not ruled out 'a coalition' to establish political stability.

On the 15th February the Group met as usual, though with several absences including Huw Lewis AM for Merthyr and his wife, Lynne Neagle, AM for Torfaen. Huw had been part of the mass Whip's resignation on the 11th February, that had included Janice Gregory AM for Ogmore and Lorraine Barrett AM for Cardiff South. Having backed Alun to the hilt, they knew they could be banished to the backbenches for good. Having lost Alun's patronage, their fledgling political careers and the chance to climb that 'greasy political pole' in the Assembly had all but vanished too. Alun Michael, now just an AM, ignored the top table chairs and slotted in amongst the Group as if nothing had happened. The transition was smooth. Rhodri took over briefings and gave us his First Secretary's report just as Alun had done. The transition of power within the Group was far less dramatic than on the floor of the chamber.

The first act was to replace Lorraine who had stepped down as Chief Whip, by telling us that as Alun's appointee it was right that she should go. Andrew Davies took the post in addition to his job of Business Manager, which involved deciding what AMs debated on the chamber floor. The post of Whip is given to favoured and trusted allies. Not steeped from the cradle in Labour folklore, I thought it was rather a boring and antiquated role that could easily have been dispensed with. Karen Sinclair, AM for \ South, clearly held an opposing view because she was like a cat with the cream when Rhodri made her deputy Whip. It was a shrewd move, as it enabled Rhodri to claim that he was supporting North Wales by empowering one of its AMs. Soon she was flexing this imprecise instrument of control – and usually in my direction.

The decision to fill the vacancy for a chair for Local Government Committee was long overdue. Yet again, I was flattered when several Labour members nominated me and it seemed the chair was there for the taking. My researcher and I were surprised when, quite suddenly, the vote was postponed and another nominee, Gwenda Thomas, AM for Neath, was allowed to enter her name although the official closing date had passed. Gwenda won by a narrow margin and my backers muttered ruefully. Another small internal Labour coup had taken place, the rules having been subtly changed to belatedly widen the field. I just shrugged and shook off the snub. My previous experience would have enabled me to do the job, but although being disappointed, the extra work would have been tricky to handle. Nevertheless, the rebuff was real enough, but the vote showed that at least some of the Labour Group rated me. Val Feld's frustration showed as Andrew's star was still very much in the ascendancy under the new leader. The Swansea East AM muttered, 'He's never had a proper job,' when I popped into her office to discuss events. I agreed that he had never inspired confidence in me and, having watched him in Group, he seemed to lack the nous to foresee pending political pitfalls. However, he was always courteous, very willing to please and never raised his voice. As Chief Whip, he also seemed to lack any real drive or toughness to make people tremble, but then again, neither had Lorraine Barrett!

Since I had openly refused to support Alun after my abstention, I dropped into Lorraine's office to make my peace, as her loyalty to Alun was unswerving. My olive branch was firmly rejected, as she was still angry and upset about Alun's treatment. I felt doubly guilty as she had paid a handsome sum for my book *No Way up the Greasy Pole* when the Presiding Officer, Lord Dafydd Elis-Thomas, had held a charity auction before plenary some days earlier. We were encouraged to offer something for auction and buy something in return. I had purchased Lorraine's signed video of Max Boyce's rugby songs and, in turn, she seemed genuinely pleased to outbid others and leave with a signed copy of my offering. Christine Gwyther's vegetarian cookbook created the greatest interest. Female and vegetarian, the First Welsh Assembly Secretary for Agriculture ensured that the bidding was brisk, with the Presiding Officer giving a very passable display as an auctioneer. He raised the bidding to one hundred pounds and the hammer fell, giving Mick Bates, a farmer and Liberal AM for Montgomeryshire, the trophy. These moments of uniting, even for a good cause, were all too fleeting. Yet this is what the Assembly had promised to deliver: less 'Ya-Boo' politics of the Westminster style and more courtesy and respect for each other. From the outset, Lord 'Dafydd El' tried hard to set the proper standard of courtesy between AMs, and he impatiently refused to accept that 'first past the post' constituency members were superior to perceived 'lower class list' members!

The Audit Committee met on the 17th February 2000: the first of the ten sessions scheduled for our second year. We were to examine why an irregular payment had been made to a National Museums and Galleries of Wales (NMGW) employee who left his

employment in dubious circumstances, with a hefty settlement of
which the Auditor General Sir John Bourn strongly disapproved.
Jon Shortridge shared the 'hot seat' with Anna Southall, the then
Museum Director who had succeeded Colin Ford, holder of the
purse strings when the payment occurred. The Assembly had
inherited responsibility for the Museum of Wales as one of its
Assembly Sponsored Bodies. Unlike a Quango, it has a Royal
Charter, but whatever its fancy status it is a public spending body
which the Assembly had empowered the Auditor General to
scrutinise.

We had to decide whether an Assistant Director responsible for
finance and personnel, accused of mismanagement by other
Museum staff, had been 'bought off' and the matter hushed up by
senior managers, rather than investigating the complaints. Tim
Arnold had signed a 'compromise agreement', thus waiving his
rights to any claim he might have against the Museum in return for a
'£31,470 pay-off plus £1,450 legal costs and an agreed Employer's
Reference.' This financial improbity went unnoticed until
discovered by a routine audit. Ms Southall's attempt to obtain
retrospective permission to pay Arnold was refused by the Welsh Office.

Matters deteriorated further when the AG reported that Mr
Ford, the outgoing Director, had failed to follow the Museum's own
prescribed standard 'discipline procedure' and although the
mismanagement was considered serious enough to merit discipline,
the allegations against Tim Arnold were not drawn to his attention.
The AG was extremely concerned that a public body had taken the
easy way out, by ignoring the discipline route and paying Arnold off
after a negotiated departure settlement with him, rather than hold a
full investigation. To add insult to injury, Tim Arnold left with a
glowing reference with no mention of his reason for departure.

Summarising the AG's findings: a huge sum of public money had
been squandered by inept managers who ignored museum discipline
policy by allowing an employee accused of serious mismanagement
to leave with a glowing reference, and then took refuge behind a

'confidentially clause'. Sir John Bourn decreed that a covert settlement was not appropriate for the public sector and must not happen again with public money at stake. Armed with the AG's probing set of questions, the Committee began to press the Museum's senior people and neither Anna Southall nor Colin Ford enjoyed the experience one little bit. Anna Southall had been promoted to Museum Director on the 1st November 1998 but had previously worked as an Assistant Director, so we assumed she should have known what was going on. Colin Ford was even more defensive over his role in the affair. Frustrated by his vagueness, I challenged his knowledge of discipline and personnel procedures. Having run a police Personnel Department I knew something about this area, and to be fobbed off was annoying. He was losing ground fast under my interrogation and his waffling and hedging, rather than admitting a mistake, was frustrating. All Audit Committee sessions were televised and the public was admitted to watch events. Grudgingly, he gave ground. Our professional duel on museum personnel procedures lasted only a few moments and the committee moved on to the next area of concern. Later, I was appalled to discover that the clip of me in 'Perry Mason' mode had been sent to the Civil Servant Training College as a learning aid for would-be aspirants to the Audit Committee 'hot seat'. It was held up as an example of what witnesses could expect when interviewed by the Audit Committee. No royalties for my bravura performance ever materialised.

On the 16th March Alun Michael announced that he would be quitting the Assembly and taking up where he left off as an MP in Westminster on the 1st May. His constituency party had cannily failed to select his successor, so the way was clear to resume representing Penarth and Cardiff South. His career as an AM had lasted less than a year. During plenary on the 23rd March 2000, Rhodri Morgan dropped the bombshell that he was postponing plans to build the new Assembly debating chamber. Worried about the escalating cost, he wanted to make sure that the project was going to be value for money. He ran into stiff opposition from the blessed

Lorraine and Alun Michael who were both very cross. Rhodri Glyn Thomas, Plaid AM for Carmarthen East and Dinefwr, accused Rhodri of indecision. After Alun and Lorraine had chided the new First Secretary for stalling, I took delight in praising Rhodri for exploring cash-saving options. I knew that as my constituents would have to share the cost of this latest Cardiff asset, delay could be justified. I had always believed that Wales deserved its own purpose-built Assembly, but not at any price. Lorraine glared at me across the chamber. Rhodri won the debate that would allow the exploration of various options including construction of a smaller debating chamber, disparagingly christened 'the Colander', to be sited in the car park behind Crickhowell House. The fate of displaced cars was not mentioned!

Back in North Wales, Chirk Castle, the magnificent fourteenth century fortress on the Welsh Marches, got its promised visit from me on the 28th March, and the roof indeed contained tons of lead. Although the Audit Committee report into our built heritage was not finalised, I got a particularly warm welcome from the local AM, Karen Sinclair, on a chilly day. She was delighted when I confided that I felt the castle should keep much of its grant. This was the last time we seemed to agree with each other. The Labour Group meeting held on the 29th March was even more poorly attended than usual, and Andrew Davies in bossy 'Chief Whip mode' complained that 'we were all missing'. Karen was now arrayed amongst the bosses on the top table alongside Andrew, Rhodri and Mike Penn, our Group Secretary. Rhodri's alternative building was up for discussion by the Group and Alun Michael and I clashed. Since losing the leadership, Alun had become quite aggressive and bullying.

Far less controversial was the Group discussion on the pending appointment of the new Assembly Standards supremo, an official responsible for advising the Presiding Officer on complaints made against Members. The only real contender, after a seemingly rigorous selection process, was a retired Local Authority Chief Executive.

I knew Richard Penn, who had moved from his Chief Executive's post in Knowsley, a deprived high crime Merseyside borough, to the post of Chief Executive again in Bradford. I felt uneasy that he left his last post with a medical retirement pension: usually the most lucrative means of leaving employment, and a popular means of escape from pending trouble in the police service. I assumed that Richard's pension would have been substantial. I shared my concerns with the Group that the proposed holder of this prestigious appointment had left a top job with a well enhanced medical pension that the citizens of Bradford were paying for. Was he fit to hold this new post? I felt that as the Assembly Standards supremo, his standards must be impeccable and must also be 'squeaky clean' in every regard. No-one was interested in my remarks apart from Val Feld. Later over tea she agreed with my logic, but as the Labour Group had already nodded through the appointment, it was all rather too late. 'By the way', she mused, 'why don't you take up a good cause, whilst you are here?' I grinned and nodded but volunteered nothing, knowing that I was already more than occupied – any more good causes would have to wait.

As if the day had not been testing enough, Rod Richards rolled into plenary reeking of ale. As usual, he stayed a short time and then left. He was not coping well with the delay before his assault trial began and I assessed that Rod needed help. I sneaked a complaint to the Presiding Officer on my touch screen, citing my concern for Rod's welfare, and an invitation to the PO's office after plenary followed. I bowled into his spacious lair and the PO offered me a drink. Thinking this was not appropriate under the circumstances, I politely declined and both the PO and Mark McGuire, his PA, kicked the sensitive problem around.

The PO felt that for his own good, Rod had to keep himself together for his trial and advice would be offered. I felt relieved and less of a sneak as a jury would surely deal harshly with a defendant who could not stand up after lunch. A few days later, I was phoned by a journalist who had got wind of my problem with Rod, and he pressed me for further details. I refused to comment, as sitting in judgement can often come back and bite the righteous! The journalist declined to name his source! I had no idea who informed the press, but upon reflection, their interest would surely have concentrated his mind on curbing his intake even better than advice from a kindred spirit.

Against this background of political shenanigans, Assembly bureaucracy droned on. My mileage claims for travelling from North Wales to Cardiff were still being rejected. It was not my fault the Assembly was at the other end of the country, and yet I was being penalised. My weekly 400-mile round trip was a huge drain. In frustration, I wrote for the third time to the Assembly Clerk explaining I could ill afford the time needed to work out what she required. The reply from Fees Office was, 'You should have got consent for the trip in advance and then have submitted Wrexham mileage on another form as it's not in your constituency.' The nature of the job was such that obtaining consent for a journey from an official in Cardiff in advance of the journey was just unworkable. Such stupidity appalled me! 'Did the Presiding Officer give himself consent to travel anywhere in advance?' I asked. Why could Peter Rogers, a North Wales list member travel from Anglesey to Wrexham, and within all of North Wales not have to complete separate forms or seek consent to travel in advance? Why then was *I* being so confined? The Presiding Officer had made it very clear in plenary on the 20th January 2000 that he considered all members, whether 'list' or 'constituency', equal. Was I being penalised by having to obtain travel consent in advance, and then fiddle around with different claim forms to recoup genuine mileage?

Under the Clerk's silly rules, I could not claim for a yard outside my constituency boundary without clearance from the Presiding Officer's staff, preferably before the journey. The rules were deeply unfair to constituency AMs and gave me more work. I asked deputy Presiding Officer Jane Davidson for help, but she seemed unwilling to understand my problem. I wrote to Jane complaining that the 'case law' approach, whereby civil servants uncertain of the way forward tested everything, was a crude means of making policy and presented an unfair burden on constituency AMs. She then invited me to her sumptuous office and coyly announced that having consulted the Auditor General, the rules were to be rewritten. The 'travel in advance consent stipulation' was to be shelved and 'list' and 'constituency'AMs would now be treated equally. I felt quite chuffed having won a small victory for common sense.

Meanwhile, Rhodri Morgan was not having an easy ride as leader. His failure to look again at his refusal to give Aerospace in Broughton the £25 million badly needed to secure 1,400 jobs, was met with angry derision, not least from Barry Jones the sitting MP. Yet Aerospace's competitors were watching like hawks as European rules had to be obeyed. It saddened me that Assembly officials were rowing over petty travel forms while Broughton was crying out for millions.

One evening, with the hills above Mold decked in snow, I attended the installation of a new vicar in Cilcain before leaving for Cardiff as a last constituency duty. The road to the church was slippery underfoot and the snow made the whole scene spookily light. Fortunately the new vicar was totally unfazed, even when the church lights failed and she had to get through a complex service helped only by a lantern and a torch. I left before the party began and by 9.00pm, bags and animals packed in the car, I headed down a snow-strewn motorway for the 200-mile trip back to Cardiff. As the Assembly sped towards its first anniversary, Rhodri's Government won applause for publishing minutes of private cabinet meetings, the first Government to open itself up for scrutiny in this way. With praiseworthy candour, Rhodri admitted that the voters still had to be 'engaged'.

On the 9th May 2000 Delyth Evans, Alun Michael's former speechwriter, took her seat under the Regional List rules representing Mid and West Wales. Unusually slim and smartly dressed for a Labour woman, with an intelligent face, and able to speak Welsh fluently, she was going to be a great asset. As Rod had been shunted to the end of the back row, she moved in beside me. We got on well from the start. The Group also liked her pedigree because a week later, she won a handsome vote to move onto the Group Executive. I was pleased that she seemed committed to being an independent thinker, prepared to be outspoken and unafraid to express an unpopular view. I saw her as a kindred spirit, happily taught her the intricacies of emailing on our plenary touch screens, and kept her up to date with gossip.

Late in May Peter Law, as Transport Minster, boosted North-South rail links by funding an additional daily service from Anglesey to Cardiff. Consumer watchdogs judged rail transport in North Wales as the worst in Europe, so Peter's train was welcomed. It was infuriating that rail operators demanded public money before upgrading service, and that the Assembly transport budget could never cope with all the demands. At a North Wales business breakfast Rhodri firmly rejected a new major road across Wales, despite eloquent pleas from the builder of the Anglesey extension of the A55 that the task was feasible. Rhodri was now doing three jobs: economic portfolio, First Minister and self-styled minister for North Wales, to curb criticism that everything was happening in the south. As Ireland had dramatically improved its economy with an ambitious road-building plan from European money, his decision was unpopular, but he would not be swayed. On the 17th May Chris Gwyther was back in the Opposition's sights over a GM crops trial, first thought to be sited in England but then discovered to be just in Wales. Farmer John Cottle caused outrage by raising the proverbial two fingers to Cardiff and Westminster, when it was discovered that Christine and the Assembly had no power to stop the trial, therefore forfeiting the proud claim that Wales would be a 'GM free' zone. Christine beat off her detractors again and said some very rude things about Rod Richards in her reply.

The Prince of Wales requested the pleasure of the AMs' company to join him for dinner at Margam Park on the 11th May. Peter York, who ran my Delyn office, and I promptly accepted the invitation as we thought it was a nice royal gesture. Only eight of the 28 strong Labour Group followed my lead and, embarrassingly, the Presiding Officer had to email all AMs and drum up a bit more support for the dinner. About 23 of the 60 AMs from all the parties eventually turned out, including every Welsh Conservative AM. The republican members in the Labour Group headed for the other big attraction on the night: a speech by Neil Kinnock, the then Vice President of the European Commission. Even the oratory of the 'Welsh Windbag' could not have competed with the sumptuousness of the Prince's dinner in the Orangery, where a long table groaned under the weight of spectacular flower arrangements, gleaming candelabras and sparkling glasses. AMs were ferried to and from the event by minibus with ministers and officials arriving by chauffeured car. This ensured that justice was done to the freely flowing drinks, without risk to our driving licences.

I was curious to know why a cushion occupied an empty chair in the middle of the long dining table. We all stood respectfully behind ours so surely the Prince knew where to sit! I assumed that the royal posterior needed extra comfort whilst he ate. When my charming neighbour Professor Cadman, who had accompanied Charles on archaeological digs, seemed short of potatoes, I generously offered him one from my plate. My skills as a former waitress left me, and the vegetable dropped between us and plopped onto the polished floor. Refusing to be fazed, I began reaching down to grab it but an attendee beat me to the task and expertly whisked the offending spud away. The Prof. remained potatoless as I lost the nerve to attempt the manoeuvre again. Neil Kinnock's admirers missed a real treat as we were enchanted by a recital by the Prince's royal harpist, who kept the diners waiting whilst she went through her pre-recital routine. After staying for the magnificent performance, the royal posterior vacated the cushion and it was time to go home.

Silly events kept the Assembly in the news during the remainder of May. A security scare was sparked when a Northern Ireland ex-terrorist was found working in the building for a month. Then the Tories were infuriated when a statue to commemorate the Greenham Women's anti-nuclear protest suddenly appeared in the Assembly's Milling area. The march had started from Cardiff, but despite the women's commendable contribution to peace, the Conservatives kicked up such a fuss it was quietly removed. The row over the shortfall of £25 million needed by BA to build its wings in Flintshire rumbled on, and the Opposition snatched a debate to censure the Assembly Government. The Administration had to weather heavy criticism over the funding issue, as Rhodri still felt tied down by European rules that would come back and bite the Assembly if he got it wrong. Meanwhile, as Flintshire called out for funding, the new Assembly building farrago rumbled on. Despite the architect's 19th January assurance and an outlay of £100,000 for a scaled mock up of the new Welsh Assembly building interior, the battle still raged over what form it should take. Rhodri strongly favoured ditching the original design for the car park 'colander' option. Later, the Presiding Officer awarded a free vote on the design, doubtless infuriating the Cabinet. The Richard Rogers design won by a clear majority, but with the caveat that costs would be capped at £27 million. Since 1999 the cost had more than doubled, but there was worse to come as Edwina later discovered, when Rhodri handed her a poisoned chalice by giving her charge of the project.

As the Assembly building nightmare slipped temporarily into the long grass, Rod Richards's nightmares also ended in June after he was cleared of assault. The jury deliberated for four hours and Ann Mallalieu, QC, battled hard for him as in her summing up he was humiliated when she stated that, 'The events of the night provide a classic cautionary tale for a middle aged man at a loose end in London!' Having lost the leadership position, Rod confirmed he would be concentrating on rebuilding his political career, but his party shunned him, consigning him to a political limbo. Now ensconced as Tory leader, Nick Bourne was not going to risk his position and Rod was obliged to stand as an 'Independent' Tory. Rod was the third senior politician to fall from grace with the Assembly barely a year old. Besides the Rogers building and the Cardiff Bay 'wind–up' scheme, yet another expensive project inherited by the Assembly was the Wales Millennium Centre (WMC). This was to gobble up another £104 million of public money and the project planning started in earnest on the 7th March 2000. Soon the National Botanical Garden of Wales, which was built largely with lottery money, would also beat a path to the Assembly seeking help to stay afloat.

Both the WMC and the Botanical Gardens cash demands were a mere drop in the ocean compared with the cost of the Cardiff Bay Barrage, all the ongoing infrastructure together with a proposed Sports Village, a project much favoured by Cardiff County Council. I worried that so much was being poured into Cardiff, Swansea and Newport, that little would be left for the sports and cultural needs of the rest of Wales.

With this background it is now hard to believe the historical fact that in 1989, Labour MPs strongly opposed the decision by the then Conservative Government to block the mouth of Cardiff Bay, and turn the area into a vast freshwater lake. Flowing into the Severn Estuary, the Bay had a tidal range of up to fourteen metres (the second highest in the world), but the scheme would greatly help the Cardiff and the Welsh economy. The original budget of £191 million proved woefully inadequate and by 1999, it was up to £197 million. When the Assembly started operating, the First Secretary increased a further capped figure to £213.4 million. Even then, the wretched taxpayer was soon to be hit again as European legal requirements would add £6-7 million to the bill for the Bay water maintenance. Although these costs were postponed for later years, it must still be found. In his first review of the Cardiff Bay Barrage, the Auditor General estimated that the Bay and Barrage costs had leapt by 15% and could even reach the tentatively estimated £220 million.

The Development Corporation responsible for overseeing the barrage construction work and improvements to the Bay infrastructure was due to stop operating in March 2000, and would be 'wound-up'. A procedure was required to pass uncompleted work to another organisation. The Assembly assumed responsibility for the 'wind-up' and took over responsibility for the ongoing re-development of the Bay.

Naturally the current First Secretary wanted to move fast to minimise any political fallout caused by overspend and to finalise ownership of Bay development, Barrage operations and water quality maintenance. Ron Davies's promised 'bonfire of the Quangos' had wrecked opening yet another, but a solution had to be found and political expediency led to an opaque partnership with a shrewd political ally, Lord Mayor Russell Goodway. A unique 'Harbour Authority' was created by a 'Memorandum of Understanding' (it will be remembered), signed by Alun Michael before the Assembly had come into being, but at a price largely uncosted. The Council was required to maintain the Bay, the water quality within the Bay and continue to develop adjacent land. It would have been unfair to load all the 'wind-up' costs on to a Local Authority, even one so large as Cardiff County Council.

Nevertheless, the Authority inherited priceless assets and the Auditor General's three reports on the Bay affair showed that Cardiff County Council did very well indeed from this 'shot gun marriage'. The mechanism used to pay Cardiff for this ongoing work was through this 'non Quango Harbour Authority'. Very soon millions were flowing out of Assembly coffers into those of Cardiff Council for Bay regeneration, and it was soon to be discovered that the monitoring arrangements between the council and the Assembly left much to be desired.

A paper on the Cardiff Bay Development Corporation 'wind–up' was discussed in the 20th January 2000 meeting of the Economic Development committee, which had twice before reviewed the wind-up. Although it is understood that the

'Memorandum of Understanding' was mentioned, briefing on the contents of the memorandum was minimal. Even if the committee had been appraised of the contents, it would have been meaningless. Auditor General's staff, whilst conducting their second review into the 'wind-up' saga, later discovered the document had no legal standing and even vital passages were open to interpretation.

On the 1st March 2000 a joint meeting was held between my Local Government Committee and the Economic Development Committee, with Rhodri Morgan in attendance. Our papers informed us of other attendees, but we had not anticipated that the Leader of Cardiff City Council himself would address the committee. He was very enthusiastic about the role his Authority would play in developing the Bay, but was vague when asked questions on costs. At that stage I didn't know that he was also Chair of the Harbour Authority, as the machinations of that unique 'non-Quango' was not yet on my radar.

He spoke eloquently of his vision for Cardiff and I recollect that he fulsomely described how the Bute Avenue scheme would 'produce a shimmering necklace that would embrace the bay.' Clearly irritated by the waffle, the practical Val Feld in the chair demanded who should pay for the Barrage scheme overspend. Russell had no hesitation in suggesting that the Assembly should naturally pick up the bill. Time would show that the Assembly was to do quite a lot of that! Unbelievably, the Assembly had already agreed to pay a minimum of £12 million a year to Cardiff Council for posterity to keep the Bay in good shape. The Assembly had not only paid for improvements to Harry Ramsden's waterside restaurant, but had apparently also given the Council a blank cheque for another £1.6 million.

Russell Goodway did not see a problem. In front of the First Secretary, with breathtaking arrogance, he felt that the Assembly had done well from the Bay 'wind-up' and Assembly officials should be accountable to their own people, rather than the other way round. Appalled that Delyn constituents had been unwittingly locked into this expense forever, I wrote to Rhodri on the 6th March 2000 asking what was going on. Should the water quality issue have been debated, particularly as the official tender winner Thames Water lost the contract to Cardiff Council? I told Rhodri that I did not like a pistol held to my head and welcomed open discussion, albeit at this late stage.

In Rhodri's 27th March reply, he said that the Bay 'wind-up' was always expected to be met from 'Central', not local Government funding and included £6.1 million for regeneration, of which £5.91 million would cover the cost of Cardiff Council's purchasing land for a Sports Village Scheme. He agreed that detailed funding still had to be finalised, but reminded me that the former First Secretary had briefed plenary on water issues on the 7th December, and that bi-lateral agreements had occurred at joint meetings of the Local Government and Economic Development committees. I backed off, confronted by this level of detail from the First Secretary, and acknowledged that Rhodri's grasp of the financial complexities of Cardiff Bay funding was superior to mine, but I was worried that Cardiff Council had been handed so many public assets on a plate. However, Rhodri was as silent on the sums 'set to be paid for posterity', as he was on whether or not Westminster would increase the Welsh block grant to cover the escalating Bay expenditure, and who paid into the 'central' fund? I wondered if we would ever know how much of the Assembly budget would end up in Cardiff Bay.

The official business plan provided by Cardiff County Council – detailing the money the fledging Harbour Authority wanted the Assembly to cough up – was long delayed, allegedly by a printing problem. Undeterred by the lack of a financial template, Assembly officials nevertheless continued to send hefty regular payments to the Harbour Authority at its bidding, and were to receive considerable criticism from the Auditor General for paying Cardiff Council in advance of work done or money spent by the Harbour Authority. This business plan eventually saw the light of day in December 2000. At first glance, it was attractively presented with pie charts and glossy pictures of the entire area, but closer examination revealed that it was short on detail and long on rhetoric. The spending assessment by Cardiff Harbour Authorities for 2000-2005 was dismissed by a senior Assembly official (Dr Emyr Roberts) as little more than a 'wish list'.

This 'non Quango', created for administrative and accounting convenience, would be initially valid for five years, and the Assembly would meet all costs 'reasonably incurred' in relation to Barrage operating costs! Up to £14 million were the first year's estimated running costs (2000-1). The Auditor General's July report assessed that the net provision to Cardiff Council from the Assembly would be £21.4 million. Maths was never my strong point but it seemed that the £12 million per year for posterity was rising inextricably, and I knew that I should have pressed Rhodri harder when I tried to clarify the Harbour Authority's overall annual expenditure in my March 2000 correspondence. There was worse to come.

Although the Welsh Development Agency took charge of managing Bute Avenue – a Private Financial Initiative (PFI) project crucial to the full development of the Bay area – the entire PFI cost, later discovered to run for 25 years at over £5 million a year, came from the Assembly. When Edwina announced large increases to various Assembly-sponsored bodies in her annual Assembly budget, these were floated as political good news stories. In reality, it seemed that Edwina had no choice but to raise sponsored body budgets so as – it seemed to me – to cover the cost of the Bute Avenue PFI and similar schemes, but in so doing, these new amounts then looked more generous than they really were. The Tourist Board and the Countryside Council for Wales also received increased expenditure with another hefty chunk of the money being earmarked, mostly for the Golden Triangle: 'Cardiff, Newport and Swansea'. The regular payments to the Harbour Authority for work and maintenance – completed or not – and the hidden extras buried in budgets of existing Quangos for Bay schemes, meant that Russell's 'jewelled necklace shimmering round Cardiff Bay' did not come cheaply. Little wonder there was no money to build a community hospital in Holywell.

The Welsh Assembly was barely a twinkle in a few political eyes when the Barrage was originally conceived as a means to transform Cardiff into a maritime city, thus greatly increasing its overall wealth by damming the Bay. True to the script, Cardiff was turning into a 'Boom Town' under our noses, with burgeoning commercial and business activity and spiralling house prices, but still the Council wanted more. Obligingly, the Assembly agreed to enter a complex financial deal with the Lord Mayor that was designed to win the 2008 bid for the Capital of Culture award. Amazingly this was the same council that had refused to make any contribution to the Wales Millennium Centre, although this building was vital to ensure that Cardiff's bid was viable. Eventually, this speculative scheme duly failed (admitted as not unexpected by the Lord Mayor), and yet again, the Auditor General's ongoing scrutiny into the Bay and its management reported negatively and gave rise to a suspicion that the agreement was all a bit of a mess. One such report seriously questioned the wisdom for hefty financial decisions that influenced Cardiff, to fall mainly on the then First Secretary, who was the MP for Penarth and South Cardiff, and whose constituency was located right in the heart of the fast developing Bay.

Despite years of planning, construction and overspends, the transport and parking needs of a fast expanding area and population had been completely overlooked, even though restaurants, shops, and office apartments were going up almost overnight. In 2002, the Cabinet was to consider a £20 million electric buggy system to run from Cathay's Park to the Bay and, for a short time, the scheme went full steam ahead. Suddenly, it was quietly shelved for no apparent reason. Well, for the time being! In 2000 however, such palaver was yet to come.

On Midsummer's Day, the 21st June, Rhodri's 'Colander' debating chamber option failed when the Assembly voted resoundingly for the now £22.8 million Richard Rogers design. 35 voted for, 22 against the Rhodri version that had been variously described as 'a toilet on stilts', a 'four-legged mushroom', or according to Lorraine Barrett, 'something to boil cabbage in'. Three AMs did not vote for anything, one being Rod Richards who was absent from the debate, engaged at the high court whilst defending himself against an assault charge, having admitted a similar conviction years ago. Peter Law voted but having pressed the wrong button, had to apologise for voting with the Tories. Rhodri took flack for delaying three months to find a cheaper alternative, which added considerably to the cost. Despite the resounding vote for the Rogers model, anxiety was still being expressed with the million pounds extra and a niggling suspicion that it was not capable of being built at all! Some of Lord Rogers's creations had experienced mixed fortunes with breaking or leaking glass panels reported on at least two of his designs, which had then required extensive repair. Our admirable Auditor General would eventually judge if the delay caused by the 'cabbage boiler' alternative had unnecessarily increased the cost of what I considered to be Lord Rogers's 'disability unfriendly' design!

Christine Gwyther's brutal sacking on the eve of the Royal Agricultural Show, announced in the *Western Mail*, shocked us and Carwyn Jones, her deputy, made the seamless transformation into the more acceptable 'meat eating' Agriculture Secretary – to the delight of the farming fraternity. Ieuan Wyn Jones won the Plaid Cymru leadership on the 3rd August after Dafydd Wigley resigned following heart surgery. Rumours abounded that Labour and Lib Dem might make a pact, fanned by a bizarre suggestion that Andrew Davies, the Business Secretary and Jenny Randerson, the Lib Dem AM, were meeting secretly in a Bridgend motorway station to re-shape the future of Government in Wales! A House of Commons envelope containing a cutting from the *Sun* newspaper dropped through my letterbox giving details of 'the long ma'am of the law', with pen-pictures of the three serving women Chief Constables. Barry Jones had written, 'Congratulations to these'. He had always admired 'my battle for justice and the part I'd played in elevating women to Chief Constables.' I was sad we had drifted so far apart.

The summer recess passed and in September after a crucial meeting in Ruthin attended by local farmers, including my constituent Brynle Williams, and Peter Rogers, the Tory AM for Ynys Môn, protests began against the high cost of fuel. Almost overnight petrol became a scarce commodity. Peter Rogers boasted on camera how he had rallied farmers and haulers to picket Stanlow Oil Refinery, and had admitted his delight when a convoy of Liverpool taxi drivers rolled up at 3.00am, honking horns in support of the blockade. In just days, fuel shortages were threatening livestock feeds and the ambulance service in my area. On the 12th September I wrote to the Presiding Officer complaining that Peter Rogers had acted irresponsibly, and may have discredited the Assembly, as he had crossed that thin line between exercising a right to picket peacefully and interfering in people's ability to carry out their lawful work. With public services suffering, should an AM be indulging in a high profile and reckless industrial dispute? Although I liked Peter, I thought it was a case for the Assembly's Standards Committee.

On Monday the 11th September I was packed, fuelled and ready to drive to Cardiff when I heard that Cardiff was devoid of petrol. A friend thought me stupid to risk being marooned in Cardiff with animals without the guarantee of being able to return home. I heeded the advice and emailed Mike Penn to announce that reluctantly, I would be ducking that week's Assembly business. The speed of the petrol paralysis was frightening and no wonder David Hanson, my Delyn MP, as a junior Welsh Office Minister, was actively courting Brynle Williams by inviting him to the House. The strategy was successful as by the 14th September, the Stanlow picket action ceased and the nation's fuel flowed again. A gratuitous email suddenly arrived in Delyn from Andrew Davies, the Chief Whip, demanding an explanation for my absence. He pre-empted my reply by lecturing me on my folly for failing to have filled up before fuel ran out. I responded to this pettiness by explaining my tank capacity and that the distance between north and south demanded a top up at some stage. My reply produced an email bearing the signature of

Karen, the new Deputy Whip, clearly anxious to show her authority. Imperiously, she stated that 'I should have sought permission before absenting myself.' Controlling the expletives, my persecutors were told to go and boil their heads and join the real world. I then got on with my constituency work unhindered, and one engagement took me to the prestigious annual North Wales Music Festival at St Asaph cathedral. As I was the only Labour AM to attend, I assumed I was not alone in having to cope with petrol shortages, and charitably concluded that fuel constraints were the reason for the absence of my North Wales colleagues. The enchanting music removed all thought of bullying whips and childish emails from my mind.

Autumn arrived with a bang! Culture Secretary Alun Pugh grabbed unwelcome headlines by taking an all expenses paid trip to Australia to watch the Olympics. Alun Cairns was forced to justify a trip to Bermuda. I was worried that AMs were going to follow some MPs who were well known as 'serial Globe Trotters'. The Assembly was unpopular enough without looking for trouble. The Labour Group winced when the Welsh papers were full of MP Barry Jones leading a farmer's deputation to Westminster for a photo call with the Welsh Secretary. Agriculture just happened to be a Welsh Assembly responsibility! By the 5th October, Wales learnt about a 'Lib–Lab coalition' and the Labour Group was told by email. Tom Middlehurst cannily jumped ship before he was pushed, his resignation closely followed by the sacking of Newport's Rosemary Butler and Peter Law. The front page of the *Western Mail* cruelly depicted their mug shots, and made me realise yet again what a dirty trade politics is!

On the 16th October 2000, fears expressed by North Wales voters in the 1997 referendum that the South would be favoured, came true. Rhodri Morgan announced his new cabinet, stuffed with people from Cardiff and the M4 corridor. Lib Dem Leader Mike German's appointment as Rhodri's deputy must have been particularly galling for Peter Law. With limited political experience and a derisory number of votes gleaned through proportional representation, Mike also acquired the Economic Development portfolio and as Deputy First Minister, held the second most prestigious job in the Assembly. Peter's ministerial portfolio had been enormous and because he was refused a Cardiff accommodation allowance, travelling between Cardiff and Blaenau Gwent had been a further burden on him. Rhodri bestowed more favours on Jane Davidson, who won the new portfolio of Education and Life Long Learning and Edwina had Local Government Affairs added to her finance portfolio. Chinese walls had to be urgently erected to head off the accusation of funding favourite Local Authorities, including her own. To counter criticism that Cardiff controlled everything, Rhodri retained his job of 'minister for North Wales'.

The following month, a new committee for Culture, Sport and the Welsh Language was formed, which gave Lib Dem AM Jenny Randerson a ministerial portfolio. The usual moans rose from the Welsh-speaking lobby that she did not speak Welsh! As a former Cardiff county councillor, she was ideally placed, in every sense, to see through to completion the highly controversial Wales Millennium Centre. I wanted to beef up support for Clwyd Theatr Cymru, desperate for better funding and well out of the 'all riches to South Wales' loop. I had to bargain hard with Andrew Davies to secure a place on this new committee, by abandoning my beloved local Government portfolio and moving to the more challenging Economic Development Committee. The last thing Andrew wanted was my presence on the committee that funded theatres and culture, particularly as the south was so generously provisioned, so he resisted my demand. Doggedly, I pressed him into capitulation by explaining the Economic Development Committee deserved a representative to speak for the business community in North Wales. I then inserted the knife by querying why I had the furthest to travel, but served on two major committees, whilst one south-based AM, with none of my travelling problems, only managed to cope with one.

When Rhodri briefed us on the reason for the pact, the shocked Labour Group reacted sullenly. With his usual bravura and charm, his explanation that the pact was the best of bad options managed to salvage Group discipline, but with gnashing teeth and openly deep contempt for the two out of the six Lib Dem AMs, who had grabbed the political equivalent of the crown jewels. The Group praised Peter for bowing to pressure and backed away from his suggested vote of 'no confidence in the coalition', accepting that it would change nothing and it would harm us more than the Opposition. Rhodri needed stability to govern, and personal frustrations just had to be stifled. We took comfort that the Plaid Cymru and Tory leaders were furious with the coalition arrangements and that Mike had great difficulty in persuading his colleagues to acknowledge their good fortune.

The newspaper page that announced Mike's elevation to cabinet status also reported that he was being urged to step down during enquiries into a £20,000 bill on a corporate credit card, drawn on by the Welsh Joint Education Committee's (WJEC) European Unit, which Mike headed. Mike vigorously denied any wrong doing, but as months passed, the allegations grew. These were fanned by Jeff Jones – board member and leader of Bridgend Council – who was regularly reported in the media as demanding answers about the WJEC's spending regime. Reporters delved into his hotel bills and the number of guests involved, and this level of interest mounted into corporate expenditure long before the police started their own enquiries into the WJEC's European Unit. Rhodri valiantly hung on to his new deputy, refusing to contemplate Mike standing down unless a police enquiry commenced. Even after police started their enquiries, the First Minister still refused to demote Mike. Opponents even accused him of making improper inquiries over the state of the police investigation, an accusation that Rhodri vehemently denied, and every time Mike took the podium he had to ride out muttering and grumbles from the frustrated Opposition. He seemed indestructible, and hung on until the 6th July 2001 when he finally bowed to ever-increasing pressure but defiantly announced that he would return when cleared.

I backed the Lib-Lab pact in the press, as I could not see that Rhodri had any other option to stabilise his Government without risking going the same way as Alun. The coalition was deeply unpopular with my constituency party but they were powerless to change it and, suddenly, severe flooding in Delyn, with Mold particularly badly affected, ensured that 'the coalition' moved swiftly onto the back burner. An inoffensive little stream, the Alyn, was hardly worthy of the status of 'river', but it suddenly turned into a raging torrent that swept into houses and left water stains as far up as sixteen courses of brickwork. Cars bobbed in the water surrounding the Mold Tesco car park, and the Flint lifeboat moved imperiously through the floods outside the Bridge pub, on the edge of the town. I waded around in wellies, to sympathise and promise help, especially as some houses had been flooded more than once in previous years.

The scenes were dreadful: sewage-tainted water remaining in lower rooms, filth trapped in saucepans and washing machines, sodden carpets and ruined furniture. Paul Murphy, then Welsh Secretary, visited the disaster area and was ferried around the floods in a Land Rover by county officials. Calf-high in swirling waters, I plodded into a small cottage I had once owned as an escape from Merseyside pressures. I was appalled at the extent of the flooding inside the building. The subsequent inquest blamed a total lack of preparation by the Local Authority and the Environment Agency, with no early warning system and a desperate shortage of the basic flood weapon, sandbags, that left victims devoid of any means of protection.

My press release praising the Lib-Lab pact shared the same page with news that only one applicant had applied for the £95,000 Chief Constable's job in North Wales. An ability to 'speak the language of heaven' was seen as a possible bar to applicants. I thought it more likely that candidates would be aware that the force had an unenviable reputation, and seemed unable to stem the continued negative leaks of still being in hot pursuit of its suspended Head of Legal Services.

I awoke early to the radio announcing that Rosemary Butler was to become the next Deputy Presiding Officer. I was surprised as the appointment had not been discussed in the Labour Group and the newscaster indicated that Andrew Davies, our business manager, had made the decision and then told the media. I liked Rosemary immensely, but I felt the post needed a tougher, more independent figure who would stand up impartially for AMs, not another Jane Davidson type, who had done little to progress my expenses problem. When John Marek sidled up before Group and asked if I would support his bid for the job, I was interested. If he could persuade just two Group members to come over, he could win. John's Assembly attendance had been erratic but he was well respected, impartial and was nobody's puppet. I made discreet enquiries of Peter Law, whom I trusted, and then made a decision. Had Andrew Davies handled matters properly, Rosemary would have walked it, but with resentment mounting, fanned by Opposition pressures that were backing John, a ballot was called. Excitement mounted as a polling booth suddenly appeared in a committee room and we milled around outside waiting to vote. As Business Secretary, Andrew had made another silly mistake by clumsily attempting to impose Rosemary, which again showed that he often had to reply upon advice from Ron to ease things along. Although a nice, inoffensive man, Andrew did not seem to possess that vital 'helicopter' vision and some felt he lacked a sharp political brain. Entering the booth, I lifted the pencil on its string and made my choice.

John Marck's victory by a solitary vote was announced in the afternoon plenary. The Opposition whooped with delight. The Cabinet looked stone-faced and the Presiding Officer appeared anxious, as if he was wondering what whirlwind he was about to reap! Peter Law and I exchanged knowing glances, and plenary continued as usual. Leaving the Chamber, I whispered my congratulations to John and commented that it was a bit tight. 'One vote is enough', he said sagely, and moved into a whole new world of privilege and status: new office and generous salary increase, elevated at last from the backbenches. John was willing and able to influence Assembly business in a capable and impartial manner and I knew that the choice was a good one for democracy. The number crunchers calculated that he had been supported by three Labour votes. Whoever could they be? John Marek took to his new role like a duck to water and became an exemplary deputy to Lord Dafydd El.

On the 25th October at 8.40pm, whilst I was poring over committee papers in Cardiff, Quince, my beloved mongrel had a seizure. I tracked down a 24-hour Veterinary Hospital and Maurice Kirk started work to save her. She was a very special mongrel, worth every penny of her £7.00 fee and the following afternoon, deeply drugged, I loaded her into my car for what would be her final journey home. By 10.15pm my own vet put her to sleep in her basket and I took her to Brynford Pet Cemetery where she finally joined her dead sisters.

On the 31st October Rhodri ditched the title of Secretary in favour of Minister, much to the consternation of Westminster chums at the end of the M4. Unlike Alun, who wrote several letters to AMs to keep them informed of policy decisions, I noted that Rhodri was not minded to follow Alun's inclusive approach. At Audit Committee on the 9th November 2000, Jon Shortridge, the Permanent Secretary, faced tough questioning in a three-hour session in the wake of a damning report from the Auditor General, showing how the cost of the Cardiff Assembly building option had soared from £17 million to £41 million. The cheapest option, Swansea's bid, had failed and the invitation to other parts of Wales to tender for the new Assembly was a costly sham. Cardiff was always going to get the Assembly even though Jon Shortridge was unable satisfactorily to explain why. Flintshire had also bid to host the Assembly and to learn that we had been duped, together with 22 other hopefuls, was frustrating and a waste of time and money. 'Ultimately, it was a ministerial decision', Shortridge claimed. The cost of hourly ferrying civil staff back and forth between Cathay's Park and

Crickhowell House had been ignored; the computer software contract had risen from £215,000 to £551,000 and no formal budget to adapt Crickhowell House, or to oversee the expenditure at a senior level, had been considered. Even the land allegedly purchased for £1.00 on which to build the new debating chamber, was too small to accommodate the chosen design footprint, and someone had conveniently forgotten that 200 parking places were to be sacrificed in exchange for the £1.00 deal. I bluntly accused the Permanent Secretary of spending taxpayers' money to preserve Cardiff's position as the Capital of Wales. 'There was a firm expectation the Assembly would be in Cardiff', he replied suavely. He did accept that 'better deals' would have been done without the time constraints! Not easy being the Permanent Secretary for the fledgling Assembly!

Weeks after its inception, the Lib-Lab pact was still a running sore and at a bad tempered, rebellious Labour Group meeting, Peter Law and Tom Middlehurst mounted an attack against the pact and demanded that a motion must be brought to plenary. Although universally loathed, no-one wanted to break ranks and openly challenge Rhodri's decision, especially as the press would make capital from it. Val Feld's complaint about the handling of the Deputy Presiding Officer debacle, yet another political cock-up presented to the Opposition on a plate, got a collective mutter of support. I glared at Andrew, having received no reply to my letter asking if he had cleared Rosemary's nomination with Nick Bourne before telling the media.

We suffered the usual rambling, emotional, long-winded speeches favoured by some of the Group's inner circle, and as I always tried to make my contributions succinct, this time I lost patience. I said that I would be voting for Peter's motion as he had been harshly treated. A front page of the *Western Mail* depicting two sacked ministers was awful, and the timing of Christine Gwyther's sacking had also been cruel. I agreed with Val that the Deputy Presiding Officer appointment had been a shambles and that those in control were making too many mistakes. The Group listened without interruption and accepted that we were giving the Opposition too much ammunition. Ron wandered over to Peter and asked him to withdraw his hostile Lib-Lab motion. Peter turned to me and said he could not do that. 'I think you should', I whispered. 'You have the Group's sympathy so act with dignity now.' Peter mouthed something to Tom, his joint sponsor, who looked relieved as both men acknowledged that the plenary motion was dead. I gave Peter a hug and the meeting came to an end.

After plenary, keen to keep informed, the North Wales AMs accepted an audience with Rhodri. We hijacked his agenda and warned him severely that if something good did not happen for the north, two AMs risked losing their seats, as the popularity battle was being lost. Flintshire's Labour administration was struggling with inadequate Assembly funding and a major flood clean up operation that did not come cheap. I told Rhodri again that he should get himself better advisers. No one appeared to disagree. Alun Pugh speculated that Gareth Thomas (Clwyd West MP), might lose his seat and the opinion was that other Labour MPs were not secure. Karen Sinclair was cross that her hard work to defuse farmers' and hauliers' anger at a Ruthin meeting had been wrecked by Gareth's highhanded attitude towards the farmers. It was suggested that he saw them as 'no hopers' and that discontent aroused at the meeting had fuelled the plan to picket Stanlow (the oil refinery), and to disrupt oil supplies. As councillors, Gareth and I had shared the back row at County Hall and I thought him incapable of saying anything even slightly controversial. However, the scenario certainly fitted in with Peter Rogers's annoyance over some incident at Ruthin, which had finally led to the full-scale fuel blockage. The Government had been severely compromised by the rapid damage the farmers were able to inflict on fuel supplies. How intriguing if one of our own had been a catalyst or the cause?

A gale wrecked sleep on the night of the 13th December and the day proved equally stormy. The Culture Committee meeting papers were a mess, having been clumsily collated by officials, and we muddled on, struggling to make sense of the confused agenda. Just before the afternoon Economic Development meeting, Val dropped by to say that the Labour Group had agreed a new plenary session programme, which we all had to obey. I was appalled because I would now have to drive to Cardiff for just one day, and all because Andrew Davies had lost some argument in the Business Committee. His failure to negotiate properly with the other parties meant also that we had a shorter Christmas recess; I was in for a nine-hour journey for just three hours in plenary. After the long term of grinding work and travel, I was close to exhaustion and refused to accept the change of plan. 'Would I go and speak to Rhodri?' I said, 'No'. Val was taken aback and I left her office in a hurry. In tears, I shot back to my office, grabbed my coat and car keys, and drove to the pier head to cool off. Bracing myself against a railing, I watched the turbulent waters in the bay as the gale blew around me. I'd known that the Assembly job would be tough, but not this tough.

Despite Cardiff being severely buffeted by gales, the evening improved with dinner with Alex Aldridge and Jeanette Antrobus, both senior Flintshire County Council members. This was only the second time I had been out to eat since I started Assembly work. The scotch flowed freely back at my pad and into every glass but my own. My afternoon pier walk had cleared my head and I wanted it to stay that way. As expected, Karen Sinclair refused my request to skip the one day back in plenary. She had already excused several members who were going on holiday, and the vote was going to be tight so I might be needed. I felt very let down and bullied by her. Karen seemed always obstructive, and a pattern was building. As a cry for help, I naively wrote a whinging letter to Rhodri on the 17th December that poured out my problems with my life as a North Wales AM. I stated 'Andrew invariably ignored emails and letters, Karen's whipping decisions smacked of bias and I felt that a business manager should be appointed from the North.' I went on to say (poor Rhodri, if he ever saw my letter) 'that office printers were too slow to print committee papers in the Constituency, and, faced with these and other problems, I was looking for a bit of loyalty and assistance in return.' Conscience told me I should have obeyed the Whip and hacked back to Cardiff for the meeting. Physical exhaustion combined with stubbornness told me that it was a journey too far for me and poor old Fudge. For just once, the Party would have to do without me while I stayed north and renewed my energy, getting on with working for people who had entrusted me with their vote.

Me, pictured during happier times, Merseyside ACC, 1988.

Monday 24th June 2002. At the Chwarae Teg office above Somerfield in Mold with Office Manager Michelle Nicholls and staff supporting Flintshire's emerging women entrepreneurs, Sue Stacey, Jeanette Miller, Dilys Leonard and Linda Young.

Me with County Cllr Anne and George Slowik at her Chairman's Civic Service, Sunday 24th June 2001. All Saints Church, Ffynnongroew.

Friday 12th July 2002. Treetops Caravan park, Gwespyr was in full bloom when David Hanson MP and I called to visit along with County Councillor Anne Slowik, seen here with proprietess Mrs Maureen Walker and son Andrew. This award winning site is in for the Wales in Bloom competition and its gardens and surrounds were in tip top condition.

Friday 21st February 2003. Me (Delyn AM), greeting First Minister Rhodri Morgan at BHP–Billiton's Visitor Centre in Talacre.

With the 'big crane' at Mostyn Docks for the assembling of windmills in the bay, 21st February 2003. Jim O'Toole was very proud to show off the 600t capacity crane that will be assisting work on wind turbine towers to be put offshore at North Hoyle. A five acre site has been cleared for Danish firm Vestas to work onshore at Mostyn, employing 60 people.

Friday 7th June 2002. Me with two of the rescued dogs and staff of North Wales Animal Rescue Sanctuary at Maes Gwyn, Trelogan.

Friday 4th May 2001. Pictured from left to right: David Hanson MP, me, Head Greenfield School, Peter Roach and County Councillor Chris Bithell with plans of new school.

26th February 2003. Jane Hutt visits Holywell Cottage Hospital and announces money will be released following persistent pressure from myself.

Pictured from left to right: Tom Middlehurst AM, me, Jane Davidson (Education Minister), Cllr David Parry, Sue Essex (Transport and Environment Minister) and Jane Hutt (Social Services and Health Minister).

Friday 26th April. Launch of Crisp (Community Resource Information Service Partnership) in Flint (also in Deeside as you know!!!).

Supporting Sandy Mewies, prospective Delyn candidate's campaign. Mold 2003.

Wednesday 11th July 2001. I welcome Sport and Culture Minister Jenny Randerson to Clwyd Theatr Cymru. Pictured with myself are Nancy Lees of Edison Mission Energy, Keith McDonogh FCC Education Director, Jenny Randerson, Terry Hands (Director Clwyd Theatr Cymru), and Rachel of Arts and Business Cymru. Edison Mission are key partners of the Theatre.

Wednesday 8th January 2003. I travelled to Wrexham to see the excellent work being done by Careers Wales helping people back into employment.

Friday 26th April, 2002. Me with Save the Family's Edna Speed dodging the drops at the official opening of the Refurbishment and Adults Centre at Plas Bellin.

3rd February 2003. Diabetes outreach day in Flint. Mr George Braithwaite is leading the push for a diabetes group in Flint, supported by Flint Town Mayor, Cllr Perfect.

The newly elected Labour women AMs and Anita Gale – General Secretary Welsh Labour party.

Oath of Allegiance/Llw Teyrngarwch

"I, Alison Halford , do swear that I will be faithful and bear true allegiance to Her Majesty Queen Elizabeth, her heirs and successors, according to law. So help me God."

"Yr wyf i, Alison Halford , yn addo trwy gymorth y Goruchaf y byddaf yn ffyddlon ac yn wir deyrngar i'w Mawrhydi y Frenhines Elizabeth, ei hetifeddion a'i holynwyr, yn ôl y gyfraith, yn wyneb Duw."

Name/Enw ...ALISON HALFORD.... Signature/Llofnod.... Alison Halford ....Date/Dyddiad .11 May 99

Witnessed by/Tystiwyd gan .... Tolley.... ──────── Clerk/Deputy Clerk to the Assembly
Clerc/Dirprwy Glerc y Cynulliad

Oath of allegiance.

Surfing new library link to WAG. Pictured from left to right: Me, Assistant Director
Libraries Lawrence Rawsthorne and Cllr Chris Bithell.

Getting ready for the 1999 election campaign. Pictured alongside myself are Barry Jones MP and David Hanson MP.

Visiting a CCTV Control Room at BHP-Billiton. Pictured from left to right: Alun Pugh (ex AM and former Culture Minister), me and Mike Kelly (Plant Operations Manager).

Ron Davies and me, Mold Market, on the campaign trail, April 1999.

North Wales Police Authority 1997. Middle row, from left to right: Leon Gibson Clerk (2nd in) and me. Far right: ACC John Cooke and Mrs J Trigger (Head of Legal Services).

Me with Fire Brigade Chief Officers, Paul Murphy (Secretary of State for Wales) and Barry Jones MP.

Martin Blake, taxi driver. *Courtesy of Vic Cleveley (Victor.Pictures@gmail.com).*

David Davies, Former AM for Monmouth and now MP. ('He of bottom fame').

Nick Bourne, leader of the Welsh Conservatives.

Visit to farm in Delyn, sheep welfare issue.

Pictured from left to right: Me, Alun Michael (Secretary of State Wales), David Hanson MP, Tom Middlehurst AM, Cllr Alf Jones and Phil McGreevy, FCC's CE.

Travelling companions, Fudge ('she of Taxi driver fame'), Quince (Mongrel) and Scrabble (Border Terrier).

2002. Fudge with new travel companions, Fidget and Figgy.

Three of Plaid Cymru's stalwarts in the National Assembly (at Dafydd's farewell party). Pictured from left to right: Cynog Dafis (Ceredigion), Dafydd Wigley (Caernarfon) and Prof. Phil Williams (S. Wales East).

The opening of the National Assembly, 1999, by HM The Queen. In this picture she is signing the formal document opening the Assembly. Also pictured from left to right: Prince Charles, Duke of Edinburgh, Rt Hon John Morris MP, Lord Elis-Thomas (Pres. Officer), Alun Michael AM (First Minister) and Dafydd Wigley AM (Leader of the Opposition).

Plaid Cymru's group of 17 AMs who formed the official Opposition at the National Assembly. *Photograph © Siân Trenberth (mobile: 0831 542275).*

Lamb to the slaughter – which matches Alun Cairns' approach to interrogating witnesses on Audit Committee evidence taking sessions! He was the other one to watch out for.

Illustration by Jim Williams as a parting gift to the Assembly on my departure.

Farewell cartoon from MUMPH (Western Mail cartoonist).

Peter Law AM Blaenau Gwent – Former Minister for Local Government, Housing & Transport (The biggest portfolio in Cabinet by far). He is now sadly deceased.

John Marek. Former MP and AM Wrexham, and former Deputy Presiding Officer, National Assembly for Wales.

My election campaign mugshot, 1999.

Police investigations and Audit inquisitions

'Birds feed on birds, beasts on each other prey, But savage man alone does man betray.'
John Wilmot, 2nd Earl of Rochester 1674

Arriving back from Goa on the 6th January 2001, I spent the following evening entertaining June who had looked after my Schnauzer, Fudge, whilst I had been away. Fudge had been such a hit with June's grandchildren that she asked if she could keep her overnight and take her to visit them the next day. I agreed unhesitatingly, unsuspecting that the request would finally lead me to standing trial in Wrexham Magistrates Court for assault and a public order offence. My alleged 'victim' was a six foot plus, heavily built, local minicab driver whom I had the misfortune to encounter when I rang for a cab at 10.30pm to convey dog and friend to her home. After considerable delay, a car pulled up outside and, although the night was cold, I neither changed my slippers, nor donned a coat as I trotted out with Fudge in my arms and began to hand her to June who had climbed into the back of the vehicle. An arm suddenly shot out of the open window towards Fudge and the driver rudely snapped 'no dogs'. Startled, I asked why not. 'She's clean and does not even moult', I explained. His response was the same and even ruder, 'No dogs, and no dogs'. Irritated by the delay in his arrival, his unnecessary aggression, and recognising an impasse had been reached, I snapped back, 'Sir, you are an arsehole.'

This is not a word that springs readily to my lips, I hasten to add, and I had not learnt such language during my convent upbringing, but his behaviour was boorish. Thus, turning away, I began to walk back to the house, but became aware of some commotion behind me. I turned again and found myself inches from the towering bulk of the driver. The angry and threatening man stood over me and breathed hard in my face. Scared that he would flatten me, I stepped back instinctively but was trapped by the dividing fence with Fudge quivering in my arms. I felt sick with shock that he might make physical contact with either Fudge or me.

The evening went into meltdown. This man had hurtled out of his car, was on my property, and was threatening me with his closeness and presence. June looked on from the back of the cab, her face registering shock and disbelief. I moved back, shot inside, dialled 999, and breathlessly complained that a minicab driver had assaulted me. North Wales Police turned up fast and in amazing strength. How many actually responded only became apparent as the saga began to unfold. I thought that only two bobbies had arrived at my front door but, as events transpired, most of the available manpower on duty that evening had been dispatched to the incident! Should I be flattered for receiving such attention? Events would show that some unpleasant hidden agenda took over and it was not designed to help me. Two bobbies wandered into my lounge. The dominant one who opened the questioning noted my bruised hand, and took June's details as she had by now abandoned the taxi journey and was preparing to walk home. I learned from one officer that the taxi driver had made a counter-allegation of assault and asked for my reply to this. I totally denied it of course, and was shocked that the driver could be so mischievous. The boss bobby yawned, gave me a visiting card and exited left, leaving me with the impression that this was a storm in a teacup that needed no further police involvement. June duly walked home without Fudge, and the grandchildren were denied the pleasure of doggy company.

As the cab driver's extraordinary attitude was unsuited to driving the public, the next day I reported the incident to the Local Authority's licensing department. I reasoned that if he could cause me so much angst, was he really suitable for his type of work? The official listened politely but, apart from telling me that dogs were carried at a driver's discretion, no avenue of redress was offered. Having discussed events with Robin Makin, my lawyer, he advised me to put the event down to experience. Although this was upsetting, I duly followed his advice. The minicab man had a vastly different agenda. Unknown to me, the following day the driver – Martin Blake – made a series of allegations against me to the police! Following a tip-off, my first inkling of his duplicity came via the *Mail on Sunday* the following weekend. It described in astounding detail how I had rained blows on a petrified man as he cowered in his taxi, fearing for his life. Unusually, no reporter had contacted me for a comment before the article appeared. An even more colourful version of our encounter, plus my photograph, appeared on the front page of the *Welsh Mirror* the following day. Again, the story bore no resemblance to the truth. I was appalled by the way the facts had been distorted to show me as the aggressor, with no mention of the assault the cab driver had made on me, on my property and in front of my friend.

On the 14th January Karen Sinclair rang to offer me time off from Cardiff! Such generosity at this time was not lost on me, but I politely declined and told her that I had no reason not to return to the Assembly. My mobile trilled as I was driving and I found myself speaking to Detective Sergeant Evans of North Wales Police, who began hectoring me as he had to see me urgently. Later, Peter, my Office Manager, confessed to being bullied into releasing my mobile number when the Sergeant rang my constituency office and demanded it. 'I'm driving, you will have to wait until I reach Cardiff,' I explained, and hung up. Tired from the drive, with committee papers to read and unhappy that the police had not seen the need to contact me before the press revelations, I was in no mood for further bullying from Detective Sergeant Evans that evening, and I switched off my mobile.

The Cardiff office phone was nearly jumping off its cradle when I arrived early on Tuesday the 16th January. A now very agitated Sergeant told me he had papers about the taxi affair on his desk.

'Am I being interviewed as a complainant or suspect?' I countered, almost as an afterthought.

'Suspect', he replied.

'Why is the CID dealing with this matter?' I asked.

'A public order offence is involved,' he informed me pompously.

'But what about my witness?' I demanded. 'And who leaked that rubbish to the Sunday paper?'

'That was unfortunate', he muttered, and refused to comment further.

Unbelievably, despite admitting to having the case papers on his desk, he knew nothing of June's presence, nor was he aware that she had agreed to make a statement to the reporting officers the following Thursday. Warning bells were ringing loudly now. The bobbies who attended the incident should have completed a written report and my friend's details should have been included, together with any follow up the officer proposed. 'How can you have the papers and yet not know I have a witness?' I asked him bluntly. He could not reply and, taking pity on him, helpfully I gave him June's phone number. Why, if the officers had done their job on the night, did DS Evans know nothing about June and the pending interview? The bobbies seemed to indicate that the matter was not worthy of further investigation, and yet the Sergeant alleged that I had committed a serious public order offence, purely on the word of an aggressive taxi driver without checking with the reporting officers or knowing that there was a witness. I snapped, 'The driver assaulted me and I made an instant complaint by a 999 call and repeated my allegation to your officers. What are you doing about that?' He brushed the question aside.

I stared in stunned silence at the notes I had just made of our conversation, trying to assess what was going on when Ron wandered into the office. He asked what had happened with the taxi driver affair. I explained that I suspected long knives were out and he nodded sagely, going on to describe an incident that had previously worried him. He had 'exchanged' words with a motorcyclist who had threatened to run over his dogs, and in defence and frustration, Ron had kicked out at the bike. Ron candidly admitted his relief that no complaint had followed. We both agreed that public figures were always vulnerable, regardless of the true circumstances. I was very relieved that my colleagues were supportive at the later Group meeting. I cheered up when Peter Law nicknamed me 'Teflon Halford' and confidently forecast that North Wales 'finest' were wasting their time.

The week moved on and, in plenary on the 18th January, as Jane Hutt was invariably taking a battering from the Opposition and I was scheduled to pose a question, I surreptitiously gave her notice of my proposed helpful supplementary question. Grinning like a Cheshire cat, almost giving my ruse away, I asked the 'loaded' question. Straight faced and serious, Jane rolled out a spectacular reply that raised approving murmurs from Labour AMs. She emailed me across the chamber and thanked me. It was nice to be seen as 'on-message' occasionally and that I had more important things to do than to fret about what Sergeant Evans was plotting!

Later that night, having driven the length of a wintry Wales, Sergeant Evans rang almost as soon as I set foot over my doorstep. He demanded to interview me the following day. I refused, telling him truthfully that my diary was too full and asked if he had completed his enquiries. 'I've just got to get the tapes of the dialogue that occurred in the taxi from the AVACAR office,' he said casually. Tired from a long day and a challenging drive, nevertheless I absorbed this snippet with interest, wondering why he had not collected what could become vital exhibits before the interview. I was sceptical that minicab drivers actually recorded all conversations.

From then on, the Sergeant became an almost daily distraction for both June and myself and I knew I needed legal protection fast. After he had rung me yet again in his demand to see me, I said, 'I'm sorry Sergeant, but I will be instructing my solicitor'. There was a sharp intake of breath at the other end of the phone. 'Someone local?', he enquired. 'Rex Makin,' I said airily. Rex's reputation in Liverpool was legendary and he had carved out a formidable career as a lawyer who stood up for justice and invariably won. DS Evans sounded very crestfallen indeed, as if things were not going to plan; a plan that surely had been devised to interview me under caution as fast as possible, even though the enquiry was not complete – and of course, without the presence of a nosy lawyer to spoil the party! A phone call to Rex Makin immediately gave me the services of Dee, a staff member and a formidable legal warrior, who was soon to appraise the Sergeant of her opinion that I had no case to answer, as the prosecution could not offer any corroborative evidence whatsoever. DS Evans gaily ignored her opinion and demanded that I report to Mold Police Station for interview under caution. With Dee as onlooker, I sailed confidently through this meeting and answered all questions truthfully. The DS lost composure when putting the questions forward and struggled to answer Dee's probing demands for information: when was he investigating my counter allegation of assault on me, and where was any shred of corroboration to Blake's wild allegations? Yet again, Evans replied that my allegation against Martin Blake would be dealt with later. It never was, of course, as time would show that was not part of the Sergeant's remit. Foolishly, I still assumed that justice and common sense would prevail. I was wrong!

In mid April a friendly journalist rang to say that the case papers were going to the Crown Prosecution Service (CPS), a fact shortly confirmed by a jolly sounding Evans who contacted me a day later. 'My witness has supported me completely', I said, 'where's your case?' 'Just routine stuff, Ma'am, as you know,' he responded jovially. It was not routine stuff at all to target June so frequently. She confided that although she had given a detailed statement to the uniformed officers, Evans continued to ring her almost every day or call unannounced at her home, begging her to make another statement. I suggested that she had cause to complain about harassment, and I wondered how a busy CID officer could devote so much time pursuing a witness who had already co-operated fully. As Evans seemed prone to making errors, it seemed sensible to keep him on the case. Cannily, June never pressed a complaint and stoically put up with his constant attentions.

When DS Evans rang to report that the CPS was issuing summonses against me for assault and a public order offence, I believed that this was serious 'payback time' by someone in high places! 'There's no corroboration', I whispered. Not his problem. The Sergeant sounded jubilant. Dee had heard the news and was brisk and businesslike when we spoke. 'We'll defend you,' she soothed. 'It's quite incredible', she ventured, 'someone is desperate to humiliate you and risk running the case with June being used by the prosecution as a "hostile" witness'. This decision had come from the CPS Yorkshire Division, who I learnt specialised in deciding the fate of high profile celebrity cases. I should have been flattered to be given celebrity status, but then I did not know that that CPS department was capable of serious blunders, however important the client!

The prosecution should never have reached court. June was the only witness apart from Martin Blake at the scene, and she supported me. The allegations were: 'kicking the driver's car' (I was in slippers, clutching my old dog and I am arthritic), putting him in fear (a huge man), assaulting him, abusing him verbally as he sat defenceless in his car – and all this under the more serious Public Order Act. The CPS had preferred to believe a minicab driver rather than me with my exemplary background, even though he had leapt from his car, pursued me onto my driveway and had so clearly lost his temper after I rudely offered my opinion of him. Wrexham Magistrates would have the task of hearing this nonsense on a day in August. Who was exacting such revenge? I had a good idea. My complaint of assault by the driver was still being totally ignored then, and forever, it transpired! Work went on, however. Weeks before, Julie Mellor, chair of the Equal Opportunities Commission, had written an apologetic letter to me as I had complained that in my quest for the release of gender balance and related statistics, I was being bounced between Her Majesty's Inspectorate, the Police Staff College and John Gieve,

CB of the Home Office Police Department. She would not have known that I had already moaned fruitlessly to Jack Straw in February, nor that 'Steve' the official had been instructed to make enquiries, but still nothing had happened. I was still convinced that unless this data was published, discrimination would go unchecked and police management in this important area would not improve. Although sympathetic, even the Chair of the EOC could not squeeze an explanation from the authorities on why EOC case notes – forwarded to assist the Police Staff College with their equality database – had mysteriously vanished. After a flurry of emails between us, the Inspector of Constabulary's staff person finally admitted that insufficient staff or resources were available to set up the planned Equality Database! He hoped it would progress when resources permitted!

At Group on the 31st January, loud cheers greeted Jane Hutt's announcement to disband all Welsh Health Authorities. I supported the move as I had never understood their purpose and thought that Health Trusts duplicated their work. Jane promised that savings would be made, but we thought that dismantling a Tory innovation was reason enough on its own. On the same day, Val Feld's attempt to finalise the report for regeneration of the Welsh economy was savaged both by Ron and Alun Cairns. Although not perfect, the document was a brave start on a complex issue and Val, as chair, had struggled valiantly every meeting to obtain a consensus for this vital piece of work. Ron ripped into the attack, mocking the fifteen times the item had been discussed by the committee, but he still believed that the document was insufficiently detailed for its purpose. He also felt that the business community and other consultees had raised too many queries that remained unanswered!

Even I, as the newest committee member, recognised that nineteen months of committee work could not be abandoned. It smacked of incompetence, as if we were incapable of making important decisions to move the economy forward. Val allowed me to speak. I said, 'The *Western Mail's* headlines that Ron is going to savage the policy are unhelpful and we have to work as a team for the good of Wales.' Hesitantly I blundered on, and although I accepted that the document needed pruning, I asked if there was general agreement on it to make progress. Ron, sitting next to me, stiffened as I spoke. Chris Chapman helpfully agreed that we had to give the economic community a lead and I rapidly scribbled a note to Ron and pushed it under his nose: 'She needs help and support, not negative vibes. Can you not find a way of making progress? I do plead with you.' He continued to talk as he observed the note and I thought he was going to ignore it. He began to scribble something on the corner of my note and then, to my amazement, began to read words that offered a way forward. Although the committee nodded in approval as he spoke, Val had not grasped what he was saying and blanked him. Ron muttered, 'She's just rejected the olive branch'. 'She does not trust you', I hissed, 'try again. Let Ron have another go,' I pleaded. Val brought me in to speak again. I spoke from my heart: 'In my long and chequered career, I have learnt that life's all compromise and now we must progress this report somehow.' Phil Williams, the lead Economic Development Plaid AM, nodded vigorously, and a cross party salvage operation was underway.

An uneasy truce was fashioned and, working as a team, the committee cobbled together the words that allowed the report to be grudgingly accepted. Val came to my office and praised me afterwards for turning things around. 'Thank Ron,' I smiled. The next day Sian, the deputy committee clerk who had been the note taker at that extraordinary meeting, stopped me. 'I should not say this, but you were wonderful yesterday.' 'He's still speaking to me,' I joked. 'I had emailed Ron and asked if any one was sticking pins into me. He replied "no."' Ron had controlled his criticism and I admired his willingness to move on.

Health expenditure had been given the highest priority by Welsh Assembly Government (WAG), yet the Auditor General's report published on the 23rd February 2001 made unhappy reading, as clinical negligence claims had increased in four years by 400%. NHS trusts had paid out £27 million in 2000, had 1,600 cases in the pipeline and £107 million was the sum estimated to settle these cases. Jane Hutt was faced with solving the problem of two thirds of the trusts being in deficit, and the Welsh health service had a £5 million shortfall. How would she ever keep money flowing into patient care with the albatross of clinical negligence around her neck?

On the 26th February, although life became more chaotic, I was happy when I added two flea-ridden miniature Dachshunds to my animal tally, since Fudge (she of taxi driver fame), had been pining as she was now alone. The animal Gods looked kindly on me again as they became instant friends, and the new creatures coped well with long hours in the car and also on their own.

By March 2001, Wales was in the grip of the Foot and Mouth epidemic that hit the rural community and tourist trade hard. Accommodation cancellations were running at 75% and the National Botanical Gardens lost thousands of pounds every day they remained closed. The ravages of the disease hit closer to home when Holywell golf club came close to bankruptcy. The course was situated on common land, its fairways roamed by sheep, and it took a day on the phone to find a responsible authority. No one would take a decision and for hours I was subjected to a cynical game of pass the parcel that moved between the Local Authority, MAFF/DEFRA and Carwyn Jones, the Agriculture Minister. My hours of probing officials led me to believe that the disease was dogged by one of the worst cases of bureaucratic incompetence I had ever met. My phone marathon succeeded. Shortly afterwards, the course re-opened and the business survived.

Anne Robinson became almost as unpopular as Foot and Mouth by sneering at Welsh people on 'Room 101', a TV chat show, and duly notched up 5,000 complaints. Some Welsh MPs even demanded her attendance before a Select Committee and North Wales Police started an investigation into her perceived 'racist remarks'. Thankfully, the MPs reconsidered summonsing her, realising that she would attract even more publicity. It was a wise decision as she had a clever knack of turning publicity to her advantage. North Wales Police chose to continue their enquiries, which of course petered out years later. Years before I had written to complain about her mean comments in her weekly column about my dress sense when attending my Industrial Tribunal. Far from apologising, my letter formed the basis of another attack on me the following week. A profile published in the *Western Mail* was kinder than Anne Robinson. I was seen 'as one of the Assembly's more interesting characters, that got knees knocking at Audit committee'. It went on to say some of my Group saw me as a 'loose cannon'. Although the Sisterhood never embraced me closely, I felt this judgement was somewhat harsh!

Rhodri summoned me to discuss the taxi saga before the decision to prosecute had been announced. His line of questioning was disappointing! 'Were you in any way "scratchy scratchy"' he asked. 'No', I replied coldly, 'it's payback time for my years on the Police Authority.' Even the Welsh Secretary, Paul Murphy, was also keen to quiz me over the incident. Invited to his suite of offices within the Assembly, I received coffee and sympathy, which was more than I could say about my meeting with Rhodri.

My meeting with Margaret Beckett, when she visited Delyn's Mostyn Dock on the 26th March was cordial and soon we were on first name terms. She then confirmed that she had been a pupil in my Norwich convent, though some years after I had passed through. I congratulated her on reaching Head Girl and she graciously accepted my praise for making better progress than me, as I had invariably been in trouble for breaching minor rules. Her two minders, sophisticated Rhodean types, deigned to accept my advice that Dee Estuary winds did not respect coiffures, and that any photos should be taken before we trundled off to inspect the dock. Photo call over, the Minister's car was soon sweeping her away with red boxes and husband Leo. Returning to my own messy vehicle, laden with old towels and dogs, I took the road back to Cardiff.

Lorraine raised startled looks at Group the next day by loudly accusing me of putting more money into our pockets rather than into the Wales Millennium Centre. The press had pounced on a comment I had made during the Presiding Officer's review of Assembly powers, when I suggested that AMs' pay should match that of MPs. We were now doing most of an MP's work and they were in the enviable position of picking and choosing what constituency work they were prepared to undertake. Larger allowances enabled them to employ more staff despite decreased responsibility, and my salary as an Assistant Chief Constable some ten years earlier was much higher than my Assembly pay, despite a higher workload. I suspected that AMs would always be inferior to MPs unless we had pay parity. Lorraine clearly did not share my views!

This Auditor General's report of the 3rd May 2001 updated the Audit Committee on the new Assembly building. Jon Shortridge led the official team again and we learnt that 'ministers make decisions; officials only recommend'! No explanation was offered as to why the Assessment Panel chose the winning design, although its footprint exceeded the allocated site boundary. Simply put, most plans, including the winner, were too big for the land set aside for the purpose. Why no contract had ever been signed with the architect two years after the design competition, and why architect's fees were set as a percentage of the final construction cost was not explained! With no incentive to keep costs down, they had increased by 73%. The Richard Rogers' design was particularly challenging, thus its construction was viewed as risky. We blanched when told that the Richard Rogers partnership was paying the Quantity Surveyor, which allowed manipulation of construction costs.

Ploughing through the questions, we learnt that the £500,000 cost to ferry officials to Swansea, had that city won the bid to host the new Assembly, had been included, making their proposal less attractive. Cardiff's £2.9 million travel costs, also for ferrying its officials, had been excluded from their calculations. 'Why did you not include them?' I asked Jon Shortridge. 'At the time the decision was made, it was thought they would not be significant,' Shortridge replied lamely. We launched into a further battery of questions but the answers became increasingly convoluted, and I marvelled at the Permanent Secretary's skill in making responses that were virtually meaningless! Had the Welsh Office been manned by incompetent officials, or was this how the system, however lamentable, was allowed to operate? Ministers made the decisions and the job of the Civil Service was to defend them. It seemed all so cosy and against the public interest! Is this how they earned their inflation-proof pay and those highly prized gongs?

On the 16th May 2001 David Rowe-Beddoe, formerly boss of the Welsh Development Agency, was appointed to salvage the ailing Wales Millennium Centre project. During his presentation to the Economic Development Committee, he candidly admitted he did not know if the plan would ever be financially viable, as success depended on attracting an audience and sponsors. As the project's advisers seemed to choose their words carefully in the reports, I thought that the Assembly was spending public money on a very shaky scheme. The only certainty was that Cardiff County Council still refused to contribute financially and if the project flopped the Assembly, or rather the taxpayer, would pick up the bill. The WMC had the making of becoming our homegrown 'Welsh Millennium Dome'.

A week later, the Culture Committee learned of the dire financial situation of the Botanical Gardens, which was blamed on Foot and Mouth and compounded by its own success with burgeoning school visits that had required more staff and accommodation, and thus more funding. I secretly believed that the Gardens were more deserving than the WMC, and had the distinct advantage of not being in Cardiff. Amazingly, despite the Welsh Office having no provision for its ongoing maintenance and no formal business plan, it had allowed the project to go ahead with public money. Apart from being told to develop a plan quickly by the Culture Committee, the deputations left empty handed. WAG had decreed that the Gardens must be funded from the Culture budget and not from the Economic Development portfolio, and as Edwina Hart struggled to curb the escalating cost of the new Assembly building, Jenny Randerson now received her poisonous chalice also! Wearing her Finance Minister hat, Edwina made a serious attempt to call the four Welsh Police Authorities to account in a memo dated 21st March. She announced that tough action would be taken against high spenders, pointed out that they were not directly accountable to the electorate and although not yet ready to cap any authority, she reminded them she had the power to do so!

The memo hinted that her powers extended to capping rogue budgets in 2002-3 cycles as well if necessary. Challenging chiefs and their compliant Authorities was so novel, after Group I congratulated her warmly on her stance. She smiled wanly and looked distinctly uneasy, almost as if she regretted putting words on paper so forcefully. It was soon leaked that the memo was either a) not sent, b) withdrawn or c) replaced by a less challenging and more temperate document. Had she been nobbled? Police Authorities were a law unto themselves and needed reining in, and she had always indicated her disapproval of vastly increasing sums of funding to the four Welsh forces, with no say in how the money was spent. The following year, some Authorities demanded as much as 20% extra cash. I would have loved to be a fly on Edwina's wall when she dealt with such impudence.

The CPS Yorkshire Specialist Squad may well have had their eyes on gongs too when deciding how to respond to the antics of a VIP: John Prescott, the Deputy Prime Minister, who was caught on camera punching the man who lobbed an egg at him in Rhyl on the 16th May. The egg thrower was instantly arrested, but all enquiries relating to John's part in the Rhyl rumble went into 'underdrive'. Time would show that very different standards were applied when judging our respective cases!

Despite Mike German's unpopularity, he handled his economic ministerial role well and was master of his brief when he addressed the North Wales Economic Forum on the 21st June 2001. He listened attentively to the business community's frustration that little attention was being paid to the needs of the north; a situation not helped by abysmal transport links. It transpired that he was hardly in office long enough to act on the Forum's wish list, as on the 5th July his enemies pounced. Plaid Cymru and the Welsh Conservatives united to demand he should 'stand aside' and the killer blow was delivered by Lord Carlisle, a senior Liberal, who finally shattered Mike's hope of hanging onto his job. Jeff Jones, the Bridgend Council leader's concerted effort to challenge Mike's probity into WJEC affairs, was succeeding. Mike's reign as Deputy First Minister in a despised coalition ended ignominiously as South Wales Police investigations into alleged fraud within the WJEC began to gather pace. My Labour colleagues exchanged spicy tales of his perceived Gulliver travel traits, his hotel and hosting arrangements, fuelled by a *Wales on Sunday* report that Jenny Randerson had denied 'a love scandal' with Mike after she was named in the WJEC report.

There was much rejoicing that the arrogant Mike had fallen, particularly by those who had been sacked to make way for the pact, but somehow the coalition was still in existence. Rhodri still had to get on and govern, and certainly did not share the euphoria. Although Mike nominated Jenny to take his place as Acting Deputy First Minister, thankfully he was sufficiently astute not to do his ex-deputy's bidding. Rhodri still saw Mike's departure as a temporary measure and in plenary was frequently forced on the back foot by the Opposition, who took delight in scoring political points over Mike German's demise. Not only did Rhodri have to endure Opposition derision, he was obliged to take on the Economic Development portfolio again. Dubbed as '3 jobs Morgan', he soldiered on until February 2002, when, under heavy pressure, he gave Andrew Davies the economic portfolio, but only after having to make it clear that Andrew should keep it even if Mike rose like a phoenix again.

July proved a challenging month for the Assembly and for more than one AM. Ron Davies stonewalled in Group on the 3rd July by refusing to admit that he had applied for a high-powered job outside politics. 'None of your business,' was his stance that produced even greater resentment within the Group, several of whom predicted that he would be ousted from the Assembly in 2003.

'Good Morning Wales' on the 4th July announced that Richard Rogers had launched a stinging attack on Edwina and her officials. He accused them of continuously attempting to disguise the true costs of the design changes they had stipulated, and suggested that the future of the new building was seriously threatened. Meanwhile, on the 5th July 2001, the Audit Committee waded into the Bay again, courtesy of the AG's second scrutiny exercise entitled 'Securing the future of Cardiff Bay.' The yearly maintenance of the Barrage and Bay was estimated now at £9 million, and Sir John was also examining the first year of operation and what had happened since April 2000 by way of operating and maintenance costs.

Doubtless enraged by Lord Rogers's attack on the 4th July, Edwina sacked his partnership on the 17th, citing 'loss of confidence' and cost pressures as the reason after what was described as a furious exchange of leaked letters on both sides. Since approving the project on the 26th January 2000, costs had soared by 93%, and more were anticipated. After announcing that new contractors would be sought, Edwina clammed up when the Group harried her for full details of what was going on behind the scenes. She fell back on the increasingly popular cabinet excuse of 'commercial confidentiality' to remain silent. Briefing and counter-briefing continued until the 17th October 2001, when all AMs received a letter from the Richard Rogers partnership, pleading that he had not being given a fair deal. Ron seemed to have his finger on the pulse of what Lord Rogers would do next and from one or two telling but vague remarks, I suspected that he was running with an ennobled hare and hunting with Labour hounds!

Sadly Val Feld died of cancer on the 18th July. She had relinquished her chairmanship of the Economic Development Committee to Christine Gwyther and I had assumed it was just a temporary measure. She shared her frustration over having to take time off through sickness with me, but I reminded her that health was more important than politics. She did not return from the Easter recess and I assumed that she was having a planned operation in England to relieve a stomach problem. Even hearing that she was in a Swansea hospital after collapsing, I did not guess how ill she was. Neither did the penny drop when the Group learnt that Rhodri and Edwina had visited her but had to wear protective garments. She despatched upbeat emails to us and I regularly responded with juicy details of what was occurring at Economic Development Committee meetings. Her researcher encouraged these communications and told me that Val appreciated them a lot. Leighton, my new Assembly Researcher, broke the dreadful news of her death as I got back to my office, and he was also juggling with the phone, whispering that David Rowe-Beddoe was on the line and wanted to speak to me urgently. Presuming I would be lobbied to support the Millennium Centre that was to be debated the following day, and too grief stricken to discuss the addition of another expensive cultural bauble to Cardiff's growing list of assets, I refused to take the call and engage in meaningless dialogue with him. Sir David's attempted personal approach was the clearest indication that the project was by no means secure and could be voted down. Assembly building flags were lowered to half-mast and the decision announced that plenary business would be cancelled the following day out of respect to Val, and AMs would be given the chance to pay last respects to her.

Thursday plenary was a sombre affair with several red eyes in evidence, including mine. Rosemary Butler had placed a rose bearing the colours of the Suffragette movement on Val's empty seat. We listened attentively to speeches, led firstly by Rhodri, followed by the other party leaders and then those of her AM colleagues who had known, worked and campaigned with her for years. I wept for her passing. When in her company, she would hold my equality achievements up as one of the Equal Opportunities Commission's finest victories, and never ceased to praise my courage in withstanding Establishment vindictiveness. She only mentioned that she was suffering some gynaecological condition that just needed a special operation, and although admitting to some discomfort, she never took a day off through sickness until she collapsed. She must have known that she was seriously ill, and yet she played it down and the cancer was never mentioned. Her political life had not been easy. She had endured a host of dirty tricks such as razor blades and nasty notes through the mail throughout her bitterly fought Assembly campaign. 'Old Labour' loathed the thought of women representing them and tried hard to see her off. She was Cabinet material but was outside the Alun Michael magic circle. Like Ron, she was a canny politician who could see the pitfalls and work out solutions. Her contributions to Group discussions were always apposite and sharp.

A day after Val Feld's political career ended, another reached its pinnacle when Barry Jones MP reaped the reward for many years of total loyalty to his Party when he entered the House of Lords. He had delayed announcing his retirement until the 16th February 2001, thus starting rumours as to why his decision to retire from his constituency was so late. The AEWU (Alliance of Electrical Workers Union, now Amicus) moved fast by introducing their candidate Mark Tami to constituency branches. Although Transport House in Cardiff imposed the short list, he won the selection contest against a strong field, which also included Margaret Hanson, wife of my Delyn MP.

Mark was well known to the Airbus workforce through his union activities and won, securing 80% of the postal vote. Mark replaced Barry as the Alyn and Deeside MP in June 2001. Coming from London with few links with Wales, his selection caused outrage in some quarters, to such an extent that several Labour councillors refused to join him on the 'stump'. Barry's ennoblement put an end to the silly game of second-guessing his title, as it was well known that he was ever hopeful of such a preferment as a fitting end to a distinguished parliamentary career.

I met the future Archbishop of Canterbury in a tent over Welsh cakes in Llangollen on the 21st July, at the 'feeding of the five thousand' event, an ecumenical celebration organised by the Church of Wales. I had been invited to the weekend of prayer, was made welcome, given a tour of the site and finally ushered into a marquee for tea. I was soon conversing with a bearded, bespectacled cleric with a mellifluous voice. Knowing nothing about the Church of Wales, I asked chattily how he enjoyed the House of Lords. 'I'm not entitled to sit', he replied patiently, 'the Church of Wales is not affiliated'. I apologised for my gaffe, and got stuck into the scones. We met again in Bangor in 2002 as he gave the sermon when the Queen visited North Wales on her Silver Jubilee. He had been shortlisted then for the Canterbury job, and he preached a thoughtful and clever homily, poised high above her majesty seated below, entirely unfazed by the grandeur of the occasion.

In another part of the country, the hapless Crown Prosecution Service was beavering away on my case. CPS lawyers turned up at various pre-trial hearings before the big day, set for the 3rd August 2001. Amazingly, at one such pre-trial hearing, the Crown lawyer knew nothing about June's statement to police, yet she was the only witness. I worried about the impartiality of the Bench and the way the case was being handled. I knew from my Police Authority experience that the JPs invariably agreed with the Chief Constable, and I was not sure that the Bench hearing my case would not be of the same ilk!

At the trial, cock-ups continued apace in the courtroom. The two officers gave evidence without the usual notebook aide-mémoire and contradicted each other badly. Although they had both arrived at my house in the same vehicle, one bobby gave his arrival time some ten minutes later than stated in his mate's sworn testimony. Giggles of derision arose from the public gallery when the officer explained he set his watch ten minutes late so he wouldn't miss his appointments. The stern woman clerk, who orchestrated events in a bossy and peremptory manner, did not falter in her note taking, despite the timing gaffe! The prosecution witnesses, including June, who was called as a 'hostile witness', took the whole day. Taxi office staff had been called to bolster the shaky prosecution and as it reached my turn to enter the witness box, the clerk cajoled the Bench into adjourning the hearing. I had two more weeks to wait before I could have my say. On the 13th August after another full day, the case collapsed like a pack of cards. I took comfort that even with the determination of the CPS to treat me differently from 'Rumble in Rhyl Prescott', the British judicial system had an awkward habit of requiring evidence to stand up in court before conviction prevailed!

Character letters provided by Dafydd Wigley and Peter Law were duly read out and with one bound I was free. Sarcastically, I bowed low and thanked the unhelpful and heavyweight clerk. She glowered, waggled her substantially sandaled feet and fiddled with her notes. My supporters in the Gallery noted afterwards that she invariably found for the prosecution when the JPs wanted guidance on a point of law. By comparison, the prosecution's barrister looked mediocre as my barrister dealt easily with her and that irritating and pedantic clerk. The clerk appeared to have eaten something disagreeable for her lunch! It had not been a good day for her either! I marched out to face the press, leaving the prosecution team looking bemused. Martin Blake had returned and stayed until the end of the hearing. An unusual practice, according to my team! In the witness box, he had denied the press had offered to buy his story. He looked crestfallen outside the court when a man, possibly a journalist from the *Mail on Sunday*, shrugged and walked quickly away from him. It was not only the police officers who had been more than economical with the truth. Martin Blake must have lost two days' wages whilst attending court, and my acquittal neatly ended any opportunity of selling his story to the press.

The court hearing revealed that four officers had been sent to my house on the night the incident broke out, and I was astonished as the number of officers available for deployment nightly across Flintshire is always dangerously low. Complaints of slow response or none at all were legion. Why then had the police managed to arrive in such numbers? I emailed the Chief Constable and asked why most of the evening's shift had been dispatched to my home. Richard Brunstrom replied that my quest for information 'could be construed as an improper attempt to influence the outcome of my case' and was therefore declined. Wearily, I asked him to reconsider his offensive suggestion. Did he not recall that officer deployment numbers were available to the public and published at Authority meetings? His memory suddenly improved and the reply was as I had suspected. Almost half the available shift had been dispatched to the incident. Should I be flattered or irate?

The *Times* reported on the 21st September that Prescott was 'let off the hook over election punch-up' after the £250,000 investigation, which had taken four months to resolve. By comparison, the taxi saga had occurred on the 7th January and I knew in late May ('charged' 31st May, according to newspapers) that I was heading for court. I wanted answers, both to the cost of my case and why the CPS used double standards for both cases, particularly as the world had witnessed John Prescott's indiscretion. So, I wrote to the Chief Constable and the Director of Public Prosecutions. I suspected that the ploy of stretching out the decision to prosecute for so long had allowed fading memories to blur the facts, and in truth, he was never going to be prosecuted. Was he even interviewed under caution? I think not.

David Calvert-Smith (plain 'Mr' at this time), got my very tough letter asking why John Prescott received preferential treatment, why the officers had not come up to proof under oath, had contradicted each other and what my case had cost? He replied that he did not like 'the intemperate tone of [my] letter and CPS staff endeavour to do their best in difficult circumstances'. The Bench had not criticised the officer's evidence and 'I am sure you will remember from your own experience that it is rare for evidence given by two witnesses to match exactly'! As he knew I had been a police officer, I wondered what else was known about me. What was stored in that large orange folder marked 'Alison Halford' that sat conspicuously with the Prosecution team's files?

For a top lawyer the Director was incredibly imprecise over the reason why I had been prosecuted under the 51% chance of success rule. He did not know 'the costs of [my] case as the CPS did not keep figures for individual cases.' 'Are you not audited or have no commitment to Value for Money principles?' I replied. CPS staff suddenly discovered a calculator and my case was estimated at £2,500. I asked why his department was suddenly able to give me a cost. With considerable aplomb, he replied that my original request had been for 'work undertaken by the North Wales Police, and that had 'been assessed as £275.77.' Amazing! Surely no account had been created of the many visits DS Evans made to Mrs Jeffreys, or interviewing witnesses, or half the night shift appearing on my doorstep, or officers' time in court etc? Chief Constable Brunstrom stuck to his guns and the calculation was £300 for the police investigation. When I again pushed for a more realistic figure, the cost grudgingly rose to £1,076.04. I gave up at that point, knowing I would never obtain the truth. I never discovered how my case covered two full days in court with witness time and expenses, and yet John Prescott's great escape from prosecution cost thousands more! Odd really, as the same force was involved! The Director had decreed my letter to be 'intemperate'. In my judgement, he should have reserved that word to describe his own staff's handling of the case!

Following Mr Calvert-Smith's suggestion, I wrote to the Clerk, Sian Jones, who had officiated in my case, and asked her to comment on my perjury allegation. Her reply on the 3rd October was wonderful 'wriggly weasel-speak'. I had no witness to confirm what PC Griffiths had said in the witness box; she pontificated and, unbelievably, her note was silent on that point, as she did not think that part of the evidence was material to the case! So, two officers arriving at a scene together can give conflicting evidence on oath, and that's all right then? She suggested options: persuade the CPS to commence a further action, or try a private summons. Although she wrote the latter was within her gift, she would not be granting one! My suspicion that she was not a member of my fan club was well and truly confirmed.

In September I travelled to the Scottish Parliament in Edinburgh for a weekend event, hosted by an American political organisation that was the brainchild of Hillary Clinton. Because the events of the 11th September prevented her from attending, she addressed us by video link and explained the goal of promoting closer links between women in politics. Plaid Cymru AMs turned up in good numbers which was more than I could say about my own colleagues, although Karen Sinclair and her faithful shadow, Ann Jones, had made the effort. We all found ourselves rubbing shoulders with Scottish women parliamentarians and Irish Assembly Members, together with a mixed bunch of UK women MPs. I was impressed with the Tory contingent, Theresa May, who had not yet developed her spectacular footwear tastes, as well as with the more down to earth, approachable Caroline Spellman. I cheekily suggested to Caroline that she should change to Labour, as it would be years before the Tories came back to power. She grinned and said the Tories needed all the women they could get, and that Iain Duncan Smith had already given her promotion by being made a Whip early and then onto a shadow position. She was staying a Tory, thank you very much!

Hungry after a long day, I found a table in a crowded Italian restaurant and ordered pasta and wine. A few minutes later a crowd of women MPs and MSPs bustled in, and, as space was short, tables were pulled together and my wine was soon refreshing the MPs' throats. Jenny Tongue, a Lib Dem spokesperson for something or other and Julie Morgan, Rhodri's wife, were particularly pleasant and I enjoyed the company of these hard working and successful women politicians. However, not having their energy, I soon said goodnight and returned to my hotel. I worked on a project required for the following day and, desperately tired, drifted into an unusually deep sleep. I was awoken by an ear-splitting sound and thought that

I had left the TV switched on or the phone was ringing. It dawned slowly on me that it was the fire alarm. Peering outside my door I heard or smelt nothing and the corridor was deserted. People appeared to be huddled together on the street far below but I was half-asleep. I was reluctant to leave my room as I was ashamed that I had scratched insect bites around my ankles, having returned from a mosquito-ridden birdwatching trip, and blood had congealed on my pyjamas. I went back to bed and eventually the dreadful noise stopped. At breakfast the following morning Julie Morgan asked where I had been when the fire had broken out. I muttered that I had chosen to conduct events from my eyrie and dashed to the servery for another helping of prunes. I felt too stupid to admit I was more worried about the blood on my pyjama legs rather than risking my life in a possible towering inferno. She gave me a sideways look and got on with her breakfast.

Recess finished on the 15th October with a bonding 'Away Day' to discuss our plans for the new term in Government. It was held in the cavernous labyrinth of Cardiff County Hall and I was surprised that this important agenda had been spurned by so many of my colleagues, mostly as usual from southern constituencies! Opening my Cardiff property after months away, I found a graveyard of dead insects and a note from the Local Authority explaining that the reason for the infestation was because the ecology of the Bay had not settled. Dragonflies, bats and more birds were urgently needed to remedy the problem. How ironic; the ratepayer had stumped up millions to remove one type of bird, only to pay again for nesting boxes to attract others to devour the insects!

The next day, the usually cagey Edwina became more talkative about the Richard Rogers affair when we met at a lunch hosted by the Governor of the Bank of England, Eddie George. She was trapped with me in a crush of people before the meal and I chided her for the growing mess and, following a steer from Ron Davies, asked who held the 'intellectual rights' to the design? She admitted candidly that she had not wanted the job; she saw it as a means of bringing her down, but intellectual rights belonged with the Assembly. 'Thank God for something,' I muttered, and we parted to sit down for lunch. With an Economic Development meeting scheduled for 2.00pm, I had to rush lunch – missing dessert and coffee – so I was in no mood to be fobbed off with more official fudge on the delays with the Harbour Authority Business Plan. I was not the only unhappy AM present at the meeting, as Rhodri Morgan impatiently dismissed the Alun Cairns demand for the appointment of a dedicated Economic Development Minister, and snapped that Alun should 'focus on results and not personalities'. Hardly any progress was made to glean the information I required and sensibly the Committee Clerks, John Grimes and Sian Wilkins, suggested a meeting with the civil servants responsible for funding the Harbour Authority. This was an excellent suggestion and Leighton set about making necessary arrangements, as I was very concerned that oodles of money could be thrown at Cardiff County Council without proper monitoring.

On that same day, the 17th October, Richard Rogers emailed all AMs, blaming changes the Assembly wanted to the building for increasing the cost. The *Western Mail* reported that legal action was being planned against each AM. Ron Davies rattled WAG's cage by seemingly siding with the Richard Rogers Partnership as he suggested the email figures were a complete rebuttal to Edwina's July statement to plenary. Who was right? Ron was so well briefed he had mentioned the 'intellectual rights' issue to me, and I wondered who Ron was really supporting – the Assembly or that controversial architect?

If Rhodri had tuned into the radio at breakfast time, that meal in the Morgan homestead would not have been particularly jovial as his wife Julie hit the airwaves, vigorously denouncing bombing Afghanistan and demanding an end to it. This was a brave comment from a Labour backbencher in conflict with her own Government. With unfortunate timing, Rhodri also had to deal with the row erupting in the Group over how Labour should respond in the forthcoming Opposition debate on the war in Afghanistan, orchestrated by Plaid Cymru. Plaid wanted to expose differences we had with colleagues in Westminster but the debate was meaningless, because security and defence matters were not devolved. As the opposing parties were free to choose a subject, we could do little apart from vote down their motion or submit our own amendments.

The Group struggled to find a form of words that would limit the damage, and Rhodri told us we could vote freely as long as we were not seen to disagree with the Prime Minister. Richard Edwards ignored this challenging instruction. He towered above us, both in height and in moral turpitude, and he raged over his hatred of the war in the debate on the 23rd October 2001. Richard supported neither Tony Blair, nor war. He denounced, 'Self righteous Western leaders in the pocket of multi-national companies that profited from third world exploitation – the West could not claim the moral high ground when they were leading exporters of arms.' It was real blood and thunder rhetoric as the front row Labour Cabinet slunk lower in their seats. I admired his honesty and passion and I happily joined in the Opposition's applause. Had I spoken in such a way, Karen would have doubtless sought to remove the Whip from me.

Swansea hosted one of the many Culture Committee evidence-gathering sessions from numerous organisations, whilst battling to find solutions to our Review of the Welsh Language. One group definitely had an Orwellian approach to the problem of only one parent speaking Welsh. Although we acknowledged learning early at home was crucial, their demands that the parent spoke only Welsh to the child reminded me of the 'thought' police in the Orwell novel 1984. Professor Howard Carter caused the most outrage by telling the Committee that 'to be Welsh is to speak Welsh', and received a severe drubbing in the press for this zany comment. Paul Murphy was also in the firing line and was branded a slow-coach by fellow MPs under a grilling by the Welsh Affairs Committee, which decreed that Welsh Office failed to pay bills and answer letters promptly.

The Assembly learnt from Carwyn Jones that Europe was threatening £300 million fines if we did not scale down our opposition to GM crops. We grudgingly approved new regulations rather than face legal action from Europe. It was generally a bad plenary session all round, as a man seated in the public gallery behind us staged a protest against Brian Gibbons AM who was defending the use of incinerators to handle waste. The protester, shouting loudly, was led from the chamber and we worried about our own security again. Police and security staff were in the chamber but it was still far too easy to jump the railing and rush at AMs from behind. I sat on the back row with my back just feet from the public, and wondered if this episode, captured on TV, would be repeated again.

Jessica Morden, the Welsh Labour Party General Secretary, had left several messages for me for days and she finally pinned me down on the 25th October. She was blunt and came straight to her point! She wanted to know, and was not prepared to wait any longer, if I was standing at the next election (some eighteen months away). She had originally started pressing for my reply in September, and it seemed to me that her forward planning was disproportionate. Although I had made an 'off the cuff' remark in *The Independent* weeks earlier that I was only going to serve one term, I was coping well with the routine, was happy with my contribution to Assembly life and work, and strove hard for my constituency who appeared to value me. I would have preferred to keep my options open and my vague response did not please her at all. She resorted to attempting to bully me, repeating darkly that '"the Party" would be most upset if I did decide to stand again after all my pronouncements and "stuff!"' I asked who the 'Party' was but she ducked the question. Emboldened, I asked if she had the decisions of all Labour AMs including Delyth Evans? Delyth was undecided about her future. She was having difficulty juggling political work with a young family, plus the added duties of a Deputy Minister role. We both knew that she was a bright prospect but she had confided she could not face a further term. As Jessica refused to answer my question,

I coyly admitted that she would be the first to know my decision. Not the reply she had sought!

With eighteen months to run and two winters to survive, I was angry that I was being eased out so prematurely. Apart from asking awkward questions and seeking to scrutinise Assembly business, I had been a loyal and hardworking member. Leighton thought the 'Party' might have been Jessica, and we mischievously discussed possible scenarios of her prematurely promising my constituency to another, and then realising that she may have overstepped the mark if I chose not to leave.

Eleanor Burnham had taken over the chair of the North Wales Regional Committee under 'Buggins-turn rules', and on the 26th October her choice of destination seriously challenged my map reading skills! The Regional Committee met in a community centre, deep into rural Wales and close to the highest waterfall in Wales. The large turnout indicated that others were better equipped at orienteering than I was! Each meeting examined a particular subject, then local groups were invited to present their case. Rhodri invariably attended and participated in a question and answer session. The entire Assembly circus included security staff, police officers, translation and sound gear and committee support staff, who all travelled north too. Beverages were supplied free and attendance at the North Wales meetings was always higher than at other regional committees. Regulars turned up at every meeting to lobby us and share views; these bonding occasions gave the public an opportunity to be heard and to challenge us in a unique way. And of course, the 'open mike' suggestion was now very much part of the Committee infrastructure.

Eleanor presided over a presentation by Brian Gibbons, a GP AM, into ageing. The report, 'Growing Old', painted a rosy picture of what the elderly could expect in their declining years. Brian was Jane Hutt's Deputy Minister and had no option but to talk up services that would be forthcoming. Jane Hutt had also commissioned a report into the funding of healthcare across Wales, and I was hostile to the plan to reduce funding in the north-east and re-distribute to the south-east and the valleys. I got a loud clap when I opposed this plan in principle, and an even greater one when I pointed out that free bus passes needed buses to board. My constituency work had introduced me to the shortcomings in facilities for the older person. I had exchanged letters with an academic charged with researching women's needs, focusing particularly on the dwindling availability of public loos. She was convinced that the closure of public toilets had contributed to an increase in urinary infections in women. When I said that incontinence pads should be free and feet and teeth moved up the priority list, I almost got a standing ovation. My Labour chums on the top table looked glum. Had they known that Jessica Morden was pushing to get me to stand down, they would have cheered!

To revitalise flagging support for the Afghan war, Tony Blair was scheduled to address the Assembly before plenary commenced on the 30th October. Many of the newspapers pleaded that the AMs should speak out against the war, but this was easier said than done from the political perspective. During a difficult and emotional Group meeting, Lynne Neagle's chairmanship was unusually brutal. She was in an uncompromising mood and I was slapped down for making a remark about increasing the Assembly budget to secure the Richard Rogers building. We learnt that Tony Blair's visit had been planned months earlier and was not a dramatic dash to Cardiff to dredge up Welsh support. It took 30 minutes to reach a shaky consensus on how we should behave when he arrived in the Chamber. Sue Essex thought she would have a problem if any part of his speech commended war, and Delyth Evans and Ann Jones were both close to tears. Delyth thought that he had the most difficult decisions to make and as he would be PM for the next fifteen years, we had to support him. Ann said that she could not bring herself to stay in the chamber, much less clap him. These personal dilemmas were very real and I was still uncertain what we had collectively agreed in Group towards Tony Blair when he arrived in the

Chamber. The very presence of him stepping effortlessly towards the podium largely resolved any dilemma. After the slightest hesitation, the Labour Group stood for his entrance, albeit slowly from some seats, and applause sounded around the Chamber. Even more slowly, the Welsh Conservatives rose for him too and then we settled to the speeches.

Wearing a white shirt, cuffs that protruded, no rings or glasses, he looked every inch a Prime Minister. Tall, slim, fluffed-up hair and bright intense eyes, he dutifully called Lord Dafydd El Mr Presiding Officer, and after twenty minutes of delivering a carefully drafted text, he bounced out of the Chamber to hesitant applause. Again, most of the Labour Group rose in deference but this time Plaid and Tories remained in their seats. I was interested in a tall, stern-looking woman with a flapping, shapeless coat who had stood with her back to the chamber door and peered watchfully at us throughout his speech. She followed him out when it was all over and I was pleased that he had a woman to guard him. Normal business resumed after five minutes. We had all behaved impeccably and the Party apparatchiks were pleased!

Although the day had been full, I ingratiated myself with Lorraine Barrett by dashing to a RSPCA reception she was hosting in the Milling area. Looking pleased to see me, she immediately took me to meet the society's president. We were soon joined by Dafydd Wigley who regaled us with stories about his long-tailed corgi. The reason for the presentation was to raise awareness of the need to change legislation to allow vets greater freedom to despatch a suffering animal, as current legislation was inadequate. Cramming a pork pie into my mouth, I bowed out as soon it was polite to do so and rushed to a clashing All Party Cancer meeting. Jane Hutt shared the top table with a charismatic Professor McVie, a world-renowned expert in his field who thought that before long, every cancer would be recognised and an antidote available to zap it. Soon cancer would be beaten, he confidently announced. A surgeon in the audience rather bluntly begged to differ, and Jane took a lashing when the surgeon crossly denounced the bed shortage that cancelled urgent operations almost at the theatre door. He described patients' frustration and said that surgery was still a major tool in fighting the disease. It was now 7.00pm and my animals had been alone for eleven hours – that would not please the RSPCA. As the cancer experts argued their corner before an implacable Health Minister, I apologised and fled. After an ecstatic welcome, a short walk round the marina and gobbling food to supplement the RSPCA pork pie, I started work again by reading papers for the economic development meeting the following day.

Val's death must have been a godsend to WMC supporters, as the moment for a full debate passed when the plenary session was given over to paying respects to Val. The Assembly then went immediately into summer recess. The chance of full plenary scrutiny of one of its most controversial projects never occurred again. That missed opportunity to probe the scheme at an early stage became even more depressing when one of the three remaining contractors pulled out of the project, claiming that the £60 million scheme was too risky to take on. That was only a fraction of the full cost – some £104 million was mostly coming from the ratepayer when private sponsorship failed finally to materialise.

On the 1st November Edwina broke her silence over the Assembly building by announcing that the bidding process had been completed and a new contract would be awarded in the third quarter of 2002. Completion was expected in the second quarter of 2004. Cannily, Edwina asked the Auditor General to review her Department's role in the Assembly building saga. Whether she needed protection from Opposition taunts or recognised that she had been handed a truly poisoned chalice was not clear. Sir John accepted the commission and as Edwina paid for his services, it was only to be expected. Sir John finally reported his findings to the Audit Committee on 'what was a very complex and technical matter' and gave the minister a clean bill of health. How could she ever be criticised when considering the weakness of the Assembly's case? The Richard Rogers (RR) Partnership had been rewarded with an undated contract that allowed costs to rise, specification to be changed and the ability to employ their own quantity surveyor. Edwina found herself still locked into the original RR Partnership agreement and still had to make an interim payment. Her officials must have been overwhelmed to come out of this report mostly with flying colours! The AG sagely warned that litigation between the parties was still an option. He was right. Time would prove that the RR partnership won the ensuing legal contest, despite the Welsh Assembly Government having consulted the most prestigious law firms for an opinion. More millions would flow into the coffers of the designer's firm and the company still had a say in its construction. The poisoned chalice overflowed heavily onto the taxpayer!

By the 7th November the Economic Development Committee was deeply immersed in budget affairs, but the lists of convoluted figures given under various headings to lend credibility to the Assembly's economic plans seemed to raise more questions than produce answers. Anxious for explanations, I sought out my faithful committee clerks and posed some awkward questions. Always the honest broker, John Grimes patiently explained that the budget merely promises that ministers will give 'X' sums to named projects, yet no way exists of matching actual spending to ministerial promises! In fact, everything was so woolly that it was almost impossible to say which ministerial budget was giving what to support the Economic Development plan. I told John not to do anything that would compromise his own career. He replied that, although a civil servant, he was on the 'scrutiny side' and it was OK to challenge officials. He said, 'We know where you are coming from and we support you'. When an email from Alun Cairns, endorsed by John Grimes, arrived stating that the 2001 budget figures were merely a re-hash of the previous year's figures, I winced. Were budget documents truly meaningless, just Ministers' wish lists to gain more votes? We need a few more people like John Grimes in the Civil Service, I thought to myself.

Plenary on the 8th November 2001 was down to 47 AMs, with the usual late arrivals drifting in at 10.00am and then leaving well before the end. I stayed, then gobbled lunch in the canteen with Leighton and was on the road for North Wales by 2.00pm. Having left Cardiff in the brilliant sun, but climbing the Brecon Beacons, my car was soon immersed in a vicious hailstorm, turning the roads white within seconds. The journey was enlivened by reports on the radio of battles raging across the Tora Bora Mountains in pursuit of the Taliban. 'Similar sort of weather here,' I mused, as I walked back into my house through remnants of sleet.

Before the Audit Committee met to examine 'The Arts Council of Wales: Centre for Visual Arts' report on the 22nd November 2001, a summary of the Auditor General's findings arrived via a press notice on the 15th November. The Arts Council for Wales (ACW) had awarded lottery money to the Centre for Visual Arts without considering the application adequately, and failed to exercise proper oversight of the project. The Old Library, a large Victorian building in Cardiff city centre, was to be transformed into a major visitor attraction — the largest in Wales — for exhibiting the best Welsh and international art. Having opened two years behind schedule in September 1999, it closed with huge debts only fourteen months later. Almost £8.8 million of extensive refurbishment, made up of £3.2 million of National Lottery grants and £200,000 of annual ACW grant, went up in smoke. This was made more galling as it was the first large Lottery grant in Wales to be awarded by the Arts Council (March 1995). The Auditor General concluded that the 'attempt to establish a contemporary art gallery had failed', that 'the project was badly planned', the 'assessment of risk inadequate' and 'the ACW then failed to monitor progress that would have headed off a crisis'. I could not understand why the individuals who had headed the project and created such a financial mess were not to be called as witnesses. We were getting Peter Tyndall, Chief Executive and Accounting Officer for ACW, but he had been appointed only six weeks previously, in October 2001. He was to be supported by Ms

Frances Medley who had been appointed to the ACW in November 2000, and yet the project had seriously begun to take shape in 1992 when a steering group had been established to assess its feasibility.

When the National Lottery was launched in November 1994, the project was well on its way to success. I asked the Committee Clerk, Keith Russell, why Sir Jon Shortridge was not being called together with Joanna Weston, who had initially set up the mechanism to obtain Lottery funding. He replied that it is the Committee's practice to call only the current accounting officer and is able to do something about past mistakes! He explained that under Standing Order 8.1, the Committee 'can invite whom they like but power to summon is restricted under section 74 of the Government of Wales Act'. Not too impressed by this response, I emailed Janet Davies on the 15th November and asked if Sybil Crouch, the current chair of ACW, could be 'invited' to attend on the 22nd November. 'I believe that she was chair at some stage during this debacle and the new CE has only been in post a few weeks.' Janet's reply was cautious but not dismissed out of hand: 'None of this mess is of his making!' Leighton emailed her again on my behalf as I was by then heading back to North Wales. Leighton suggested that the Audit Committee could call anyone it desired; summonsing witnesses is a different issue but 'it seems fundamentally wrong to spend time talking to someone who was not responsible for the ACW at the time, and why do we have a chair (Ms Crouch), if she takes no control over financial decisions?'

Having received more waffle via email from the Clerk, emboldened, I emailed Janet on the 20th November and asked if she would allow chairperson Crouch and the former ACW chief executive, Jo Weston, to appear before us. Janet sensibly decided that the 22nd November should go ahead and then members could decide the way forward. Peter York, my valiant office manager, on my behalf sent Sir John Bourn an email that pulled no punches. 'I do not wish to make waves unnecessarily but I am sure you will agree that the Committee must he seen to be fulfilling the duty with which it is charged.' He went on to say, 'I am concerned that the Committee should be able to interview the people who were responsible at the time that errors occurred, so as to determine who was accountable for any breach of conduct or policy.' I wince now when I re-read that email to such a distinguished and competent civil servant as it was very challenging, but I felt strongly about the principle of obtaining the best possible evidence from the most appropriate persons. The email bluntly continued: 'interviewing the current post holder is akin to hearsay evidence, and I do not think it right that the Committee can only summon those who are now and only recently in authority, when predecessors can give us the fullest account of what happened. The rules of engagement will result in a fudge if appropriate witnesses are left immune!' I asked for his view before the committee met on the 22nd November.

Peter Tyndall gave a spirited and well-briefed performance when he came before us, but he left many areas that needed further probing. My colleagues agreed to widen the net and call those who had made the decisions that had led to such an unmitigated financial disaster. The Clerk was instructed to seek the attendance of Emyr Jenkins, Chief Executive Arts Council of Wales 1993-98, Joanna Weston, Lottery Director ACW 1994-98 and its Director, 1998-2000, Sir Richard Lloyd Jones, Chairman ACW, 1994-99, one other and finally my good natured adversary, Jon Shortridge for the Assembly. As usual, Sir John Bourn and the team who had compiled the report were present and, as usual, Janet extended the usual invitation to speak in Welsh or English, that translation was available as would be coffee at about 3.00pm. Each witness was then asked to introduce themselves and at 2.00pm on Thursday the 13th December, we were off on a really exciting voyage of discovery. Sir Richard Lloyd Jones opened for the witnesses, apologised for a really stinking cold and a cough and hoped he could be heard. 'I was Permanent Secretary, Welsh Office, 1985 to 1993, and chairman of the ACW from 1994 to March 1999.' Having thanked Madam Chair for the invitation, Emyr Jenkins introduced himself in Welsh as chief executive of ACW from 1993 to 1998, then retired. He wanted to give evidence in Welsh to the committee but would use English, so as to quote and discuss them but would answer questions in Welsh. As father to William Hague's wife, whom she had taught Welsh when he was a former Welsh Secretary, Emyr was naturally accomplished in both mediums.

Jo Weston batted last. 'I was lottery director from 1994 until 1998 and chief executive of the ACW from 1998 to 2000.' She candidly admitted that although she had started work in September 1994, the Lottery commenced in November 1994 and the new unit was working from a blank piece of paper. Emyr Jenkins described how arts were facing the uncertainties of local Government re-organisation and the whole process would be handed over to a shadow authority, as yet unelected, and matched funding from Cardiff City Council, lost unless the project could be finalised to meet the 1995-96 budget. 'We know the problems of Clwyd Theatr Cymru caused by local Government re-organisation', he replied archly. Then Ms Weston made Audit Committee history by announcing 'there was an important error in the report in front of you! I just wanted to point out one of the errors'. There was much foot shuffling under our tables. No one had ever challenged accuracy of an AG's report before. Alun Cairns cut in, 'Would you be kind enough to highlight them and give them in writing so we can consider when making our deliberations.' Jo Weston thanked him for the opportunity.

Sir Richard added fuel to the flames. 'We were not consulted at all during the report's preparation and we could have helped materially. If we undertook to tell you about all our concerns, we would be here until tomorrow.' Alun briskly told Sir Richard that there was no point in going over old ground – we had to use the information we had, but 'if we are questioning you on incorrect information, then you need to advise us.' Sir John Bourn was asked for a comment and, unfazed, stated that the 'usual arrangements had been followed and the current accounting officer consulted'. Mr Jenkins was in no mood to be silenced. I recollected that when responding to the Clerk's invitation to give evidence to the Audit Committee, he had written, 'The report is now in the public domain without my being given any opportunity to contribute to its contents or to check its accuracy. The AG adhered to a convention that such investigations did not involve persons who were no longer in post. My first contact with this investigation is your letter (Clerk's 23rd November). I must add my voice, and say that the convention had not served this committee well.' He told us bluntly that he agreed with Sir Richard and he too began to describe what he considered to be further mistakes. It was a tricky moment and our loyalties were being severely tested. However, I agreed with every point the witnesses were making, and that was the reason I had so doggedly pressed to call the people in charge at the time. It was inexplicable that the AG's team had not checked with the hands-on officials, rather than rely upon the newly promoted Peter Tyndall's six weeks' experience in post. Janet made soothing noises and then asked me to ask my questions. 'Thank you so much for coming', I cooed, 'sorry you are not well, and would it be impertinent of me to ask how you got the job? I was interested in exploring "jobs for the boys"'.

Sir Richard Jones, 'Me?'

Miss Halford, 'Yes'.

'The Secretary of State for Wales appointed me and then extended the period.' 'I can probably be blamed for the fact you are sitting here this afternoon', I murmured. Emyr Jenkins butted in immediately and I asked him to continue. 'I was going to respond to you Miss Halford, and thank you for raising the point to invite us.' I smiled blandly. Although we batted questions and answers back and forth until 5.03pm, we failed to establish how £107,000 worth of assets were not accounted for, why valuable IT equipment was sold off cheap to staff or who had removed the expensive custom built reception desks.

Having no natural affinity with a male Welsh Office Permanent Secretary, whom I assumed was probably a significant mover and shaker in the Cardiff and County club, that Val Feld had derided months before, my desire for justice pushed me into thinking that Sir Richard and his team had been given a raw deal as the public criticism had been damning.

We now knew that in those early days, sophisticated mechanisms to manage risk and to accurately determine visitor numbers just did not exist. I wanted to be fair to both sides and after the meeting, he and I continued a dialogue by phone and letter, thus giving Sir Richard's people every chance to exonerate themselves. He hinted that he did not understand why I seemed to be on his side! In my view, the former Permanent Secretary had a grievance. An extract from his letter dated the 7th January 2002 to the new Audit Committee Clerk said it all. 'Four former ACW servants, now private individuals, have in effect been subjected to what amounts to public condemnation in the press. Sentence was passed before any plea was entered.' This manifestly unfair treatment raises questions about the procedures employed by the National Audit Office. I respected and trusted the Auditor General in a way I had never trusted the establishment before, but clinically linking the facts together indicated that for once, the well-oiled cogs of the Auditor General's review team had grit in the wheels, and that the mode of Auditor General's operations needed more careful scrutiny. The Assembly broke up on the 18th December and I was well on my way through my stint as a Labour AM.

Murky waters and the rise of the Millennium Two.

'Laws are like cobwebs, which may catch small flies, but let wasps and hornets break through.'
Jonathan Swift 1709

When the 1st January 2002 dawned, the Assembly entered into its final full year before the compulsory election scheduled for the following May. The Assembly was still in recess, as most of continental Europe filled their wallets with Euros for the first time. Wales was allowed no such choice as national details of this magnitude were firmly in the hands of Westminster. The 'Today' programme ran the story on the release of Stephen Downing after 27 years' imprisonment for a murder he did not commit, and I listened with contempt to the soothing platitudes uttered by my old adversary David Calvert-Smith, the Director of Public Prosecutions. Not one word of apology, nor even the suggestion that Steven Downing had never been guilty – just that now the evidence was considered unsafe. Yet another prosecution gaffe and another life ruined, but so what? I turned off the radio in disgust.

Just before Christmas (the 19th December 2001), Jenny Trigger had rung my office and spoken to Peter, who reported that she sounded distressed and wanted advice. Having won a partial victory in an Employment Tribunal with her union's help, Mr Dent, the Clerk to the North Wales Police Authority had recently faxed her (27th November 2001), demanding that she should return to work at once, as her suspension was lifted. Her union representative, Elaine Boniface, had asked Mr Dent for an urgent explanation and whether the discipline case against Mrs Trigger had been dropped. On the 7th December, Mr Dent had faxed Jenny Trigger again, and ordered her to return to work on the 10th December. This had so unnerved her she sought medical help and had immediately been placed sick for a

month, as her GP had been monitoring both mental and physical
health for the two years she was in dispute with the Police Authority.

Dent's fax revealed that most of the discipline charges had been
dropped but Jenny Trigger was then uncertain if any action was to be
taken against her, nor was she told the reason for this amazing climb-
down. Naturally, Elaine Boniface pressed to know why Mr Dent was
back-peddling so fast. Unison lodged a complaint against Mr Dent
to Cllr Malcolm King, Chair of the Police Authority, in a very
detailed letter dated 15th January 2002. 'Why', she demanded to
know, 'did Mr Dent and the Chair review the discipline evidence on
the 10th April 2001 and decide to continue the case against Trigger?'
What had altered since April 2001 for the charges to be dropped?
Unison had every right to complain, although I suspected that such
action was a waste of time as Authority and Clerk had been hand in
glove over the treatment of their employee and would continue to
support each other.

Why had Mr Dent insisted, since the 15th September 2000, that
he had been right to use a procedure relating to Mrs Trigger's
contract and yet, twelve months later, had been forced to concede
before the Employment Tribunal that this procedure had not been
correct in law? 'An extraordinary state of affairs from a man who is a
practising solicitor', she wrote to Malcolm King, the Police
Authority's Labour Chairman. She was concerned that Mr Dent's
legally incorrect procedure had caused Mrs Trigger great stress and
had resulted in a gross waste of public funds. Unison had even more
worrying complaints. Cllr King was informed, 'having taken a note
of a letter which was highly detrimental to North Wales Authority's
case against their employee – both in respect of the employment
matter and the disciplinary allegations against Mrs Trigger – this
highly relevant letter to her case was missing from the copy file
Unison had requested.' Unison believed that this letter strengthened
Mrs Trigger's case and undermined the whole basis, 'on which any of
the discipline allegations have been made.' 'Why', she asked, 'had this
missing letter suddenly arrived with no explanation from the Clerk?'

Elaine Boniface asked how Unison could trust the Authority if papers could be removed before inspection, and she indicated that such conduct appeared to be unbecoming of a solicitor and Clerk to the North Wales Police Authority.

Had Elaine Boniface read my book *No Way up the Greasy Pole*, she would have been unfazed by Mr Dent's behaviour. I had personal experience of files being filleted, documents and minute sheets removed or partly re-typed, and Special Branch going into overdrive to make an old police policy file look genuine and not tampered with. Ironically, the same law firm – Weightman-Rutherfords as they were known in the 90s – had acted very vigorously indeed for the Chief Constable of Merseyside when defending him against the Equal Opportunities Commission, who had represented me. What a coincidence that the same firm was acting for the Authority against Trigger. All those years ago I had examined official files and documents, used by me in my job as head of Personnel and Training on Weightman's premises and found that the files had been severely tampered with. Snopake was used on some pages to blot out the proper chronology in the original page numbering, together with other oddities. Was history repeating itself ten years on in another force and with another Police Authority? Surely not?

I had warned the Police Authority colleagues in January 1999 that unless handled carefully, the Trigger saga would cost the taxpayer dear! No one had bothered to listen, not even Malcolm King – who had moved effortlessly from being a stern critic of the force and had willingly signed our 'concerns report' to Jack Straw – to the position of friend of the chief and chair of the Authority. After weeks of negotiation with Stan Rupa, Unison Deputy Regional Secretary, in September 2002 the Police Authority and Kelvin Dent, their Clerk and trained lawyer, managed at public expense to terminate that expensive mess of the Trigger saga. The *Daily Post* headed, 'Trigger Happy' and 'Police lawyer settles £500,000 dispute after three year battle.' This was only an estimate and we learnt that so keen was the Authority to keep outsiders in the dark, the minutes and agendas were numbered and had to be returned. Lawyers had worked on the case for three years – Mr Abraham's report (he who excluded me from his witness list), was just one of the reports called for by the Authority together with the need to instruct counsel. Meanwhile the work that should have been undertaken by Mrs Trigger had to be covered, as the force needed legal advisers. Her union estimated that 'well over a quarter of a million of public money had been wasted.' I was asked to 'put pressure on David Blunkett to order an investigation as to why the Head of Legal Services is suspended for over two years on full pay, by the unqualified acting clerk, Mrs Few, and then on the whim of the current Clerk, the bulk of allegations are dropped?' On the 15th January 2002 Mrs Trigger's Unison rep had written to Cllr Malcolm King, the Chair, to complain about the conduct of Mr Dent.

Mr Dent refused to disclose the full costs. A 'Confidentiality Clause' was the excuse, even though the Auditor General for Wales had specifically outlawed this practice in 2001. I had written regularly to Ceri Stradling, the District Auditor, begging him to involve himself and save public money, but he refused, stating he had no powers. I met with him on the 28th October 2002 and was appalled to learn that although he was finalising a report on how North Wales Police had dealt with their employee – who had outlived her usefulness to the then Chief Constable – only the Police Authority would receive his report. The Authority alone could decide to release it to the public that paid the District Auditor's wages too!

I knew that Elaine Boniface's complaint to Chairman King about the role Mr Dent had played would be a waste of effort, as was mine when I complained to the Local Government Ombudsman and the Law Society over Kelvin Dent's seemingly incompetent handling of the Trigger saga. Why had he allowed the Authority to fight the case, even when advised that she had a genuine grievance and the case should have been settled months earlier, rather than allowing her misery to drag on since January 1999? Mr Dent was on record to suggest that Mrs Few, the acting Clerk, had suspended Mrs Trigger prematurely, this fact having been supported by Chairman King in a letter dated 19th November 2002. He wrote, 'The decision to suspend Mrs Trigger was taken by the acting Clerk', (legally unqualified) 'and was not, and could not, be a decision of the Authority itself.' Diane Few had suspended Trigger on the 16th November 1999, employed Mr Abraham to build grounds to discipline Mrs T, and then found other employment. She left the Authority on the 20th February 2000, making way for the new Clerk Kelvin Dent: a qualified lawyer. Why suspend her before starting a disciplinary investigation? Rather cart before the horse, I thought.

Although Trigger was suspended when Dent became the Clerk, he was still Mrs Trigger's line manager and should not have participated in Mrs Trigger's disciplinary problems, yet that he was actively orchestrating disciplinary action against her was unethical! It was wrong that he was both poacher and gamekeeper and she had no one in either force or Authority to lend her support. I had communicated with Dent, advising that the discipline case would not stand up as most of the charges smacked of a desperate trawl to pin something on her. Unison believed that no senior officers would be called upon to give first hand evidence against her, and the case against her was to be presented by Mr Abraham, who had recommended disciplinary action. How was it possible to conduct what was ostensibly a court action against her if the main witnesses were missing, and therefore their truthfulness could not be challenged? To rely on nothing more than second hand 'hearsay' evidence was completely contrary to natural justice. Neither the Ombudsman nor the Law Society felt able to intervene. The Ombudsman could not accept a complaint from me, and how Mr Dent gave his professional advice to the Authority was a matter for him and not his governing body!

With charges dropped without explanation and an expensive settlement reached months later in August 2002, the saga ended. It was not only the Clerk that I knew was culpable. John Anderson was a long-standing Authority member and experienced chair of the local Magistrates' Committee. His decision to chair the Grievance Sub-Committee that dismissed her complaint for discrimination from her Chief Constable (against external advice from the Devon and Cornwall Clerk who had suggested a settlement) showed bias! The failure to support her grievance opened the door for her suspension. Authority member Barry Harrison was another powerful friend of the Chief, and he too stood by and allowed the wheels of injustice to turn against her. He then moved on to take up the chair of the new local health trust under Jane Hutt's new health scheme.

I wrote a furious letter to her officials suggesting that with his background, his judgement, lack of impartiality and personnel management skills were open to challenge his suitability for this important post. Officials visited me in the Assembly and expressed concern and sympathy with my point of view, but weeks later the capitulation letter arrived. Barry Harrison was judged as a fit and proper person to chair Jane's new Health Trust, and Mrs Trigger's treatment at the hands of Police Authority was quietly ignored. I recalled that Jane announced in Group that finding suitable chairs was proving challenging against a tight deadline! How sad that a recruiting shortfall propelled a dubious candidate into a position that demanded total trust and integrity!

As John Gieve headed the police department in the Home Office, I thought he might be interested in the North Wales Police debacle! His lack of interest was conveyed by a courteous letter dated 30th October 2002: 'The Department cannot comment on personal matters in another organisation. Police Authorities are bodies corporate and not derivative of the Home Office.' He advised that if concerned 'about misuse of Police Authority funds, then you may wish to contact the District Auditor.' I did not bother to write and inform him how I had failed to get support from the Distict Auditor (DA) either! Game, set and match to 'Bodies Corporate'. Tough though on the public purse! Malcolm King, his Police Authority, a permanent secretary, the Ombudsman to whom I complained on the 12th March 2001, Paul Murphy, then Welsh Secretary to whom I wrote on the 30th March 2001 and a District Auditor (having lost count of the letters I wrote imploring his intervention), all sailed serenely on, unscathed and ineffectual. The reason why the discipline case collapsed, why proceedings had taken so long, the reason for the Police Authority to humiliate its former faithful servant and end her career, and the financial cost to the public who paid, remained unanswered, and a Police Authority and its Clerk are unaccountable to law.

Although silent on the settlement detail, Mr Dent was shamed into providing some of the costs incurred over the Trigger debacle. The cost of the Devon and Cornwall report advised that Mrs Trigger had a grievance to be settled – £1,360, excluding VAT. The Abraham's discipline action report: £9,422.47. Representations from three barristers: £8,169 (excluding VAT). Two legal firms involved: Messrs Hammond Suddards, £7,266 (excluding VAT) and Messrs Weightmans, employed by Mr Dent: £31,192.20. As Weightmans had presumably been instructed in 1999, after Mrs Trigger received the ACC John Cooke's constructive dismissal memo, their bill for legal services seemed very modest indeed.

On the 2nd October 2002 I asked Mr Dent to confirm the names to be called as witnesses against her. On the 4th November 2002 he wrote, 'The witnesses whom I would have called had the disciplinary hearing proceeded, were still under review.' She had been suspended in November 1999, the Discipline Panel had met on at least three occasions, and yet the Clerk in charge of the discipline procedure still had not decided whom to call as witnesses? Very odd!

The Wales Millennium Centre debate, cancelled the previous July out of respect to Val Feld's death, was discussed in Group before the plenary session scheduled for the 22nd January. Frustrated, I had to leave to participate in a radio phone-in whilst discussions were in full swing. Many callers were as hostile as I was to this new cultural palace; many complained that evening return journeys by public transport were impossible and that public transport, even from so close as the heads of the valleys, was not feasible. The Centre for Visual Arts had failed due to lack of visitors and I was even more apprehensive that the project would become a constant drain on the Assembly culture budget.

I dashed back to Group only to learn that the vote for the WMC was to be 'whipped', which meant that together with other Labour members I must vote for the scheme, regardless of my personal choice. The demand for a whipped vote came from one of those AMs, who in my opinion, was very close to a conflict of interest, having Cardiff based connections she shared with Alun Michael. Both Ron Davies and Peter Law had challenged this decision but their objections had been ignored. I had just filled the airwaves with my contempt for the scheme and now I was expected to register publicly that I was voting for it after all. £104 million to build and millions needed yearly to keep it afloat: a project that even David Rowe-Beddoe was unable to guarantee. I was mortified. Recalling that I had promised my selection panel that I would take the whip or find a way of compromise, I asked John Marek for advice. He told me that the Westminster procedure was to ask permission to abstain. I duly asked and was refused as 'the Group had spoken'. Peter Law agreed that he could not vote for the Centre; his constituents would revolt! I respected Peter and told him that I too would either abstain or vote against the motion. I was very undecided and worried that Peter would change his mind and I would be on my own in voting against a Group decision.

Plenary started with hushed expectation. Many people, particularly the Cardiff and South Wales contingent, wanted a WMC badly, however risky and expensive. John Marek was in the chair and allowed us more than the usual three minutes to make our speeches. I wobbled through a mixture of my thoughts and those written by Leighton. My only controversial comment related to the Assembly being seen as behaving like a backwater County Council, that had to pander to the wishes of a powerful South Wales minority. Leighton had written the line, which I churned out dutifully: 'Are we to behave like some backwater council, pandering to the wishes of certain south-based Members, or are we going to set proper priorities for the benefit of Wales as a whole?' I then sat down hastily. John Marek gave me a small nod of approval.

The result was not surprising. 50 voted for and two against. Peter and I had stood firm and praise for our stance began to roll in from all quarters. Peter and I left the Chamber together and walked though a chorus of congratulatory chatter from WMC supporters. At last, Cardiff was to get a prestigious new cultural centre that would greatly enhance its chance of winning the European City of Culture bid. I should have rejoiced as it was going to be a cultural icon for the capital, but I kept thinking of how it was ever going to succeed without regular injections of public money. The more that flowed into Cardiff, the less that would ever come to North Wales.

On the 28th January I wrote to Jenny Randerson about the Wales Millennium Centre Funding issue again, as I was genuinely concerned how the project had come before plenary while the Culture Committee had received no indication of budgetary implications. We had been given two presentations and general discussions but no proper financial detail. I wrote that the first time the Culture Committee heard of the general cost was during her ministerial statement on the 22nd January and when she was asked for clarification, emails arrived two days later laying out basic facts. I explained that the Local Government Minister had always shared proposed budgets for general discussion with his committee, although accepted that the Cabinet would make the final choice.

I felt that the way the Millennium project had been handled was a worrying and detrimental decline in the Assembly's scrutiny and general powers. The total project was estimated at £104 million, up to £37 million from the Assembly, Arts Council £10 million and Millennium Commission £31 million, with another £6 million being chipped in from the WDA, Tourist Board and the Cardiff Bay

Development Corporation. Additional funding of £20 million plus was expected from the private sector and some £11 million had already been promised.

Jenny Randerson replied graciously on the 14th February, noted my concerns and knew I would understand the need for commercial confidentiality and that we had seen the Business Plan. She agreed plenary had been told that if some of the perceived risks materialised, the item would be brought back to plenary. She said it was right and proper for Peter Law and me to raise concerns – a smooth conciliatory touch – followed by a final sweetener by referring to a plan by the Arts Council to raise Clwyd Theatr Cymru's funding by 15% next year!

I headed for Pontypridd by 8.20am the next day, as the Culture Committee was to take yet more evidence for our Welsh Language review. The Community Centre had seen better days as the loos were dreadful and the entire building was as drab as the weather. Dafydd Wigley suddenly left the members' table and took a seat in the audience, drank a glass of water and then loosened his tie. I was concerned that he was having a further medical problem and sent a note to Rhodri Glyn Thomas, our chair, pointing out that Dafydd seemed unwell and should he summon medical help? 'He suffers from claustrophobia', the note in reply stated and as soon as the meeting ended, we were assured everything was under control. As Dafydd had announced earlier on the 9th January, his intention to stand down at the next election together with colleagues Cynog Dafis, Plaid's Policy Director and their highly cerebral colleague Prof. Phil Williams, I just wondered if claustrophobia was Dafydd's only problem. Leaving his party so bereft of talent to defend a crucial second term seemed extremely risky, and the *Western Mail* had suggested that PC would be in 'free-fall' if all these stars departed simultaneously.

I left quickly after the session as I had arranged to meet officials who understood the mysteries of Harbour Authority funding and my list of questions was growing. Dr Emyr Roberts introduced his team including David Powell, who had worked previously for the Welsh Office. He had taken retirement, but as he was the man who understood the system, he had been re-employed again by the Assembly to continue the process of funding the Harbour Authority. The meeting was frustrating but good-humoured, with official wicket keeping at its best as so many of our questions were deftly parried. 'We'll come back to that one' was the usual response, particularly when details of cost were required. Emyr admitted that the much-delayed Harbour Authority's glossy report was a 'wish list' and that in truth Russell Goodway had not wanted responsibility for the Barrage. The inference was clear and not fully in the public domain that a very hard deal had been struck by Cardiff County Council for it to be swayed. Leighton and I learnt very little about hard figures but we were told that the Oval Basin, a prominent area of the Bay ripe for new development into an eating and leisure area, was very much part of the financial demands that Cardiff was making. So, WAG-funded Harbour Authority funding would be used to greatly increase revenue and value for the City, but not for the rest of Wales. That hastily signed Memorandum of Understanding (Agreement 165) was, in my words at least, even more closely resembling smoke and mirrors. There had been nothing sinister, we were told, in dumping the successful Thames Water tender in favour of the Council's allegedly cheaper option. By then, Leighton and I were uncertain if any savings made by Cardiff taking responsibility for the oxygenation water work could be kept by them or returned to the Assembly coffers; nor were officials sure if their calculations would attract a large VAT payment.

Officials agreed however, including the rather mournful Keith Parsons and David Powell, that the Cardiff Bay Development Corporation document was legal and although the audit trail was proving difficult to track down, nothing had been wrongly paid and everything was generally OK. 'Even the glaring conflict of interest between the Chair of the Harbour Authority being the same person as the chairman of Cardiff City Council?' I enquired. My notes to cover a response to that particular question mentioned the words 'waffle waffle'. I felt sorry for the officers. They were only trying to execute decisions of the former First Secretary. Although I told Emyr of my serious reservations over the ease in which funds poured from the Assembly into Cardiff – a happy situation not enjoyed by the other 21 Local Authorities in Wales – I promised that I would not lay traps for him at subsequent meetings. I knew he had done his best to disclose as much information as he dared and I resolved not to abuse what little trust he had placed in Leighton and myself. He seemed pleased with my frankness and secretly I marked him up as a future Permanent Secretary, somewhere, sometime, in the vast empire of officialdom.

Leighton and I were undecided if the two hour meeting, attempting to make sense of the Harbour Authority's capacity to spend vast sums of Assembly money, had been worth our effort. Some small consolation for our dedication to detail occurred when EDC next met on the 30th January, as my beacon of knowledge about Bay funding was glowing just a little brighter – in fact, even enough to recognise discrepancies between some information given to us at our meeting and further information given to the committee. In one breath, the claim that savings made by the Harbour Authority by taking over the water oxygenation deal could be kept by them, was contradicted when it was reported that any savings would be repaid to the Assembly! Yet again, no one else seemed to have noticed that the facts did not always match.

I turned my attention to Rhodri Morgan, holder of the Economic Development ministerial mantle again. I admired Rhodri enormously and he headed my list of ethical MPs, but I asked how he was able to support so much money being paid to the Harbour Authority when he was the First Minister, the Economic supreme and also a Cardiff AM. By holding so many positions of power, did he not think that he risked being accused of stifling open scrutiny of Harbour Authority accounts and affairs? He looked very rueful at such a suggestion and coldly dismissed my fears by reminding me that he had voted against the Barrage when he had been an MP. I dared not press my point further apart from muttering that 'we had already seen one controversial decision taken last week', meaning the WMC vote. Was he not concerned that he was too close to funding Cardiff County Council by using Welsh Assembly money? Doggedly, I queried the weakness in the Harbour Authority Business Plan. I did not mention Emyr by name, but disclosed that the document was regarded as a 'wish list', hardly worth the cost of production. Rhodri looked pained; I knew I was making no friends at court so ended by asking, 'Was it sensible to employ the District Auditor to audit some of Assembly sponsored accounts, as well as the Auditor General who was the main player in auditing Assembly expenditure?'

My jaundiced view of the function of District Auditor arose from my North Wales Police Authority experience when Mr Stradling continued to tell me that he could not involve himself in the ongoing Mrs Trigger saga – regardless of the cost – until the matter had been settled by the Authority. Even then, his report would go to the Police Authority who had the right not to disclose it. Of course, I made little progress in putting forward my points and finally, at 6.00pm, the meeting finished its business.

Jane Runeckles, a senior Labour Group flunky, was hovering in the corridor clutching a white envelope that was pushed at me with an apology that Karen Sinclair was unable to deliver it herself. I smiled graciously and beetled back to my office to read that I had contravened National Assembly Labour Party Code of Conduct 1 (d) and 3, when the vote was taken on the 22nd January. My crimes – 'not acting in harmony with the Group by voting against it, and making a speech that attacked the resolution and has caused public difficulty to a number of your Labour colleagues.'

If, on the 5th February, the Group accepted the Group Executive's decision to withdraw the whip, then I would lose the benefits of Group membership for a week. Failure to abide by the whip during this period may result in 'a further review of the suspension period.' Of course, I should have laughed at this officiousness but I was upset by this development. I wrote back seeking information about my attendance and voting record and asked for comparisons with other AMs; what part of my speech caused offence and was this the first occasion that removal of the whip had been proposed for a Group member? I needed this information to defend myself.

No reply was forthcoming apart from the formal confirmation of the whip being withdrawn on the 5th February. The letter was signed 'Karen' rather than her full signature she had used in her earlier correspondence, so perhaps things were softening a little. I moaned about my proposed suspension to a friend who found the situation very amusing and could not understand my chagrin. 'You are always complaining that Karen refuses you any time you want in the constituency, and she's handing you a week off on a plate! She's doing what you wanted; grab it and be pleased.' I giggled and cheered up, particularly when Peter York told me that the newspaper coverage in North Wales was good and my Delyn Party people were proud of their AM. Even so, the Group meeting on the 5th February was an ordeal. I have always been a team player and have lived within rules and codes of conduct all my life, and I found that I was forced to defend myself to people I hardly knew. The turnout was exceptionally good but Jane Hutt and Edwina Hart were missing. Karen shared the top table with Mike Penn, Lynne Neagle, our chair, Rhodri and Andrew Davies.

The first step was to propose the motion to suspend Peter and myself. We were to be dealt with individually and I was first in the dock. Karen nervously read out the evidence against me and invited me to respond. I did not know if I wanted to laugh or cry. Expecting that we would be dealt with together and that I could rely upon Peter's greater Party knowledge and better oratory skills, this threw me, as I had not prepared anything of importance to say. Somewhat emotionally, I gabbled about my dedication to Delyn people whose mandate I had followed and that my objections had been consistent.

Suspending me must surely increase the problems of the perceived 'North-South divide'. Was I to be penalised for taking an ethical stance? As soon as I had spluttered to a stop, Ron Davies firmly stated he would not be supporting the motion; nothing like this happened in Parliament and everything went against Labour Party ethics of keeping to one's conscience and valuing democratic freedom. Lorraine Barrett put the boot in hard. 'Whips have to be obeyed; Alison's done a lot of damage to colleagues' – apparently I had not helped the North-South divide and was not interested in my credibility with my constituents. Peter and I muttered about vested interests and how she had much to gain, being Cardiff based and with a husband actively involved in the Arts.

John Marek was equally swift in denouncing the motion and felt that the Executive's decision was fundamentally flawed. He told Lorraine that she was wrong to criticise me and told the top table to 'get a grip'. He thought the press would have a field day if we were suspended and demanded that the vote be recorded. Tom Middlehurst and Ann Jones were in the Lorraine 'out-to-get-her camp', as was Carwyn who felt some reprimand was necessary, although he acknowledged the building was not popular in North Wales but on occasions, hard decisions have to be taken or nothing gets done. As the vote for the Millennium Centre had been overwhelming, Peter's and my votes counted for nothing: this line of argument seemed thin. Rosemary Butler was definitely a friend and talked about draconian measures and that it might not be right to demand suspension. Lynne quickly headed off her request to amend the motion, as forgiveness seemed not to be on our Chair's agenda. Sue Essex vacillated between her respect for hard working members and a need for discipline. I felt that if she had not been in the Cabinet, she would have joined the Ron and John support for clemency. The Halford-Law duo voted against the motion.

Huw Lewis launched into a convoluted diatribe that amounted to the need for a whip or we would end up like woolly-minded Lib Dems. Was this the same Huw who was ordered to stand down as a deputy minister or be sacked for his attacks on fellow Labour AM Minister Carwyn Jones? Rhodri Morgan immediately agreed with him and then Peter's indictment was read out. His indiscretion attracted fewer contributions and by now it had all been said. Delyth spoke finally that the motion was wrong and we were entitled to stand by our consciences, and even Tom toned down his demands to just suggesting a reprimand. Only Rhodri and Andrew Davies did not speak after Peter had made his reply, but their hands were amongst the first to shoot up when the vote was called. The very first raised hand belonged to the individual who led the charge to have the vote whipped in the first place: the Arts loving Lorraine. I felt humiliated. Jane Davidson abstained and bashfully admitted that she had once been suspended years ago for six weeks. She acted bravely. In Cabinet and very ambitious, it would have been easier to have voted with her masters. I mentally thanked her for her independence.

Nine AMs voted against the motion to suspend, twelve supported Karen to have me suspended and fifteen indicated that Peter should also lose the whip for a week. I was surprised that I had won more support, as he was the Party man. Perhaps that was what had swayed them. He knew the rules and I was still a learner, so consequently more easily forgiven. As the Group moved onto the next agenda, I collected my papers and walked out. There seemed little point in remaining if they had just voted for my temporary exclusion. Peter soon followed and we trotted to the Members' Tea Room for coffee. Within minutes Karen and a minder bowled in. What were we going to say to the press? Minder's pen was poised to take the note. Peter chatted amiably and pointed out that the Group had brought trouble on themselves. I sat stony faced and when she asked me what statements we were making to the press, I snapped. 'You would hardly expect me to answer that?' She left quickly, mission unaccomplished, and came to my office to deliver her letter confirming suspension later that evening. This time I was far more gracious and accepted the document without rancour. 'I really did not want to do this', she moaned. 'I hear you Karen', I countered politely and she crept out looking dejected. I felt mean afterwards for my huffiness. She was doing her job and may just have been the messenger for others who wanted us punished! The suspension rankled because we should never have been whipped in the first place, and therefore my wrath should have been directed at the Group and not the poor, zealous messenger. The suspension seemed a hollow gesture as it was over and lifted almost as soon as it had seemed to begin. I enjoyed a robust note from Glyn Davies that described my lot as 'farts', and not for the first time I noted a greater affinity with the other parties rather than my own.

As John Marek had forecast, the press had a field-day. 'Stick it up your Arts', raged the front page of the *Welsh Mirror* on the 25th January. Our readers' verdict on the Cardiff Bay Millennium Centre, followed by the headline on the 7th February: 'Dictator Rhodri's rebel art attack' by Paul Starling, the *Welsh Mirror's* political editor. Peter nicknamed us the 'Millennium Two' and we swapped letters and press cuttings applauding our stance. Clive Betts, the *Western Mail's* WA journalist, made a telling comment that our suspension was a sad sign of Labour intolerance and that the Centre could be compared with the £700 million Dome. He wrote that AMs, as MPs, have sufficient wit and intelligence not to suffer council style tactics where any dissent is rigorously crushed, and that other AMs used the collective whip as protection from constituents who saw no use for another cultural centre. My Constituency Party wrote to Labour Party Cardiff supporting me and telling them politely to 'bog off'.

A letter dated 22nd January from the Presiding Officer on the mysteries of the Short Debate did little to cheer me up, although it was confirmed that I was not alone in my failure to secure precious debating time on a topic of my choice at the podium, with the added zest of forcing an immediate ministerial reply. Lord Elis-Thomas gave a breakdown of AMs' success rates and explained that I was one of four members who had entered the contest over 30 times and had not been drawn. 'In short, you have been unlucky', but he urged me to keep on entering and hoped that 'my luck would change'. It didn't, and I suspected that the system could be tweaked to be more inclusive and reduce the luck factor.

'Police too sick to work cost taxpayer £10 million' made the *Western Mail's* front page on the 12th February. This was just days before Edwina wrote to the Chair of the North Wales Police Authority, expressing pleasure at the constructive meeting of other Welsh Police Authorities that took place on the 2nd February, but hinted that she would not want to see 'budget increases greater than that suggested'. She accepted that funding anomalies existed between English and Welsh Police Authorities, but thought it vital to obtain solid evidence to help establish a case. I believed that the Assembly should take over full responsibility for policing in Wales, and even Richard Brunstrom concurred later at a Regional Committee.

Funding was a mess with the Home Office slowly reducing its grant to police forces from 51% to 48% of total expenditure, thus increasing the burden either to the Assembly or onto Council Tax. The Home Office were crafty too. Announcing a 6.1% increase in 2002-3 sounded fine, but after top-slicing (taking back part of a promised sum for another purpose), the average increase shrank to less than 3%. With police sickness rising and even larger sums required for sick and regular pensions, police forces were struggling to make ends meet. However, the Police Authority could determine what budget it required. It then fell to councils to collect any shortfall from the Home Office and Welsh Assembly funding, by the mechanism of their Council Tax. Edwina had a good grasp of the problem and had policing been devolved, she could have made a substantial contribution to challenging high spending Police Authorities, who, as was the case in North Wales, seemed unable to refuse the Chief Constable's voracious demands.

On the 15th February Edwina was in the firing line as 'the Assembly received a further slap in the face over the Assembly Building row' when the Assembly lost a claim for £6.8 million damages against sacked architect, Lord Richard Rogers. The public also would pay more than £430,000 in disputed fees for the design of the stalled Assembly chamber. Edwina had not been at fault: a fact confirmed when the Audit Committee picked over the entrails on the 19th December.

It seemed very clear that 'Lord Rogers had significantly underestimated the cost of the building. Although he had effectively got it wrong, the Assembly is not due any damages or repayment of fees.' Ron Davies told her bluntly, 'we have to accept that this is a major embarrassment for the Assembly. We have fought on two cases and have lost on two cases and the result has been self-inflicted and very regretful.' No one thought to remind him that the Assembly had inherited the scheme and its failure should be laid at his ministerial door. In picking the winning design, neither officials nor the Welsh Secretary had foreseen the true cost of construction or architect's fees, originally unrealistically set at £11.5 million in 1998. Ron had been Welsh Secretary until he hastily resigned on the 27th October 1998 so he must have been in the know? In November, barely three weeks into his new job as Welsh Secretary, Peter Hain hit out publicly and 'demanded an end to Assembly HQ mess'.

The Auditor General's report into the fiasco suggested that the chamber design should have been immediately rejected as too expensive; a statement confirmed by Sir Jon Shortridge in yet another appearance before the committee. 'If the true costs had been known at the time', he mused, 'their entry should have been rejected from the competition as non compliant.' Why the Assembly had lost their claim was difficult to understand. The best lawyers had been briefed and there could be no defence to the architect's original costing that spiralled to £47 million. The construction would be complex and the costings were woefully wrong. Maybe officials had been foolish to allow the judicator to be a Quantity Surveying expert rather than a judge, but the Auditor General's report was weighed down with mild rebukes for official inability to check exactly what they were getting for their money. The Assembly watchdog concluded that Edwina was right to challenge a claim; our top official agreed that our reputation had been damaged and yet again we nodded sagely, collected our files and wound up another Audit session. The project would be finished, but at what time and for how much was still not known as the 2002 term ended.

On its front page on the 27th February, the *Welsh Mirror* printed what it perceived as Labour's two big problems. The top half depicted 'Spinnochio' Stephen Byers, sporting an elongated nose and accused of lying, whose position was slowly disintegrating under the weight of the Jo Moore ('a good time to bury bad news') email fiasco. Featured below, cruelly pictured looking dozy whilst adjusting his specs, came Andrew Davies, below the headline 'NO HOPE-IO. Does he have a clue?' The paper railed at the fact that having been handed the £70,000 a year Economic Development job, serious doubts were expressed about his experience and ability to transform the Welsh economy. Not an easy start for Andrew who had to share a page devoted to his own derided suitability for the job with that of Alun Cairns, who described Andrew's performance in the Assembly as 'amongst the worst in the Cabinet'.

Further indignity followed when Paul Starling's comments column showed yet further remarkable contempt for Rhodri. He announced, 'the Cabinet is on trial and under his control, not fit to run the Assembly.' He ranted on: 'Eight months ago Rhodri's mate, Mike German, left the Cabinet because of police enquiries into 'irregular' expenses and Rhodri had stumbled around in the dark proving himself incapable of dealing with a small issue. He then threw the hottest political potato in town to Andrew Davies, a man who has run a team of four people, done a bit of lecturing and who once worked for Ford.' I winced at the brutality of the attack, although I had not been overwhelmed by Andrew's general performance as Business Minister. Being charitable, I felt he never inspired confidence and his plenary performances were adequate but fell far short of Rhodri, or Edwina, or frankly the rest of the Cabinet.

In my political naivety I still assumed that ministers would not blatantly reward their own constituencies with special grants and there I just noted that Edwina Hart, Finance Minister, had announced the previous November that she had set aside £150,000 per annum for the Chamber Orchestra for Wales. Jenny Randerson followed up this good news in her culture statement on the 5th December that the grant was for a number of orchestras and musical projects. On the 27th February 2002 I attended Edwina's launch of the Chamber Orchestra of Wales, with Owain Arwel Hughes as its Principle Conductor in the Assembly Milling Area. The string section serenaded us, speeches were made and I learnt that the fortunate orchestra was based in Swansea. Edwina represented Gower and from the gist of the compliments flying about, she had played with the National Youth Orchestra.

The *Western Mail* ran a story the following day asking why the Assembly had directly funded the new Chamber Orchestra, as it was 'the only artistic ensemble to receive from central funds rather than from the Arts Council for Wales.' Edwina was quoted as 'strongly denying suggestions that she had given the grant to help her constituents.' The row rumbled on and into Culture Committee deliberations as Owen John Thomas, the Plaid Cymru Culture spokesperson, clearly suspected Edwina of patronage and expressed concern that money would be allocated without proper consideration. He had made his suspicions known to the media and to the plenary debate on the 28th February, and the story gathered momentum. BBC Wales's 'Dragon's Eye' – the hard-hitting and generally unbending watchdog of political events within the Assembly – also waded in and eagerly ran their version of the row later that week.

Ever loyal Lorraine Barrett, one of the formidable 'Sisters' (my description of course), led by Big Sister Edwina Hart, stepped smartly to the rescue. She welcomed the Government's 23% arts funding for the next financial year and openly declared an interest as her husband was applying for an Arts Council grant. Her intervention had moved things on and Edwina was back in command. Thursday morning plenary – changed to that day months ago – was a chore as it delayed an early return to our constituencies, and I had idly noticed that several AMs were missing part or all of Thursday morning sessions. The absentees or late comers invariably included Ann Jones (Karen's bosom pal), Janice Gregory (Lorraine's soul mate) and Tom Middlehurst, all best mates of Karen, keeper of party discipline. Surely she was not favouring her friends, I thought uncharitably. Knowing that such patronage never came my way, I emailed Karen and hoped that they were not ill?

I could not remain aloof from the orchestra row as on the 4th March, two constituents came to the Delyn Constituency office representing Ensemble Cymru, a small chamber group based in North Wales. Learning of the Swansea grant, they were concerned that their application for funding had suddenly been turned down by Margaret Evans, Jenny Randerson's senior Culture official, and their business plan surprisingly dismissed. Treading carefully, the Ensemble team did not want to start an arts funding row but they wanted an open procedure and fair treatment, as they did not know if any other musical body had won the jackpot, even though the Swansea orchestra had only been established in 1999. Despite Jenny Randerson's scathing dismissal of the *Western Mail* article as largely inaccurate, it was odd that Edwina should make a grant directly from central funding, when the Culture Committee and the Arts Council were all to receive increased budgets to distribute to deserving causes. I promised help and pondered how to get them funding without upsetting the holder of the purse strings.

I wrote to the Culture Minister on the 5th March 2002 under the heading 'Funding of the Chamber Orchestra of Swansea'. I asked which other orchestras benefited and by how much; who decided to release the £150,000 to other benefactors and did a bidding process exist? After a fulsome reply from Jenny to the Culture Chairman Rhodri Glyn Thomas, she stated that the money was available to support various groups other than Swansea. The Arts Council did not consider it had a monopoly as provider of arts in Wales, that my North Wales Ensemble's business plan was under consideration and it was all a storm in a teacup. Suddenly, a grant to the North Wales Sinfonia, 'Ensemble Cymru' was agreed and after a culture meeting had finished, I quietly thanked Margaret Evans for this change of fortune. I quite forgot to formally declare the CD presented to me by my Ensemble in recognition of a successful conclusion.

The same day, Jenny thanked me profusely for attending a lunchtime launch of a scheme to encourage parents to speak Welsh to their children. Ample proof existed to show that early home conversations are more likely to ensure Welsh survived than other more exotic schemes. Only recently, the *Western Mail* Yearbook arrived, giving thumbnail vignettes of all AMs. I was amused to read that I 'asked quirky questions, was not afraid to admit less-than perfect-knowledge, can then ask a scathing question' and that I was 'an independent-minded AM whose contributions were unpredictable. She will step down in 2003; the Assembly would be poorer – more of her ilk is needed on the back benches and her unique character enriches the Assembly.' I could have written it myself but being serious, I regarded anything to do with the Culture Committee as my duty to support, and although welcome, Jenny's thank you was unnecessary as I had a genuine regard for all Assembly activities, and where possible always showed up. Jenny's handbook entry afforded her the rank of acting Deputy First Minister and responsibility for sorting out Millennium Centre and Arts Council funding problems, so it was important to keep me on side.

Rhodri had jetted back from a trip to the States in time for the afternoon plenary on that same busy day, 5th March, and walked into two big controversies! The Opposition were furious over Andrew Davies's Economic Development appointment and were ballistic that Rhodri had not disclosed that Jon Shortridge, the Permanent Secretary, had been making regular contact with the police over Mike German's expenses investigation. At the podium,

Rhodri coolly faced down Nick Bourne's and Ieuan Wyn Jones's joint wrath. 'Had the cabinet known of this liaison?' The questions demanded answers as rumours abounded that suggested contact had been made since January, and that Jenny Randerson was in the knowledge loop. Matters were complicated by Andrew Davies's appearance on 'Dragon's Eye' on the 28th February, who totally denied that the administration had attempted or had knowledge of any contact with the police.

It was clear to all that Rhodri had his back to the wall. Rhodri defended himself vigorously but the facts just did not stack up. Delyth Evans and I watched our leader with quiet disgust. We both agreed that he had held up well publicly but we feared that his credibility was holed below the water line. We could not understand why WAG had tried to suppress contact with the police, as for good governance and an ability to plan ahead, the return or otherwise of Rhodri's deputy and Economic Development Minister was important information. No one had suggested that any pressure had been brought on the police to terminate or rush the investigation. Had Andrew made a different statement to 'Dragon's Eye', would Rhodri not have been so wrong-footed? Although this episode paled into insignificance when compared with 'Spinnochio' Byers, compromised civil servant Martin Sixsmith and Ms Moore, it left a nasty taste that openness and transparency had begun to wilt badly in the Assembly.

I read my Economic Development Committee papers very diligently for the 6th March meeting, as it would be Andrew Davies's first appearance in his new job. Alun Cairns and I had already agreed to support each other in continuing to prise open the mysteries of the Harbour Authority that had now moved to Andrew's portfolio. I had received confirmation from the Assembly's Consul General, Winston Roddick, that the EDC had the right to scrutinise payments, call for monthly updates and even invite the First Minister to attend before it, although it could not compel. At least I knew the extent of our powers: an important position when attempting to scrutinise the wily administration that controls the Harbour Authority.

Andrew's entire staff seemed to have turned up at his first outing and sat squashed in behind him. Emyr (he whom I had tipped for great advancement), flanked his right and Derek Pritchard, very senior and very languid, sat on Andrew's left. The Wales European Funding Office's supremo and other officials spilled over into seats normally reserved for the public. The meeting went well with Andrew speaking to a detailed brief and not ashamed to call officials to deal with the more probing questions. No one tried to jump him or score points. We all knew it was a difficult job and, collectively and without conferring, we would ease his passage – for his first meeting at least!

The next meeting, on the 20th March, was less successful and Andrew seemed like a fish out of water, despite being surrounded by his usual army of officials. I passed Ron a note wickedly wondering how much the taxpayer was paying for such a plethora of officialdom taken from other duties to baby-sit the new minister. He giggled then stepped in to rescue Andrew from Alun Cairns who had clearly decided to abandon the 'let's-be-nice-to-the-minister' truce.

As Rhodri was due to speak at the North Wales Economic Development Forum the following morning in Wrexham, I hoped he had chosen a different route from the A470 as I had encountered seven sets of temporary traffic lights the evening before. Shelia Drury, a major player in the business and industry world, was Chairperson, and dealt effortlessly with my frustration at being denied a place around the table, being forced to sit behind the delegates, yet Eleanor Burnham's nametag was on the table. The penny dropped. Although the newest AM, Eleanor rightly claimed her place to sit with Forum members as she had assumed the chair of the North Wales Regional Committee, that post being rotated yearly between the parties. Silkily, Mrs Drury gave me a special welcome and then, exuding teamwork vibes and 'lets-get-the-job-done', we galloped through the agenda in readiness for

Rhodri's arrival. He was given a tough time with CBI (Confederation of British Industry) members, who quizzed why no European Funding Office was sited in the north-west. When could the area expect quality Government jobs to be relocated to North Wales, and why were the five richest areas all located in South Wales?

Rhodri's response to job location surprised me, as he seemed unwilling to commit himself to this policy. Edwina had started an embryonic relocation process, but jobs lasting five to seven years would be difficult to relocate, and union consent was needed. A loud snort of disbelief arose from one member and clearly, Rhodri was not amongst his strongest supporters. As his answers had obviously caused surprise, I decided to write seeking clarification and shared my intention to do so with Shelia Drury. Just for once, the quick-thinking articulately-gifted and well-briefed Rhodri could not produce all the answers on cue!

I too got things wrong and was left in no doubt by Martyn Jones, Clwyd South's Labour MP, when he sent me a letter on the 15th March, denouncing my weekly column in the *Flintshire Evening Leader* as over the top! I had criticised MPs for heftily increasing their salaries and pensions, having read a report by a special committee on pension remuneration. He challenged my statistics, felt I had been unfair to imply that the public would pay for the upgrades, believed that police and fire service pensions were more generous and costly to the public than MPs, and generally had a good rant. Martyn was a very experienced chair of the Welsh Affairs Committee who had always been amiable whenever we had met and had not intended to offend anyone. I replied giving him my sources and thanked him for flattering me by even bothering to read my scribblings in the local rag.

By mid March 2002 the Culture Committee's Welsh Language Review was moving towards completion, as the report had to be signed off by the 27th June before the summer recess in July. The Clerks began the challenging and complex task of drawing together all the evidence we had taken from a myriad of groups across Wales. Deputy Minister Delyth Evans, with her advantage of speaking

Welsh, worked hard to lay down a definition of a 'bilingual Wales' that would placate the Labour Group and yet be acceptable to the other parties. As Plaid Cymru – mostly driven by Dafydd Wigley – were actively pressing for a new Welsh Language Act, and other extensive demands that had worrying cost and administrative implications, it was important that we were not railroaded into recommendations that would compromise WAG when the review was published. By April, the first draft of 'developing a strategy for the Welsh language' gave us something to get our teeth into at last. The strategy was placed under various headings: culture, education, economic development, housing/planning and heath and social services. Some of the proposals were innovative and were accepted within the Review.

The encouragement of welcome packs distributed by estate agents to people considering relocating to Welsh-speaking communities was one. The establishment of a regulatory body for translation companies and taking positive steps to make housing more affordable in Welsh speaking, if not all communities in Wales, gave a flavour of the many issues the committee had addressed. It was vital too that Welsh speaking communities were not seen to be singled out for preferential treatment and yet, the proposals should be strong enough to keep the language at the forefront of modern Welsh life.

Used to drafting and dealing with precise language, I read every draft produced by the Clerks with infinite care and made suggestions that invariably found favour with the whole committee. I knew that the Clerks were secretly pleased with my contributions and my ability to see a problem before it occurred. Until May, all parties worked well together with minimal argument between our respective viewpoints, but consensus ended at the Culture Committee on the 15th May when Dafydd Wigley read out a much-extended wish list, demanded by Plaid Cymru for inclusion in the official draft. I well understood Plaid's passion to progress the language, but I saw pitfalls in allowing Plaid to bounce the committee into important recommendations not previously sanctioned by the majority.

The only time a new bill had been raised by Dafydd and Owen John was at a culture meeting on the 27th February. Delyth thought it would be a distraction and that neither Plaid Cymru members had thought the proposal through. Jenny Randerson thought it was too soon to decide; a case had not been made and she worried about the cost. Abroad, she knew that Basque language expenditure was vast and diverted funds from other deserving areas. I mildly suggested that Dafydd should formulate what he wanted and why we needed fresh legislation. He did not look keen but agreed, as Rhodri Glyn liked that suggestion. Nothing more was said on the subject at that meeting.

On reflection, the committee had previously been invited by Plaid to explore reasons for a new Welsh Language Act and, knowing that achieving one was a main Plaid Cymru goal, we should have anticipated that a late charge would be forthcoming. By the 21st May, the pressure for one was still on with Rhodri Glyn, admitting that seeds were being sewn in the media mind that the Labour members wanted to wreck the entire review. Had we agreed with PC, only Westminster could write new legislation and we were unconvinced that the case for new powers was proven. Nevertheless, as PC continued to press their case strongly and other members would not support Plaid's demands, for the first time since the review started – when all agreement was consensual and not decided by a vote – we were almost forced to abandon convention and use our Labour's majority on the Committee to defeat Plaid's proposals.

At the following meeting on the 29th May, Plaid Cymru mounted a further attempt to re-present the evidence painfully collected over the past twelve months. We were swamped with a flurry of new papers passed around the table by Jon Owen Jones. Labour AMs protested. Rules demanded that committee papers were circulated within agreed timescales. Only by agreement could new material be 'agendered'. Poor Rhodri Glyn Thomas as our chair and top Plaid member was performing linguistic gymnastics to try to give Dafydd and Jon their way, and yet adhere to proper committee rules of engagement. The new papers included Dafydd's all-Welsh speaking juries, yet another area we did not control, and we had already discussed the practical difficulties in an earlier session as only the Lord Chancellor could make this proposal happen. I threw him a lifeline and suggested the Assembly should ask for a pilot scheme to examine all the options. I said that I could not support any recommendation that was not workable or we could not realistically achieve. I thought it would undermine all our good work. All sides working hard, we agreed to include some of the new proposals but to reject others. During the coffee break Rhodri Glyn looked physically relieved, was outstandingly pleasant and whispered that he would try and get Dafydd to drop the new language bill completely.

We resumed the meeting and moved onto the next item on the agenda. One Labour member was furious that we had almost been bounced into unrealistic last-minute proposals and had muttered loud protests. I was more sanguine. Welsh language development formed the backbone of Plaid Cymru's reason for being and I enjoyed the special buzz that went with the bilingual aspects of Assembly life. I adored the Welsh National Anthem 'Mae Hen Wlad fy Nhadau' that was sung before the British National Anthem and, for a time, my mobile played it when it rang. I did not blame Dafydd for trying again for the new act, particularly as he had been asked to give us his views, albeit months previously. Not only was he standing down, but he had also made bravura statements to the press promising much, and his chance of shaping Welsh language policy was slipping away.

Delyth and I whispered urgently to each other as a debate droned on during the 31st May plenary. She was feeling the heat as Jenny's deputy and was frustrated that although the Cabinet had been asked for a steer, the committee had received only a deafening silence. The Labour Culture AMs were on their own against the heavy pressure for Plaid's ostentatious language demands; we were powerless to meet as an Assembly even if we had wanted to. I muttered that we – Labour – would be painted into a corner and lose the high ground if we rejected Dafydd's belated demands completely; a year's successful teamwork would falter and Labour would be blamed for wrecking the review. Delyth muttered that she was disappointed that Rhodri had ignored her request for guidance, and I suggested that she should email him and give him a further chance to reply. She nodded and as she busied herself with her task, I busied myself drafting words that might satisfy Plaid and all culture Committee members of our commitment to exploring a need for a new Welsh Language Act, without actually promising we would ever press Westminster for new legislation. Unless this issue was resolved, the stalemate would continue. After much scribbling, I suggested that recognising a promise made by the minister to push current legislation to its limits, if events proved it was insufficient, then the committee would support the suggestion to seek further clarification for the need of a new Welsh Language Act. Delyth read and approved and I casually wandered across and laid my scribblings before Rhodri Glyn and Dafydd whilst plenary debate rumbled on. My effort was soon receiving approving nods from across the chamber. An elated Dafydd sidled up to my seat. 'If you'll give us that, I'd be delighted.' I whispered that I could not give anything but I genuinely wanted to find some way to make progress.

As the *Western Mail* had given extensive coverage to Dafydd's demand for new legislation, it occurred to me that it was important to leave room for compromise, as he may have needed to save face. I suggested to him that we could formally launch the finished report with the help of those who had given evidence. Turn it into a celebration and ensure everyone had ownership in it, I muttered. Both Dafydd and Delyth agreed. 'We should do more of this sort of thing', Dafydd remarked and returned to his seat. Having fiddled further with the draft and then typed it in my office, I returned to plenary with the text and gave it to Lorraine to read. She approved it by writing her support on it and handed it to Delyth. I started my next task of finding a form of words to appease Jon Owen Jones's demand for Welsh medium classes for three-year olds. That proved even trickier and after kicking the text around with him in the Members' Tea Room, we ran out of time and had to return to vote. Delyth asked why I was being so helpful. 'It's my job to solve problems, find answers and make progress. I've been doing it all my life', I growled. She thanked me for this help in getting the committee back on course. I smugly congratulated myself. The following day, Delyth emailed that she was worried that my draft would be seen as a U-turn. Leaving another committee meeting early, I dashed to her office to explain that far from changing our minds, we were taking back the high ground by admitting that Jenny Randerson had already recognised possible shortcomings with the present Act. We also said all we were doing was to look fair and reasonable by not shutting the door completely.

My draft did not feature fully in the final recommendations but the exercise had built vital bridges. Although it was a year in the making and the May meetings had been challenging and difficult, by the 19th June the horse-trading had finished and on the 27th June, 'Our Language: Its Future' was born. My suggestion to widen the audience had been accepted and when Jenny Randerson unveiled our plans on the 9th July, I felt immensely proud that the recommendations were realistic recommendations if approved by WAG fully, and would make great strides for taking the language forward. I watched the Presiding Officer's obvious deep and emotion-charged pleasure and that of an enthusiastic mêlée of Welsh Language aficionados, who clapped ecstatically at every speech. Delyth expressed her warm appreciation of the ability of AMs from four parties to work together. I felt that not only had I been part of history, we had in fact achieved a small miracle in bringing together a consensus report on such an emotive and sensitive topic.

Taking the story back a notch, Rhodri Morgan had a very rough time in plenary on the 2nd May when he was 'accused of dictatorial behaviour and lying: one of the most serious instances that an

Opposition leader had ever seen.' Having announced on the 18th April that WAG was withdrawing from the Wales European Centre in Brussels, and had discussions with Tom Middlehurst who was involved in European affairs, both Opposition leaders were furious that Rhodri had failed to consult fully and had shifted his position significantly. The Wales European Centre was the 'Wales Office' in Brussels and Rhodri decided to withdraw the Assembly's contribution claiming financial prudence. In a classic power struggle both Nick Bourne and Ieuan Wyn Jones realised that they would lose any say in WAG affairs in Brussels. It was one of the most acrimonious debates ever held. Tom Middlehurst's name was mentioned during the row and Rhodri used Tom to reinforce his argument that he, Rhodri, had acted and consulted properly. I saw Tom looking angry and sent him a message inviting him to drop out and come for tea. The drinks dispenser in the Milling Area was a favourite watering place. The usually totally loyal and laid back Tom was livid. Rhodri was wrong to divulge a private conversation between them, and had not been totally frank in what he had told plenary. Tom felt that Rhodri had let him down badly and he muttered that his own loyalty was being tested to the limit. He complained that Rhodri's arrogance over appointing Mike German to the Cabinet and his shabby treatment of the Group was becoming far too frequent. I sipped tea and nodded sympathetically. 'He's making too many mistakes', growled Tom. I had to agree. Alun had excelled at keeping the Group informed and Rhodri shared little with us.

My Delyn constituency was selected again only to 'shortlist women.' Although happy that I must be pleasing some of my colleagues, I was disappointed for Peter York who, having run my office since May 1999, knew the ropes and was immediately barred from contesting Delyn. I was even more disappointed when I discovered that Bryan Grew, my agent and County Secretary, had organised a 'Meet the candidates' event and I had neither been invited nor informed. He told me he had done so 'at the express instigation of Pauline Jones, the Labour Regional Secretary based in Rhyl, as there was a risk that I might influence any decision.'

I was rather hurt and wrote to Pauline and presumed that I might be expected to endorse the selection of, and to canvass with, the successful candidate, and surely potential candidates could have learnt something about the job I was performing had I been present at the selection process. Pauline replied, somewhat officiously, that she had informed Bryan that the rules did not permit me to attend as 'you are not a member of the Delyn constituency and therefore have no claim to take part in the selection process for a new Assembly candidate for Delyn. Once Delyn have selected their candidate on the 19th July, I would hope that you would co-operate with the new candidate and work hard to ensure that Delyn once again elects a Labour Assembly member.' I did not bother to reply but the double standards and party officialdom left a very sour taste indeed.

On the 19th July Leighton sent an interesting email covering items found on Cardiff County Council website to Lew Hughes, Deputy Auditor General, and a very approachable officer of Sir John's team. Russell Goodway and his Cabinet had been addressing what the Authority had given to the Millennium Centre project. Leighton wrote that 'the key concerns stem from two Council Cabinet meetings on the 9th and 11th February 2001 that do not seem to square with a statement made by the Culture Minister on the 23rd April 2002.' Cardiff County Council's much earlier position was to make no contribution to the Centre, but the minutes showed that the land was transferred 'with no charge', and there was a discrepancy over the price they had paid originally: either £2.5 million or £2.6 million. Whatever the cost, it was to be transferred to the Assembly for no charge.

Extracts from the 9th January minutes stated:

> 'Cabinet member sought further clarification
> on the related issue of the National Assembly's
> future contributions to the Capital of Culture

project, and considered it would be preferable for a letter of understanding to be received from the National Assembly in this respect prior to the formal exchange of contracts regarding the Wales Millennium Centre site.'

The 11th February minutes read:

'Cabinet was informed that the District Auditor had expressed concerns as to the tension between the capital city role and service delivery role and queried whether the Council should be undertaking the capital city role. The Lord Mayor confirmed that he had made clear to the Minister for Finance at the National Assembly that the Council would not make any further contribution towards the cost of the European Capital of Culture bid (apart from that included in Council budgets), until such time as the input from the NAW matched the value of the land transferred. The Lord Mayor had indicated that he would welcome a confirmation letter to this effect.'

How could the land be transferred 'with no charge', as we were led to believe in the Minister's statement, and why link the sale of land to the level of 'input' from the Assembly to the capital of culture bid? No such link was mentioned in any Culture Committee discussions on the Millennium Centre in Jenny Randerson's 23rd April statement. As a member of the Auditor General's team, did Lew Hughes think the matter was of further investigation? Letters to Jenny produced responses, but no clear or easily understandable explanations. Sir John's team agreed to take on the investigation and determine if Cardiff County Council had obtained a commitment from the Assembly to provide a financial contribution to the city's 'European Capital of Culture bid equivalent to the value of the land transferred.'

By August, Sir John was able to say that:

> '[His] staff had obtained specific confirmation from the Assembly that no written commitment of financial assistance for the Culture bid has been given by Welsh Assembly Government to CCC by way of compensation for the transfer of the land.'

On the 4th September poor Jenny was sent another probing letter asking her, yet again, to explain why a connection had allegedly occurred between the land given at peppercorn rent that had become tied up with the Capital of Culture bid. I reminded her that an earlier briefing from Sir Alan Cox (his role now undertaken by Sir David Rowe-Beddoe), had reported on Cardiff's reluctance to give the Millennium Centre any tangible financial support. Jenny replied on the 30th September and her understanding was that Cardiff had bought the land for £2.5 million and transferred it to the Assembly for 'a nominal consideration', and that the Assembly leased it to the company constructing the centre. Cardiff undoubtedly recognised that the WMC represented a major contribution to their Capital of Culture bid. She agreed that having already given Cardiff £500,000 towards this bid, it would be match funded up to a ceiling of £1.1 million. As Edwina had been cited in Cardiff's minutes, I found the chance to talk to her when leaving plenary in early November, as she had made it very clear that Jenny Randerson was dealing with me and she had nothing useful to add at that stage.

Accepting that official Local Authority minutes involving funding and personal comments regarding the Finance Minister could not go unchallenged, Sir John's team pressed on with enquiries. On the 24th October, Mike Usher collared me as an Audit meeting concluded and said that all their research indicated that the minutes were incorrect. No evidence of any supporting documentation within the Assembly had been found and therefore, there was no connection between land transfer for the WMC and funding the Capital of Culture bid. 'How could they be wrong?' I argued. If the largest Council in Wales, with the highest paid local politician was able to place inaccurate minutes on its official website, surely that was unacceptable and made a mockery of accountability and openness. Jenny Randerson wrote again to me on the 20th November, but apart from going over old ground, I thought it was hardly worth the ministerial effort.

I had spent hours trying to unravel why Cllr Goodway's Executive had allowed the wide circulation of 'incorrect minutes'. I should have backed away but I had a job to do and owed it to my constituents to ensure that public money was not being spent profligately. I knew that Russell Goodway could unlock the key, and despite having failed to get him to answer, I thought it was worth one last attempt. So I wrote to him on the 2nd December and reminded him about our earlier conversation over the 9th January and 11th February minutes and asked for clarification. By this time I had gathered a lot of information about the Harbour Authority spending demands, and I had discovered why Cardiff had attempted to pass the bill for the city's Christmas trees on to the Assembly, but I will refer to this fully later. I certainly knew in December that Russell and his chief executive's refusal to allow independent scrutiny of the Harbour Authority by the Auditor General had created distrust, but happily the dispute was now resolved and surely the public was entitled to know how much Cardiff was contributing to both the Capital bid and the WMC. Although the Lord Mayor's private secretary promised me a reply, things just went from bad to worse and eventually, receiving no reply despite sending two reminders, I finally made a formal complaint against Russell Goodway to the Bishop of Llandaff, Cardiff's Standards Committee chairman, but events would show: to no avail!

Only in October would we know if Cardiff had made the culture capital shortlist. With no proof but a shrewd hunch, I just assumed that if the Lord Mayor could make funding demands of the Finance Minister, boldly announce this fact on his council website, duck my questions, initially refuse to open Harbour Authority accounts for audit and lead the Auditor General's staff a merry dance, I needed to know what the Assembly would have to contribute to secure the bid for Cardiff. If it was true that Cllr Goodway had little hope of winning, yet used the bid as a means of improving Cardiff's facilities thereby squeezing capital and revenue funding out of the Assembly, I thought that unfair to other Local Authorities. I could do nothing until I received Russell Goodway's reply, but realised that I must ask Edwina herself about the reference to her in the council's minutes!

That meeting with Edwina duly occurred on the 14th January 2003, in the presence of an official in her ministerial office and was cordial enough, accompanied by cake and coffee. What was not forthcoming was any constructive explanation as to why Russell Goodway appeared to be holding her to ransom over the Culture Capital funding and recording this fact in official Council minutes. Plucking up courage, I asked her to explain how the Lord Mayor had specifically mentioned her in the 11th February minutes. He 'had made it clear to the Minister for Finance that the council would not make any further contribution towards the cost of the European Capital of Culture bid, until the input from the National Assembly matched the value of the land transferred.' Edwina denied any knowledge of such an agreement. 'How could the Lord Mayor make such misleading statements to his Cabinet and even have them placed on the website? Was there any documentation to prove the minutes wrong?' Edwina would know surely that all local Government procedures invariably required that all minutes were validated and signed off as being a true record of the minutes, if not (cynically) what had actually taken place at a meeting. Totally unfazed by this battery of information, she coolly countered, 'Minutes not true; the Lord Mayor had been mistaken and that's all there was to it.' The official shuffled and we were being dismissed. Humiliated, we were ushered out in silence, and my last memory was of a composed Edwina lifting the previously uneaten cake to her mouth with her elegantly manicured nails.

Outside, Leighton and I were dumbfounded. No notes were made throughout the meeting so to be fair and honourable, I drafted my perceptions of the dialogue once back in my office. On the 20th January, I emailed the result to her official, asking if they could agree my note. On the 22nd January, Owain Lloyd, Private Secretary to the Minister, responded haughtily by letter. 'The Minister does not think it appropriate that an official should be asked to indicate whether they are content or not with a note taken at such a meeting. The Minister's recollection of the points made at the meeting does not fully concur with the account you have outlined.' Owain did assure me that the Minister would write to the Minister for Culture, Sports and Welsh Language and would contact me when she received a reply. Therefore, another line of enquiry had firmly hit the buffers.

Another doughty scrutinizer, Paul Starling, the *Daily Mirror's* political correspondent, had also appointed himself to keep an eagle eye on the 'powers that be' within the Assembly. He had already shown his extreme dislike of Rhodri in an earlier column, and on the 9th July 2002 he struck again! The journalist wrote the stinging headline – 'Rein in or dump arrogant Rhodri' and suggested that he was in danger of being dumped, as his style of leadership and cosying up to Lib Dems could spark a potential palace revolution. Cruelly, he exposed Rhodri's ownership of a million pound detached country mansion in a hidden valley, a stone's throw from Cardiff, and berated him for 'giving most of the plum Assembly Cabinet jobs to his closest friends.' He ended with a dire warning that if he did not lose his arrogance, then 'a full leadership challenge could dump him.'

Weeks later in August, Ron Davies took up the same theme and blasted Rhodri's style on an HTV programme, describing his 'maverick image' as not in keeping with New Labour and as the reason for Tony Blair twice rejecting him as a Westminster Minister. 'Rhodri wouldn't know the working class if he bumped into them' he complained. Ron dismissed the Welsh Government calling itself

'WAG' as 'nonsense', described the Assembly building chaos as 'an embarrassing failure' and confirmed that he, Ron, was 'interested in becoming the First Minister.' When I read the coverage in the *Daily Post*, I then understood why Rhodri rejected calling Ron into his Government, despite his enormous talents. Some of Ron's criticisms were justified. The Opposition had great sport with teasing the Cabinet over the acronym for their new title, Welsh Assembly Government. 'Had no one realised such a glaring error?' chortled Nick Bourne. In my back row, I squirmed. Delyth and I secretly agreed the word order had been unfortunate and of course, the Group had not been told of the new collective name either.

Ron's high ambition staggered me. At 56 and married twice previously, he announced in June he was wedding a 35 year old woman on the 5th August, that they were trying for a baby and he was still interested in the First Minister's job. It seemed that Ron could bounce back from anything, for he had such talent and scintillating capacity to look ahead. Even when the *Guardian* ran a detailed interview on the 'moment of madness' incident in November, he rode it out without giving an inch! On the 21st May 2000, during a Sunday Group Away Day at Transport House, he made several cogent and perceptive comments. He raised the spectre of three eighths of the entire Assembly budget going to the NHS in Wales, and of the dangers of allowing healthcare to gobble up everything. He pressed for a strategy to deal with events on a weekly basis, (a polite way of telling the Group that the Government was making too many decisions on the hoof), and the indecision and haste showed. However, he admitted that MPs sometimes were guilty of similar failings.

Carwyn Jones also impressed me with his thoughtful comments, recognised that Westminster needed to be challenged, but realised the risks, and suggested the Assembly needed five new major schemes with which the public could identify. He had only recently assumed a Cabinet post but he had 'Future Leader' written all over him.

On the 25th April, having had a question tabled for Jenny Randerson, my supplementary was to seek her support to have the Mold Gold Cape, a unique and ancient artefact, returned to the constituency from the British Museum. It was a hot topic as local hoteliers and tourist leaders were pressing hard to get it back as it was a tourist attraction. I then headed for the launch of the Economic Development Committee Energy review with Christine Gwyther and Dafydd Wigley. Somewhat uninformed on the subject, I made a few scathing remarks about the United States being the main polluter of the planet, which went down well with the assembled media. The event was over by 4.00pm and I fled back north and settled to watch Question Time, in which Alun Michael took a lot of criticism from the audience over the part he played in the Welsh Assembly.

Catching up with constituency correspondence, a letter from Richard Brunstrom, North Wales Chief Constable, irritated me as he refused to divulge the cost of policing to the newly opened private port of Mostyn Dock. The Home Office gave a grant and surely I, of all people, realised the importance of security. I was annoyed when a junior officer had assured me originally that all port officers were the responsibility of the Home Office, something I did not think true. John Denham, Minister of State at the Home Office, confirmed I was right when he wrote on the 7th May 2002. 'Mostyn derived funds from three sources: grant from the Home Office, contribution from the host force and from the ferry operators.' The police precept had more than doubled in the last six years, more than five times the rate of inflation. Part of the police budget must surely fund some port activity and yet the taxpayers were denied information about the cost to us to police a private dock. Why did South Wales and Southampton Docks Company pay a private security firm and not use police officers? Why was Mostyn Dock so favoured? Mr Denham or local MP David Hanson, whom I had already approached for help, were unwilling to say!

April ended on a sour note. I was leaving for Cardiff on the 29th when my Labour Party neighbour popped over to chattily inform me that she would be suing me for compensation. Weeks earlier, whilst canvassing for Labour, she had broken her arm tripping between my property and next door. She gushed on that she was only doing it because it would not cost me any money! The following day, a shockingly abusive letter arrived from a solicitor demanding immediate compensation. I could not believe that a Labour Party colleague would try such a thing, and passed the letter to my insurers who happily refused liability. My next door neighbour May, on whose property Margaret had actually fallen, likewise suffered a spate of bullying letters from the same firm and a year later, incredibly they were still pursuing her for compensation. I told May to ignore their letters and if we were taken to court, we would surely win. Labour Party canvassing rules had been broken by crossing over a boundary wall and the Party had also refused to compensate her. I wrote a witty piece in my next column despairing of the greed of compensation grabbers and warning that a similar fate could easily befall my readers. I had mischievously suggested that we should put up notices disclaiming any liability for people coming to our properties. The column was well received by everyone it seemed, apart from the compensation seeker and her councillor friend. I was not forgiven, was called vindictive and lost myself two friends.

My stormy relationship with Karen nearly erupted again when I discovered in Group on the 4th June that, although the North Wales AMs had been invited to the Queen's Jubilee celebrations visit at Bangor cathedral, she would not automatically release me from Cardiff duty. Cabinet members were planning to go north for the event and Karen decreed that 'the numbers had to kept up for plenary'. 'I've already accepted my invitation' I growled, 'and for the record I will be there.' It seemed mean for the Cabinet to come north and I would have to travel south and miss it. The top table stared hard in front of them but no one challenged me.

On the 11th June, Peter and I took our seats early in Bangor cathedral and sitting with Ann Jones, had to duck the extensive brim of her hat, which was amongst the best on parade. The sermon preached by Archbishop Rowan Williams from a pulpit high above the Queen and the Duke's twin chairs, was dignified and awesomely clever. He was being tipped to become the next Archbishop of Canterbury and pressure to impress must have been great. Outside the cathedral, we mingled with the dignitaries. Russell Goodway looked impressive in his chain, the sun shone and the crowds roared approvingly as the royal party left. Grasping Rowan Williams's hand, I stuttered, 'you don't know me but I wish you well'. He had an impeccable pedigree and the appointment would be wonderful for Wales.

Two days later, the Queen visited the Assembly for the second time in its short life. Plenary commenced early with a shortened agenda but Eleanor Burnham still spoke to her 'Short Debate'. Incensed she had won it despite her limited time at the Assembly, I marched out. At 3.40pm the Royal visitors took their seats and Lord El, the Presiding Officer, and Rhodri Morgan both spoke well. The Queen's comment that Rhodri the Great had once ruled Cardiff raised titters, but I winced when she praised the Capital's new developments and was pleased that the site of the new Millennium Centre had replaced old rail tracks. The Duke giggled at Rhodri's witty speech and even the Queen managed a smile when he spoke of our 'Anthracite Anniversary' as a new Assembly. Speeches over, we divided in two groups and the Royals split up to meet us. Her Majesty was enchanted by Lib Dem Kirsty Williams's baby. Proud father was called forward through the crowd by the Presiding Officer and chatted nervously to the Queen, who seemed unable to stop caressing the child's tiny wool encased feet. She agreed with Alun Cairns that the Bangor sermon had been good. It seemed that Rowan Williams might get the Canterbury job after all!

Returning to the Assembly on the 12th June, the press began to contact Leighton about the pending launch 'of the Labour Group of

North Wales MPs'. We were not aware of this event neither, we discovered, was any North Wales AM, including John Marek, the deputy PO. The ever-watchful press soon picked up our ignorance, particularly as the Mission statement promised to develop a Labour agenda for North Wales and working proactively with other elected Labour representatives. I refused to make a TV comment as I did not want to risk another fallout with my MPs, but they were certainly intent on holding onto power. The Grand Committee had not been disbanded and another Welsh 'talking shop' seemed unnecessary. Had my little column that had so irritated Martyn Jones meant that the idea of this new forum had been spawned? After the launch, I heard nothing more of it meeting again.

Ron Davies shared front-page coverage in the *Welsh Mirror* with the Queen's triumphant journey round Wales but the comments about him were far from favourable. 'Wrong again Ron', Davies lied to win Assembly. '"Yes" vote says MP.' Llew Smith, who shared his Blaenau Gwent constituency with Peter Law, had told Paul Starling in an 'exclusive' that Ron Davies made promises that he knew he could never keep when he pledged to shut down Quangos. Ron's suggestion that disbanded Quangos would pay for the Assembly and that £20 million would amply fund it with a lot to spare was a lie. The truth: 'Just two Quangos were abolished and Assembly running costs were up to £148 million and rising. The National Assembly for Wales' – concluded Llew – 'has been founded on a lie.' There was no love lost between Ron and Llew for sure, and reports circulated that Ron was taking legal action for being called a liar.

Next to share the front page with the Queen's historic Welsh tour was a snap of a red-eyed Mike German with the 14th June headline announcing 'German cleared of fraud', and that he was back in the Cabinet last night. After a thirteen-month investigation, there was insufficient evidence to bring charges. Almost running into him in the Milling Area, I said I was very pleased for him and understood what he had gone through all these months. He had struck me as cold and arrogant but I hardly knew him. It had been rumoured that he had given Christine Humphreys, the first North Wales Lib Dem AM, little consideration despite her irksome journeys, and she had been expected to do as much as her South Wales colleagues. She retired after a long period of sickness offering stress of the job and travel as the reason. Later, an effusive Jenny Randerson told me that Mike had been thrilled with my kind words on the enquiry verdict.

Rhodri infuriated the majority of Group members by reinstalling Mike as Deputy First Minister. With the rural affairs portfolio and Minister for Wales Abroad, that automatically gave him the chair of the European Committee. Cynics believed that these appointments were clumsy, as having been cleared of credit card misuse and financial mismanagement, Mike was being handed an even bigger credit card with which to gallop off to Europe all over again. Peter Law asked Rhodri if he had the right to make this appointment and thought it should be put to the vote. He bluntly warned that Rhodri was pushing his luck too far and with some members looking mutinous and angry, Peter had spoken for the majority. Peter Law dropped into my office as I was clearing up for the night. I was asked, 'Would you sign a letter to the Presiding Officer challenging Mike's appointment to the European Committee?' I agreed as I felt the appointment should go to a vote. 'I'll miss you, Teflon', he joked. 'If I had gone to another AM's office so close to home time, I would have been given the bum's rush.' I laughed and joked, 'I'll be the next Paul Starling and spend my time writing nasty articles'.

Peter's anger carried into plenary on the 20th June and he and other AMs were queuing up to ask probing questions of the Mike German new portfolios. John Marek apologised that the Presiding Officer was indisposed. Small titters followed with remark when some wag whispered, 'Was this a case of an Almanac too far?' Ron Davies demanded a statement and Nick Bourne launched into a scathing attack on the Minister for Wales's abroad proposal. Peter Law followed with an even more stinging criticism and asked why

Rhodri was 'prostituting himself' with the Lib Dems? Rhodri kept his cool but regretted that sort of language. Mike German sat quietly on the front row, seemingly oblivious to the row raging over his head.

After plenary, Peter confided that Edwina had warned him to back off from attacking Rhodri as he was in danger of being disciplined. 'What have I done wrong?' he asked plaintively; 'we were denied a vote, and I have an opinion.' I kept quiet. I guessed that even the loyal Party man, having delivered a 61.8% majority from Blaenau Gwent, was not entitled to challenge Rhodri's autocratic decisions, particularly when the Lib Dem pact was involved. Less colourful language was used on 'Dragon's Eye' later that evening. All who took part in the programme were equally scathing over Rhodri's decision to give Mike German power over those who had pressed for an investigation, and for placing him in an arena where his corporate competence was on trial. That exact point had been made by Ron during the first Group discussions on Mike's new portfolios. 'Charges being dropped for insufficient evidence are not the same as going to trial and being acquitted', he argued, looking straight at me and winking as he spoke.

On the 25th June I listened to further Group mutterings over Mike's control of the Rural Affairs portfolio. Now that Labour policy was beginning to deliver, no-one wanted Mike German to grab all the credit with his powerful job. 'Would he ever do that?' came the mocking chorus. Carwyn Jones gave a good rural affairs presentation, and Ron made several excellent suggestions about giving voters 'open access' to Forestry Commission land and banning fox hunting across these areas. I whispered praise for these sensible and vote appealing suggestions. He nodded and whispered back, 'I knew more about agricultural issues than my officials.' I believed him. Rhodri left the meeting and Edwina vigorously prophesied that 'we are going to have trouble with Mr German.' Described as the strong woman of the Cabinet, she always dressed immaculately and Delyth and I frequently commented that she seemed able to conjure up a new outfit for every day of the year. Her manicured hands stabbed the air. Even the indestructible Mike German would be no match for those nails! Peter announced that he would not vote for Mike's Chairmanship to the European committee and Tom Middlehurst asked mildly when the item would be brought back to Group. 'Next week', Rhodri snapped coldly. Someone mentioned that newspapers had begun to speculate on Tom being offered the Euro chair, and what was Rhodri's position? Tom shuffled his papers diligently. Rhodri snapped again, 'that's private'. His discomfort was obvious and finally he was rescued by the chairperson, who refused to allow any further discussion.

Later, Tom admitted he was delighted his own interest in the Euro chair had come up. I assumed out of loyalty to Rhodri, Tom had kept quiet, but newspaper speculation seemed true; it seemed incredible that Rhodri would snatch a half promised position away from an already aggrieved ex-ministerial Labour colleague, and reward his disliked Lib Dem deputy leader. Somehow, Rhodri's political acumen was failing and yet we were supposed to support his mistakes without protest.

Bowing to criticism that the Assembly needed to get out of Cardiff occasionally, the whole Cabinet went to Llandudno on the 18th July for its first WAG question and answer session. Infuriated by a decision to build a school on previously contaminated land, 25 parents grabbed the chance to protest and marched out crying 'shame' and 'waffle'. Taking this all in his stride, Rhodri declared later than he had no regrets about the 'fantastic' open Government meeting, and that the idea would be copied throughout 'the Western World'. I smirked at the *South Wales Echo's* mockery of the second four minute public meeting presided over by the Lord Mayor of Cardiff. Local Authorities were forced into holding Cabinet meetings in public, and Russell Goodway was accused of 'fiddling with democracy' by Opposition politicians. A Tory councillor complained that a 116-page Social Care Plan had come before the Cabinet and questioned the quality of decision-making by councillors. Unfazed, Cllr Goodway denied that 'there was any substance or justification in what they are saying, that everything was totally open and transparent and not there to entertain the Lib Dems or the Tories.' The *South Wales Echo* suggested a list of things you can do in four minutes: boil an egg or prepare yourself for an atomic bomb, being just two witty comparisons with how Cardiff's Cabinet chose to spend its time with the public it represented.

My frustration with this arrogant politician had sharpened during the Audit Committee meeting back on the 16th May, when the main item was a third report into the 'Continued Regeneration of Cardiff Bay'. We then discovered that Sir John's staff had been denied access to financial records and accounts by the Chair of the Harbour Authority (Russell Goodway) and his chief executive Byron Davies. We were further astounded when Jon Shortridge, as Principal Accounting Officer, admitted that he too had not been able to prise open all the Harbour Authority accounts.

I recollected how the Harbour Authority's Business Plan was finally presented to the EDC committee on the 30th January, with much of the financial and other information out of date, after inexcusable delay. The Economic Development Chair, Chris Gwyther, was pressed to write to Russell Goodway on the 6th March 2002. She expressed concerns about the lateness of the Business Plan, that membership of the Authority 'is entirely Cardiff based' and that she was concerned about a potential conflict of interest – 'the public perception of the closeness of the Authority to Cardiff County.' She felt that wider representation would make it easier for people outside Cardiff to 'accept the expenditure of £20,000 on Christmas trees'.

I still suspected that the Assembly had paid the bill for Cardiff's Christmas decorations under the guise of Bay regeneration when the council should have picked up the cost, but at that stage in the year, Sir John's audit team were still clarifying the facts. Several suggested questions supplied by the Auditor General's team were worrying, 'Why have officials yet to put in place an agreed financial memorandum for the Harbour Authority and with this deficit, how can satisfactory financial controls have been operating over the past two years?' Jon Shortridge was also asked 'if he felt comfortable that figures presented to his officials by Cardiff County have not yet been audited by the District Auditor?' Leighton's ferreting indicated that Cardiff County were more forthcoming with Cabinet and committee minutes on the web, then they were with their time at public meetings and with access to Harbour Authority accounts to Auditor General's officials. Minutes of the 15th April showed that the 'District Auditor did not enjoy a warm relationship with the Cabinet'; the inference being that he was asking too many questions about members' allowances claims.

The Harbour Authority had received millions since its creation in 1999. The financial memorandum had no legal status and Assembly scrutiny seemed minimal, now relying upon a Welsh Office official brought back from retirement to untangle the complexities of Harbour Authorities finances. The Audit Committee was enraged that the Assembly Accounting Officer and the Audit General could be denied access to its books.

The Auditor General's report on the wind-up of the Development Corporation was accepted, but after an 'off-camera' conversation I wrote to Sir John in mid March. 'Your report raised worrying issues over conflict of interest, particularly when the former role of the "First Secretary" and the location of the constituency are taken into consideration.' I said that I had interpreted his report to suggest his concern over the Permanent Secretary's unease. This was about the 'decision making process being vested in one individual (Alun Michael), particularly as ministers are responsible for interpreting the Codes that bind them, and that certain official advice had been offered on more than one occasion.' Although any perceived conflict of interest was safeguarded by the involvement of Cabinet members, I noted that a statement made to plenary on the 20th October 1999 gave the Economic Development Minister responsibility for overseeing the Harbour Authority agreement (then Rhodri Morgan), but this instruction was not followed. It seemed that no monitoring had occurred until I joined the Economic Development Committee and asked the Assembly Consul if this Committee could scrutinise what the Assembly was paying to the Harbour Authority. The answer was 'yes'. I was making no allegations. I only sought assurance that procedures and policies – created probably under enormous pressure in the frantically busy early months of the new Assembly – were now appropriate and afforded the taxpayer proper protection and value for money. I recalled that Peter Law, who had been a cabinet minister at the time, had privately disclosed to me that he had no recollection of any involvement in 'wind-up' discussions. In fact, he seemed to recall that the Cabinet had been generally excluded from the debate. Ever diplomatic and careful in his choice of words whilst giving evidence before the Audit Committee, Jon Shortridge agreed that ministers make the decisions. Permanent secretaries can only advise!

Loud warning bells were ringing in my head having learnt that Russell Goodway, joint author of this unique 'non-Quango', and his Chief Executive both felt that the Auditor General was interfering in Harbour Authority matters. Objections to the District Auditor were one thing, but then to the Principal Accounting Officer and now the Auditor General – it seemed very fishy. 'How can you compile a report without all the financial information?' I complained. Sir John agreed that it had been difficult. The Committee unanimously instructed Jon Shortridge to get the books open and fast, if necessary by taking legal action. He frowned; a gesture I took as calling intransigent politicians to account by threatening the lawyers. This was not how the Civil Service did things. Nevertheless, Jon Shortridge was left in no doubt that the committee would not tolerate further nonsense, even from the Lord Mayor of Cardiff.

Russell Goodway's response to the Chris Gwyther letter was masterful fudge! 'Printing problems had delayed the Business Plan, and Assembly officials received detailed and open financial and technical information on a monthly basis.' He was surprised with Christine's concerns, as all accounts were regularly audited (the

District Auditor with whom relations were sour would have undertaken this task). He saw no sense in widening membership of the Harbour Authority, and was confident that 'the Bay's incomes would soon increase, his Authority had made a saving and no extra scrutiny was required.'

In July I emailed Jon Shortridge and asked if the Authority's books were yet open. A series of letters between his officials and Byron Davies were produced, but Cardiff County still refused to budge. The District Auditor audited their accounts and they (Lord Mayor and Chief Executive) were not prepared to allow further scrutiny from a different body! With the Harbour Authority refusing most external scrutiny, the AG suggestion that 'Assembly Government monitoring and overseeing arrangements were not fully effective' was spot on. I thought that he was being unduly patient!

In truth, Assembly Government could not offer assurance that the considerable resources pouring into the Bay were being used for the purpose intended, because the Harbour Authority were calling all the shots and were determined to keep it that way! Leighton tabled a flurry of probing questions about Harbour Authority costs. On the 15th May Andrew Davies, now the Economic Development Minister, responded to:

Question: How much money has been paid to the Harbour Authority since 2000-1?
Answer: £54.28 million.

Question: Is the minister confident that existing auditing arrangements associated with payments to the Harbour Authority are adequate?
Answer: It's up to the Auditor General for Wales, as the auditor of Assembly accounts, to reach a view whether these arrangements are adequate.

I felt like giving a quick rendition of 'there's a hole in my bucket' as the scrutiny parcel was passed back and forth. Months later an uneasy truce was reached. The Harbour Authority graciously allowed AG staff to attend meetings. No mean victory, I thought! Wading birds, as well as Cardiff dwellers, were also racking up large bills (excuse the pun).

Draining of 200 acres of reclaimed land farmed since Roman times to accommodate displaced Bay waders had always been controversial, and with little evidence of relocation to the wetland reserve and spiralling costs, the Audit Committee was briefed to probe the Gwent Levels Reserve at its 16th May session. Leighton's questions were coming thick and fast to Andrew Davies:

Question: How much has the Assembly paid to the reserve in finance years 2000-2?

Answer: First year, £1.406 million in capital costs to meet inherited liabilities and then, adding up all the years, £420k had been paid for liabilities and managing the reserve. The reserve could have been costing over £440k a year and was just one of the additional items that WAG had to fund yearly.

The final report on our 16th May findings was frankly damning and, surprisingly, it took some fourteen months (24th July 2003) before the Auditor General's final report, based on the evidence gathering session, was presented to the Assembly. Although I had left the Assembly by then, curiosity made me obtain a copy. The Auditor General reported on his 'considerable concern that the principal agreement governing the operation of the Harbour Authority (the Alun Michael/Russell Goodway pact), should be open to interpretation on such a basic issue as the timing of grant payments.' That was unusually stern language and rarely seen in previous AG reports. He stated 'that it was simply unacceptable for over £45 million of public money to be dispensed by the Assembly without a suitable detailed financial framework being formally agreed.'

The Assembly was exposed to unnecessary risks as the dispute with Cardiff County Council drawdown (of £3.3 million) demonstrates, and 'we expect Assembly Government to ensure that future funding agreements are supported at the outset by suitable detailed financial agreements…and monitored closely.' He was surprised and disappointed that monitoring key performance indications, a basic element of good programme management, had not been written into the more comprehensive 165 Agreement. The point was that some targets had been set, but no-one was collecting the data needed to judge if they were being met or if the public was getting value for money.

The Auditor General was generally upbeat in other parts of his report and the transition from the Cardiff Bay Development Company was never going to be straightforward. However, he agreed that 'the absence of a legally agreed financial memorandum – the failure to complete an independent audit of grants to the Harbour Authority – are serious gaps in the framework of control for such a large amount of public money.' He felt that 'being denied unfettered access to Harbour Authority records was particularly worrying, as was the long delay in the production of the Business Plan and lack of clarity about monitoring arrangements.' The Auditor General was 'disappointed that although the Assembly continued to provide transitional funding of £12 million to continue regeneration work in the Bay and to complete unfinished projects, a full Cardiff Bay regeneration programme had yet to be agreed.' He also said that 'project proposals funded directly by the Assembly were to be approved in advance of expenditure being incurred.' I could not conceive the same loose funding arrangements being applied to any North Wales project, and I felt my probing and questioning had been fully justified and that I had been right to press for proper scrutiny of the Harbour Authority.

A deal was struck between Alun Michael's Administration and Cardiff County Council. However, it was strange knowing that Local Authorities are legally obliged to monitor their performance and ensure all expenditure was fully justified, yet this important requirement had not featured in the devolution of the Bay to Cardiff Local Authority. Aspects of the report presented a slap on the wrist, not only to officials but also to Rhodri who was instructed to monitor expenditure from the beginning and to Edwina, who held the purse strings. The Bay agreement and the secrecy surrounding it was a poor start for an institution that had canvassed on the mandate of promising openness and transparency.

Alun Michael featured again in another Audit report 'The Disposal of the Mid Wales Hospital', when the committee examined how the Dyfed-Powys Health Authority had sold the site jointly to Doctor Bailey, a former Chief Medical Officer of Powys and his wife, who used her company to assist with the purchase. Dr Bailey bought the houses within the substantial grounds of the now surplus to requirements mental hospital for £55,000 and sold its constituent parts for £335,000, thus realising a substantial profit. The actual price Dyfed-Powys sold the site for in a questionable tendering procedure was £355,000, inexplicably ignoring a higher bid of £365,000.

The *Wales on Sunday* newspaper ran three articles on the 18th and 25th November 2001 and on the 13th January 2002. Various challenging allegations of impropriety were outlined. The site was offered as one unit and the 'split conveyance', (splitting the site into two tranches) to the eventual purchasers was improper. Dr Bailey's substantial profit in reselling the houses denied the Authority value for money on the hospital's disposal, and less to reinvest back into the NHS. Mrs Bailey had allegedly claimed 'the slates alone were worth £2 million', which was a further indication that the sale price was too cheap. Furthermore, the Authority unduly favoured Dr Bailey as a former chief medical officer, and Mrs Bailey was favoured by being 'tipped off' by the Authority's agent about the level of the highest bid. The last allegation that caused the paper to give the hospital's disposal so much prominence was because the Secretary of State, Alun Michael, had offered

Mrs Bailey an extension after the deadline advised to all bidders, and that had unduly favoured her.

On the 18th November 2001 *Wales on Sunday* printed 'exclusive' details of the 'controversial property deal' story together with the 'Assembly's and Mrs Bailey's responses' to various allegations. The chief reporter, Martin Shipton, wrote that the north part of the estate that contained houses, chapel, cricket pitch and acres of land was sold to Dr Neville Bailey for £55,000. The south part of the estate was sold to Chancefield Estates Ltd, of which Dr Bailey's wife was a director for £300,000. The sale of the north and south parts of the hospital estate was completed on the 22nd October 1999, with the National Assembly as vendor and Dyfed-Powys Health Authority as its agent. Alun Michael became First Secretary in May 1999. Martin Shipton also alleged that the remainder of Dr Bailey's piece of real estate was sold on the 6th May 2001 to another company; this time the chair was Dr Bailey's wife. The by-line read, 'How ex-chief made 500% profit in public property deal', and showed photographs of Dafydd Wigley with the caption 'concerns' and Alun Michael's mug-shot with 'authorised' under it. The paper reported that the site had been sold separately, thus ignoring original Health Authority policy, and printed that Land Registry papers showed that it was in fact sold in two parts. The paper repeated this claim in a question to Assembly officials: 'Who was responsible for authorising the sale in two sections?' The official reply was 'the entire site was sold in one unit.' (Totally untrue!)

In Mrs Bailey's statement printed by the *Wales on Sunday*, she admitted that she found that the estate was for sale at very short notice and there was urgency as it was about to be purchased and demolished. The agent handling the sale informed her it was too late to put in another bid because decisions had been made and recommendations were going to the Health Authority. She was told the highest bid was £365,000 and she offered another £5,000 but the agent told stated that it was too late. Mrs Bailey proffered the following: 'I sent a fax to Alun Michael, whom I have known for some time, explaining what I wanted to do.' He sent a letter saying it had been in the market for so long that a decision to sell could not be deferred any longer and that the Authority was meeting soon. He nevertheless suggested that I could put in a bid, providing it was done within the timescale.' She then gave a detailed account of how a company called Chancefield Estates had been formed and how the doctor (her husband), had purchased the houses as an emergency measure for £55,000. This was to keep them in a separate mortgageable sized unit, which he then transferred as soon as possible to a separate company called Chancefield Gardens Ltd. The two companies were held by a holding company Pyra Trust, of which she was the chief executive. There was no denial that the transaction had netted someone or some company a huge profit from a public asset. The article ended with a comment from the UK Rural Affairs Minister, Alun Michael, that he had a 'vague recollection' of the hospital sale but did not wish to comment before he had read relevant official papers.

The Auditor General report found that 'as far as evidence is available, the handing of the disposal was regular and there was no evidence of wrongdoing on the part of the Health Authority.' This was a curious statement when compared with Martin Shipton's detailed version of events. The Auditor General's report concluded that 'certain aspects of the sale fell short of good practice', and a comprehensive audit trail was not possible because the Authority did not fully record all its decisions and actions respecting the disposal. The NAO must always be obliged to err on the side of caution and be able to fully justify any criticism with benefit of the doubt always given. However, the *Wales on Sunday* newspaper did seem not only 'to stand up', but also to provide a powerful, compelling and worrying slant on this 'unique' disposal.

Only one of the three witnesses arraigned before the committee on the 24th October had been involved in the disposal transaction: Neil Jones, senior surveyor in the Assembly Estates Division. Still feeling unhappy that we invariably took evidence from witnesses who could only give 'hearsay', rather than speak from first-hand knowledge, I had written to Dafydd Wigley on the 2nd October and repeated some of the difficulties that had arisen over the Centre for Visual Arts fiasco. I still thought there was merit in taking evidence from people who are actually capable of giving it. In his capacity of Chairman of the Audit Commission, would he consider that Sir John should go to people in charge at the time and not reply upon people who played minor roles years later? Lacking the teeth of the Westminster Select Committee, and taking evidence from witnesses not previously involved in any policy decisions, just struck me as very unsatisfactory. The goal was to elicit the truth and learn from mistakes, not shield those who possibly had got things badly wrong.

During the interviewing session, Alun Cairns asked if parts of the disposal looked 'fishy'. Mrs Ann Lloyd, by now head of NHS Wales and usually very well briefed, believed that no bid was sent to the Secretary of State. She did not know why the Health Authority had no record that a 'split conveyance' could proceed, nor any record of the fact that the Authority would not reject Welsh Office advice to obtain an updated independent valuation; nor could she explain why the Authority ensured all potential purchasers had not been informed about the proposed lucrative change in planning permission. She could not be expected to know! It had all happened years before she was promoted to her present post. Unimpressed, I asked how an agent and a Health Authority could work on disposal and yet 'a stranger can fax the secretary of State for Wales at the eleventh hour and the bid succeeds.' I demanded an answer. Mr Jones replied lamely, 'Yes, it is certainly very unusual for any bid to go to the secretary of State. We had no control over where the bidder sent her bids, but we were prepared to accept her offer.' 'I would not even know the fax number of the Secretary of State' I retorted. 'It is most unusual', the official agreed. The 'split conveyance' (disposal arrangements to ward off the entire estate being 'cherry picked') had been previously totally denied by officials according to the *Wales on Sunday* article. One nil to Martin Shipton!

The evidence we took on the 24th October raised more questions than answers. I was not fully aware of various complaints that had been lodged with Assembly personnel by frustrated bidders including member of a Taliesin Project and local builder, Jim Morris. The Taliesin Project, (all volunteers having attempted to create sustainable and environmentally attractive development), were invited in 1996 to mount a full public presentation by the then chief executive of Powys Health Care NHS Trust. Ten other organisations had given support, including Prince Charles. The former company secretary of the Taliesin Project, John Rogers, felt that the AG's suggestion 'that the proposed change of restrictions was in the public domain and serious purchasers were likely to have been aware of it in any case' contained 'breathtaking assumptions'! Another aggrieved individual, Neil Bally, submitted a detailed dossier to the Assembly suggesting that the AG's 'report began to collapse around one point of misinformation', and concluded that the AG and his staff were misled. Martin Shipton of the *Western Mail* reported on the 10th January 2003 that the 'Auditor General for Wales confirms that he is to re-open his enquiry into the sale of the former Talgarth hospital.' This article mentioned that crucial written records relating to the sale of the hospital could not be located by the investigation team. He wrote that an investigation that lasted the best part of a year published a report stating that he (the AG), had failed to find evidence of impropriety but nevertheless, the AG identified a number of areas where it 'fell short of good practice'.

The final report following the re-opened enquiry was finally presented to the Audit Committee on the 2nd March 2004, months after I had left Audit duty. I wondered about the long delay before the report was signed off. The Auditor General had been very concerned with some of the witness statements and that 'the handling of bids had potentially been undermined by the receipt of a fax on the 17th May 1999 from the eventual purchaser to the Welsh Secretary requesting an extension of the deadline, which was on that day.' Sir John stated that 'although the purchaser made no actual use of the twelve hour extension of time that was granted to her, the information was supplied on time. We [the Auditor General's team] consider that it was inappropriate for that extension to have been made to only one of the prospective purchasers'. He recommended that in future, 'public officials needed to demonstrate a "level playing field"'. This final report, presented to the Assembly seventeen months after evidence was first taken, confirmed that Alun Michael's office had replied by fax to Mrs Bailey, thus lending credence to her earlier statement to the *Wales on Sunday* newspaper, that Alun Michael had indeed responded to her fax and offered her advice as to how to assist with the purchase of the hospital. Because the other tendering parties were denied the chance of raising their bids once the Baileys had entered into the sales (just days before the closing date), it was tendentious to suggest that the Baileys were the highest bidders.

The AG's final report – now based on his unprecedented re-opening of enquiries – was now more critical over many of the aspects of the disposal, including use of a fax giving advice that had come from the Welsh Office on the 17th May, the last day allowed under the tendering procedure. He was concerned over the absence of comprehensive documentary evidence and with other shortcomings discovered by his team. The AG's view was that there was no evidence of impropriety, 'although certain aspects had left much to be desired.' The report agreed that although the Secretary of State did indeed offer an extension, no unfair advantage was actually obtained. Martin Shipton's view was that as Mr Michael was ultimately responsible for authorising the sale, his involvement seemed irregular. All the allegations made by various complainants were found to be unproven by the AG's team. Humm! However, a fat Welsh Health Circular was rapidly written and widely circulated. Hopefully the disposal of NHS estates will never be so haphazard again! The speed of the response to Mrs Bailey's faxed cry for help, even from the workaholic Alun Michael, must have set a new ministerial record.

I recalled how, years earlier, Alun Michael delayed weeks before replying to our report to the Home Secretary when we sought help to do our job as Police Authority members, and I wondered how ministers chose their priorities when asked to intercede! Just a week after the tense Audit Committee session, Jon Shortridge's well-deserved knighthood was announced in November. Overseeing setting up the Assembly from scratch could not have been easy. Having been to the Palace to collect it on the 13th November, Sir Jon received a drubbing from the Audit Committee when we learnt how unprepared the Civil Service was for the Welsh Assembly's IT needs, despite clear warnings that an Assembly would be formed. A Tory-run Welsh Office had tendered for a new computer system for its own Welsh Office between 1994 and 1996, and a contract for Welsh Office requirements was signed in January 1997. Failing to foresee that a 'yes' vote would turn a dream into a reality and the fledgling Assembly would also need an IT system, nothing had been included for an expanded contract. When Siemens Computer Services won this PFI funded Welsh Office contract, based on numbers using it and times of logging on, the company was firmly in the driving seat when the need for extra hardware was belatedly recognised.

The Welsh Office contract was very inadequate to service the needs of 60 AMs, support staff, constituency offices and for a growing army of officials, but unwilling to risk legal complications with Siemens rather than tendering competitively, the company was offered the task of providing the new equipment. It did not come cheap, although Sir Jon Shortridge refused to tell us details of Siemens' profits from the deal. In fact, he was very unwilling to talk about money at all, but the AG's report was more forthcoming. The committee learnt that originally the cost for computer provision was £20 million over a 7 year PFI agreement plan. However, the total current expenditure projections 'rocketed to £64.4 million, some 39% higher than the £46.1 million which the extended contract was originally expected to cost'. Specific functions of the renegotiated contract proved costly, with the example that so few calls to the help desk, provided for Assembly members on evenings and weekends, meant that the cost of each call was effectively £6000. Choosing the PFI funding mechanism rather than conventional funding could cost as much as '£2.2 million more that non-PFI procurement.' Siemens was not blamed on the desperately slow connectivity to far-flung constituencies, and Jon Shortridge had not been party to negotiating with the company as far back as 1994.

The Culture Committee agenda for the 6th November 2002 promised an oral report on the European Capital of Culture bid, and the unannounced arrival of Russell Goodway and his team took most of us by surprise. He enthused about the bid's progress and felt confident the judging panels' concerns could be answered. Looking slyly at me, he emphasised 'the importance of good transport links between North and South Wales', as he 'wanted to use them to assist taking Cardiff around Wales.' His vision and commitment for the event resonated strongly with the Committee and I felt a real 'party pooper'. The dry run in 2005, when Cardiff would celebrate its anniversary as the capital city, would focus on organising theatrical events in the Bay. Having experienced the flying insect problem that prevented Bayside residents occupying their balconies all summer, I suspected that unless the problem was solved, the dry run events would be uncomfortable for all spectators. Russell had thought that 'success was improbable'. I thought that with so much new infrastructure and improvements being poured into Cardiff, courtesy of WAG generosity, the Lord Mayor Goodway was in a 'win -win situation' whatever the outcome.

With the presentation over, questions were usually invited and I stepped smartly in to ask if the Lord Mayor could explain who was contributing what. I suggested his own county minutes 'wanted a note from the Finance Minister before a further contribution was made, as his Authority had already bequeathed the land on which the WMC was being built.' As Rhodri Glyn had told the previous Culture Committee that 'no figure had been set for how much is to be given to the Capital of Culture bid', the financial situation was looking muddled. Explaining that the only certain thing I knew was that land had cost someone either £2.5 or £2.6 million, and had been transferred from the County to the Assembly to meet tight building deadlines, I asked if the Lord Mayor could clarify. Before he could utter a word, Rhodri Glyn suddenly ruled that pressure of time excluded questions. This was even more surprising as we then broke immediately for coffee and I found the Lord Mayor flanked by his team, Lynne Williams and Yvette Vaughan loitering in the foyer. I barged into the group and repeated my question. The Lord Mayor beamed at me. 'What you really need to concentrate on is getting another North Wales AM back into the Cabinet', he countered loftily. I took his reply as conversation closed. I was foolish to attempt to obtain a straight answer from such an accomplished politician who held such sway, even, it appeared, with the Chair of the Cultural Committee and with the Finance Minister herself.

I should have been supportive of the Cardiff bonanza more readily, and would have been if other parts of Wales were being offered some sort of sliding scale in arts and cultural funding. Four committee members made regular declarations of interest: Dafydd, who received Welsh Books Council funding, and whose wife was a major player in Welsh Arts; Lorraine representing Penarth and Cardiff South, whose husband was seeking an Arts Council grant; Rhodri Glyn Thomas, a member on the shadow board for the Cardiff Culture bid, and Rosemary Butler who chaired the Swansea National Waterfront Museum project. Was this the reason why Andrew Davies had not wanted me on that committee? Surely not, but it all seemed too cosy for comfort! Jenny Randerson and Owen John Thomas both represented Cardiff and South Wales respectively and Delyth, as Jenny's loyal deputy minister, was effectively muzzled, I was really the only truly impartial member with no vested interest in Cardiff's wealth gathering regeneration.

Looking at that year's budget revealed similar shortcomings. An additional £45.5 million was added to Jenny Randerson's original baseline budget settlement, which appeared not to include a generous £250,000 given to the Welsh Books Council halfway through reviewing all aspects of this unique Welsh Council. That meant she would continue to support the Cardiff Capital of Culture bid, with more than a million convinced that it would put Wales on the European map. Despite some projected £15-16 million left over in the 2002-3 calculations – these under-spends known as 'End of Year Flexibility' – Clwyd Theatr Cymru's needs were being examined but no guarantees were forthcoming. By comparison, Sue Essex's road transport budget did not fare nearly as well and only small improvement schemes were envisaged. Russell Goodway's desire to cascade Cardiff's cultural gems around Wales and share the capital's good fortune on an enhanced transport infrastructure began to look bleak indeed. Ignoring my frustration at uneven funding, the Culture Committee's budget would make a significant impact on what we were seeking to achieve. The Welsh Language project was to receive £16 million over three years and by securing Heritage Lottery funding, Swansea was set to move smartly up the cultural ladder, thus reducing the earlier disappointment of losing their Assembly Building bid to Cardiff. A new Olympic-size pool and now the go-ahead for the National Maritime Museum had definitely sweetened the pill. Even the struggling National Botanical Gardens were thrown a financial lifeline, thus making the original decision to develop them without having a properly structured long-term investment strategy in place very peculiar indeed!

During the Group meeting on the 12th November, Ron Davies quizzed Rhodri on the terms of reference for the forthcoming Richard Commission. Lord Richard had been a former Labour leader of the House of Lords, but had been sidelined after the Labour House of Lords membership scheme went wrong, but was now rewarded with the challenging task of examining Assembly powers and recommending changes. All parties had made various demands for a wide-ranging review on Assembly responsibility for months. Did we need tax raising powers, or taking control of policing and possibly increasing the number of AMs? For some reason, Rhodri bridled at Ron's comments and began to get cross. Knowing the Commission was up for discussion, John Owen Jones, MP for Cardiff, had joined the Group and sourly forecast that this review would return to bite us. Rhodri muttered that Ron should not believe all he read in the *Western Mail* and disagreed with John Owen Jones, but admitted that his Cabinet held no collective view on the merits of establishing the Commission. Just as things were getting quite tetchy, Edwina Hart broke our concentration by bowling in with a tray of coffee for 'the Sisters'. The agenda moved on to blame BT for a shortage of high-speed Broadband facilities across Wales, and as we lagged behind England, it could turn into an election issue. Having finished with the cups, Edwina vehemently demanded that Freemasons should declare their membership. Events would prove that nothing was simple. To declare or not to come out had become a political hot potato, and the Assembly was seriously wrong footed when its demand for disclosure was ruled unlawful. When David Melding's proposals were rejected by the majority, he resigned his chair of the Standards Committee. The *Western Mail* was right to regard the handing of the Freemasons' issue as a 'total mess'. As the meeting ended, I offered Sue sympathy that her transport budget had been slashed by £5 million. She looked surprised and said she knew nothing about it. 'My researcher's got it wrong', I muttered apologetically as she headed away to quiz her officials. Later, Phil Williams confirmed that the research was correct and any memory shortfall rested with the Minister.

The 128th Group meeting on the 19th November was only slightly less confrontational. Alun Pugh ruffled feathers by asking Rhodri's consent to float his backbencher piece of legislation to ban smoking in public places. Alun rarely missed a chance to demand a smoke free Wales, either by raising the topic in plenary or circulating one of his numerous press releases. His crusade did not square with all AMs, who accepted that the smoked filled rooms were beloved of many of their constituents, who would not take kindly to the loss of their long-held social amenities. Ron Davies expressed his ongoing concern over Cardiff University hoovering up £9 million of Objective One money by winning research contracts, despite the fact that Cardiff was not a socially deprived area. He was right to sound warning alarms as much of precious European money was being directed towards supporting bureaucratic infrastructures, private business and public bodies, rather than being directed towards creating sustainable jobs lower down the workforce chain.

Ann Jones was appalled with Westminster's refusal to resolve the Fire Brigade Union's pending 48-hour strike. She emotionally told us how their employers refused to return her calls, and how she wept when she walked with their picket marshalled outside the Assembly Building. Her solidarity with the fire brigade was understandable. She had been a Fire Control Room Operator and had invited Andy Gill and other senior Union luminaries to an Assembly reception, weeks before the dispute had escalated. At the event, although I clapped politely after Andy had confidently explained that firefighters were right to demand a huge hike in pay to £35,000, and Ann had stood shoulder to shoulder and agreed with every word, I thought the demand was just too excessive – much as I valued their dangerous job and gruelling shifts.

Although most of us sympathised with the fire brigade, it was clear that few had much of the same for John Marek, who was locked in mortal combat with his Wrexham executive and his only option was to seek re-election rather than have been returned unopposed as the candidate. Ron mouthed to me that John had a fight on his hands. Long-winded discussion was followed up by more of the same from the usual Group 'windbags'. 'Why do they rabbit on', I growled under my breath. 'Why use twenty words when a sentence will do?' 'They don't think clearly', was the tart reply.

Plenary on the 20th November was greatly enlivened by Rhodri Morgan telling Peter Rogers that he was 'talking bollocks' from the sedentary position, as Peter stumbled through his speech, demanding Government action on delayed sheep subsidies. 'I'm not talking bollocks at all First Minister', Peter lamented. 'You know very well that payments have not been sent to farmers.' John Marek, in the chair as Deputy Presiding Officer coolly appealed for brief contributions and reminded members to watch their language. 'I do not want to hear such words whilst I am in the chair', he ordered sternly. Unbeknown to Rhodri, the 'B' word had been captured by the ever-present note takers and duly appeared in the official record the following day.

The press ran the story and Rhodri was embroiled in a war of Spherical Objects. 'It's "talking b*ll*cks time" was what I said', protested Rhodri. Karen Sinclair, ever faithful to her leader, railed against John Marek over the precedent set by the Deputy Presiding Officer regarding language reportedly spoken by the First Minister. Poor John had not even made a ruling. Rhodri apologised later (27th November) for his comment and for what it's worth, that word is in the record for posterity.

Even before the spherical objects row, the *Western Mail's* article of the 21st November quoted John Marek of accusing Rhodri as being behind 'a plot to get me out and for quashing open debate within the party.' John had challenged for the Deputy Presiding Officer job as a protest of Rhodri control freakery and patronage, but he blamed Tony Blair for many of the Assembly problems. Ron's forecast that John had a fight on his hands with Labour colleagues in Wrexham, began to materialise when his executive started enquiring into his Party activities, claiming he was 'a party wrecker' whose career was over.

Undeterred by the brewing constituency storm, John chided Karen at Group on the 3rd December for complaining about his handling of Rhodri's now infamous 'B' remark. The record was accurate and Assembly procedure followed appropriate Hansard rules. John was a stickler for adherence to proper procedures; one reason why he was as good as the Deputy PO. I was appalled how Labour people could turn so quickly against a long serving, experienced ex-MP and exact revenge if a member showed the smallest degree of independence and integrity. Rules were not evenly applied either, as I knew to my cost. A good example occurred on the 19th November. Peter Hain, now the Welsh Secretary, had berated AMs in the *Daily Post* for the mess over the new Assembly building. He demanded that we should get a grip and implied the project could be dropped as it was too expensive.

Such disloyalty to the new institution who had inherited the problem, was conveniently forgotten when Peter Hain addressed the Labour Group on the 26th November. He made no mention of the building, was warmly congratulated on his new appointment and no-one breathed a word about his treachery.

Whilst I basked in the last days of the summer recess, North Wales Police Authority finally threw in the towel in their indefensible dispute with their own employee, Jenny Trigger, and agreed to settle on the 23rd August 2002. The *Daily Post* featured a smiling Mrs Trigger under banner headlines 'Trigger happy. Police lawyer settles £500,000 dispute after three year battle.' Perhaps she should have accepted the money offered her to dispense with her services, but why should she end a lucrative career when she had really done nothing wrong? Accepting that the decision would have been collective, but concerned that some members also held other influential public positions and therefore should be even more accountable, I wrote to JP, Mr J. V. R. Anderson, who had chaired her grievance procedure against chief officers. I had to write twice before a reply was forthcoming. I simply wanted to know why he, as the chair of the Discipline Panel, had declined to accept the Devon and Cornwall Clerk's recommendation that settlement was the right course, as he felt her grievance had been proved and should be resolved.

My first letter of September 2002 was ignored. Emboldened by this rudeness, I fired off another letter dated 18th November, repeating the question and asking if he had actually undertaken the training required of magistrates. Fearing for possible bias and lack of impartiality which might extend to his work on the Bench, as he was a chair of Magistrates too, I stated my intention of seeking advice from the Lord Chancellor, should Mr Anderson feel my letters were not worthy of a reply.

Despite the time it took, but convinced that Mrs Trigger had been badly wronged, I penned a letter to Lord Irvine of Lairg. 'How', I had asked, 'could a magistrate member chair of the Authority and Mrs Trigger's grievance panel ignore such a crucial recommendation from a professional who had been tasked to examine the facts of her grievance and make recommendations?' Lord Irvine pleasantly surprised me with a personally signed response, but it was not his Department's problem. The Home Office was in charge of Police Authorities. At least the Lord Chancellor replied, but I could not challenge his logic. So I wrote to the Commissioner for Public Appointments, Dame Rennie Fritchie's Office, a Cabinet appointee herself. She had seemed most approachable when making a presentation on her official duties at an Assembly Equal Opportunities meeting, and as the Assembly had promised proper attention to how public appointments were awarded in Wales, I hoped she could give me some advice. I wrote that I was also troubled that Mr Barry Harrison, another senior Police Authority member who had also participated in the Trigger saga, could be seen as suitable to be chair designate of a newly proposed Local Health Board in Flintshire. Although he always supported the Chief Constable at Authority meetings, I was not mounting a personal attack on Barry, but I knew that fairness, impartiality and well-attuned personnel management skills were crucial for this very senior NHS appointment. I felt right to warn those who were to appoint him that he could be a liability.

I drew a blank with Dame Rennie's office too. She could only become involved if senior officials in the Welsh Assembly had examined my concerns. Doggedly, I pressed on and wrote to Jane Hutt who dispatched a senior department head from Cathay's Park to talk over my concerns. The official listened hard but seemed genuinely confused as to how to deal with my complaint. I guessed no-one had ever raised such a challenging problem, but she did not deny that I had raised a serious point or that I was wrong to raise the issue. Of course, she agreed that chairs of the new Health Board should have impeccable credentials, but she also knew that her minister was under pressure to complete the appointment of all the chairs and chief executives and the starting date was approaching fast. Finding a replacement would not be easy. She must have had much to dwell on during her journey back to Cathay's Park.

Already under extreme pressure with Welsh waiting lists rocketing and the promised panacea being the new Health Boards, Jane wrote some weeks later confirming that Barry Harrison's appointment would stand. Meanwhile, the Home Office wrote in reply to my JP Anderson concern. 'Dear **Mr** Halford' – Not an auspicious start! – 'The Home Office is unable to assist as it is a matter for the Police Authority itself.' A 'how to complain' leaflet was helpfully enclosed with the suggestion that this was the way forward. Nothing changes. The tricky question of 'who guards the guards' remained unanswered yet again. Why waste all that time and effort? Because I had unique knowledge of how the Police Authority behaved towards an employee, and it was important from my own sense of duty to prove yet again how untouchable Police Authorities are. Although the Home Office would never admit this, I presumed that every time that great department of state knocked me back, some official was noting a problem and would be working behind the scenes to find a remedy. Was I reading too much into the change of law around the same time, that gave the Home Secretary stronger powers to challenge decisions made by Police Authorities? Pure coincidence of course!

On the 4th December Jenny Randerson made a fascinating Cabinet Statement, part of which seemed mindless 'gobbledygook'. A newly created Swansea Waterfront Museum Company would take charge of co-ordinating the financial package for it to be built, plus another £6 million. Jenny's statement pronounced she was issuing a 'Letter of Comfort'! I was intrigued, especially as this cosy document accompanied an email stating that ten AMs had ten days in which to table a notice, requiring the minister to seek approval of this transaction from the Assembly. If at least ten members had not tabled a notice requiring the minister to seek Assembly approval, the minister would approve the transaction on the 19th December, in compliance with Standing Order 19.14. The only chance of proper scrutiny would have occurred at the 18th December Plenary, just before the Christmas recess. Cynically I guessed that officials had cannily utilised Standing Orders and other clever administrative ploys, knowing AMs were tired and distracted by other issues before the long break. This 'Letter of Comfort' mechanism ensured that the Assembly was committed to underwriting the company's entire losses, should things go badly wrong with the financial arrangements. The maximum amount could be £11 million but the risk to the Assembly was judged as far less than that. Yet again, this substantial expenditure seemed geared to miss being 'put to the vote'. As only Peter Law showed any willingness to seek a debate, let alone 9 other members, Jenny was 'off the scrutiny hook' and free to do exactly what she liked with yet another sum of public money that would soon flow into the 'Golden Triangle'.

On the 5th December 2002 I had emailed both Jenny and Edwina, who still held the finance portfolio. I pointed out the various unquantified cost implications for the scheme, such as £6 million being set aside for cash flow and other financial needs, and as the project (yet unbuilt) has already been given 'National status' surely there must be a plenary debate. Jenny had replied on the 17th December that she would release a copy of the 'Letter of Comfort' and silkily pointed out that the NWMS was being planned in such a way that would be of benefit to the whole of Wales!

Cynically, I compared the speed of organising funding for the NWMS with the immoral delay to Holywell Hospital (some 27 years and rising). Announcing the plan just before the Christmas recess was a clever ploy, and lessened the risk of debating the museum, thus enabling Jenny to authorise the deal with nothing more transparent that her official 'statement' and emails. I had long ago realised that a 'statement' offered far less opportunity for probing the facts and was frequently used by ministers to avoid a challenging debate. I wondered how the Auditor General would judge the securing of the NWMS or what secrets and connivances might be exposed when the accounts were audited.

I have a vivid recollection in the dying days of the term in 2002, looking over the first floor balcony on the 17th December, when Rosemary Butler honestly and truthfully spilt the beans about the Museum's set-up problems. Rosemary, the Museum's chair in waiting, had confided to me that 'contracts should have been approved months earlier but officials messed up the contract months ago!' 'So we are accepting something that's still not fully sown up?' I asked with incredulity. 'If Jenny hadn't moved, the delay would be costly,' Rosemary replied evenly. I shrugged, wished her a Happy Christmas and walked back to my office to leave for my last Christmas recess. It was clear to me that the Assembly was now legally committed to underwrite any financial shortfalls. All these decisions were to be made without the opportunity of full debate, despite the expenditure of so much public money.

Jenny had written to me on the 17th December and graciously agreed that it would be useful to provide members with a full opportunity to discuss this project. She would support me if I wanted a Culture Committee discussion in the New Year when Museum representatives could brief us. She reminded me that other museums, two in North Wales perchance, had also received Assembly Government support. Rolling over on the metaphorical ministerial tummy, she assured me that the museum was being planned to benefit the whole of Wales and she would be happy to see me and discuss any aspects of this topic I wished. Jenny was probably blameless and only obeying the demands of Cardiff AM's plc, but once again, under her supervision, a 'project costing £30.8 million, plus generous Assembly support, had been approved without plenary discussion or vote. Should I feel a rat for making life difficult for the minister, or should I boast that I was one AM doing the work for which I was being paid? With a most welcome Christmas recess upon me, I really did not care. Another year had ticked by and I had kept faith with my community. I was doing what was required of me. On the 19th December the minister approved her 'Letter of Comfort', and my zealous scrutiny had come to nothing.

Curtain call on three careers.

'He was an unzipped fly, caught in forever amber.'
Richard Condon 1967

By January 2003, the Assembly had just four months to run and I knew that I was over the worst. The previous nine frantically busy weeks from the 14th October to the 12th December – plus driving through some of the slowest roads in the UK – were particularly challenging, but the countdown had begun on the 30th April 2003, when the first historic Assembly term would end. As seven of us were not standing for election again, the 1st May election would produce a new crop of AMs. My achievements had been minimal, apart from entering the fray to assist the security staff on duty in the Assembly when, on the 30th October, five protesters leapt the railing between the members and the public gallery and charged down the main walkway towards the Presiding Officer's desk, waving a flag and a blood covered T-shirt. Jane Hutt's departure from the podium was less rushed than that of her cabinet colleagues and the Presiding Officer, who retreated fast though his official door. No police officer was in the chamber and it was left to a security officer to attempt to grab a man who was shouting noisily, and had managed to drape himself around the Presiding Officer's desk. He was soon joined by a WPC who strove diligently to break his grip, but the protestor doggedly hung on and, in the impasse, I feared someone might get hurt. Concerned that the man could grab the water carafe and glass on the desk above him and use them as weapons, I sidled up and removed them from his reach. 'Stop abusing the lady', I hissed, 'You've made your point, now behave'. Several more officers had now piled into the chamber and the reinforcements managed to untangle the man who was led, still protesting, out of the chamber.

Instantly, plenary resumed as if nothing unusual had happened. Calmly, Jane remounted the podium and took up where she had left off. Inspector Ian Pepeloe stopped me later in the Milling Area. 'Thank you Ma'am, for your help', he said respectfully. 'Much appreciated by the WPC'. I giggled, 'Makes plenary more exciting', I countered, 'Nice to get in on a bit of the action once more!'

That small drama counted for nothing in comparison with the Penarth Marina incident! Whilst exercising the animals after work, Fudge, my elderly, blind schnauzer, toppled into the Marina one winter's night. My first reaction was to go in, as I could not leave her paddling in icy water. Fortunately, she was still attached to an extending lead; pulling her up by her neck would have garrotted her, but I had to do something. Realising the stone steps that ran down to the water's edge were close, I tottered down to the water, managed to manoeuvre her around a jutting out stave and to guide her close enough for me to lunge down and pull her out. Triumphantly, I staggered back up the steps with a wet and shivering dog and heaved her into my car. She seemed unaffected by the dip and gobbled the best supper I could find. Not only had she survived being assaulted by the ignorant taxi driver, she had even coped with the black water of Penarth Marina.

Cardiff County Council's minutes mystery remained unsolved, and, just before Christmas, Mike Usher, one of the Auditor General's audit team made a welcome U-turn when he implied that they were 'not wrong', only that there was an 'inexplicable discrepancy' between them and his review of Assembly files. I was beginning to wish that Leighton had never found them on the County's official committee website. Why had Finance Minister, Edwina Hart, during that 14th January meeting, denied knowledge of a connection between the WMC land and the Capital of Culture bid, and yet Russell Goodway confirmed to his executive that there was one? Steve, her official, had really rocked Leighton and me when he confidently announced that he saw 'nothing wrong with the Lord Mayor embellishing his minutes, as Local Authorities do it all the time'.

Nor did he 'have a problem with Cardiff Council attempting to prise as much finance as possible out of the Assembly'! Was Steve trying to minimise the Lord Mayor's odd minutes and if so, why? Surely an official should not condone a Local Authority's attempt to circulate contradictory minutes and fleece the Assembly? Why did Russell Goodway refuse to answer my questions and fail to answer my letters? The executive minutes indicated that the District Auditor did not enjoy a warm relationship with the Lord Mayor, and I suspected that he was having a very hard time endeavouring to monitor every aspect of the County's accounts. I was wary of confronting that strong minded and very powerful council leader. I have already stated my extreme frustration earlier at having hit a brick wall, and knew that my last option was to ask the Chair of the Council's Standards Committee, the Bishop of Llandaff, to investigate my concerns. I hung back from this irrevocable final step, but there were more than worrying concerns about probity and accuracy of public records that Leighton had unearthed and, to be fair to all parties, I was unwilling to walk away.

The Labour Group was in full swing when I arrived from our chats with Edwina and Steve on the 14th January 2003. Ron was pressing for the Group to demand more powers, even though turning the Assembly into a Parliament, similar to the Scottish model, was high also on the Plaid Cymru agenda. Immediately noticeable was a dramatic change in the great love affair between Rhodri and his deputy, Mike German. With the election just over the horizon, Rhodri announced that, 'It's open season on the Lib Dems and Labour will contest all their seats.' The pact that had so upset staunch Labour people was well and truly over. This fact was confirmed two days later when the *Welsh Mirror* reported that Rhodri Morgan declared, 'I aim to sweep the Lib Dems out of the Assembly.' I had watched Rhodri frequently humbled by supporting Mike German – knowing he had courted the contempt of disaffected Labour colleagues – and ditching Mike so clinically amazed me. I was being naive!

The pact had delivered for WAG by giving the ruling group a majority but the ground had shifted significantly. Now, Rhodri had no option but to put clear red water between himself and his former political enemies, or risk a leadership challenge from disgruntled colleagues. Both men had seemed inseparable friends. Not when an election has to be fought!

Ron made no comment about the demise of the pact, preferring to concentrate on winning the election. He favoured an international mandate for the Party, surmising that a low turnout would be a major problem for us. He suspected that Group needed to urgently establish its own position on Iraq, as Blair's Government seemed determined to support the USA's demand for war. Every AM seemed totally hostile to it, and both Sue Essex and Brian Gibbons thought it must be the last resort. Most AMs agreed with them, but only Rhodri remained silent. Martin Shipton, the *Western Mail's* Assembly journalist, had sought to canvass the views of all 60 AMs on the Iraq situation that pushed our Labour 'High Command' into a 'control freak' flap. Having been elevated to Chief Whip when Andrew Davies gained his Economic Development portfolio, Karen Sinclair was always pressing the need to support Rhodri's administration. Her 'Round Robin' email on the 10th January, reminding us it 'has not been policy to respond to press-initiated blanket surveys', was not well received by Peter Law. He accused Karen Sinclair of gagging the Labour Group as he felt free to disagree with her approach and he would be communicating with Martin Shipton. Karen looked miffed and I thought it wise not to admit that before I had seen her email, I had already responded to Martin's quest for our opinions. It would have been interpreted as yet another rebellious act against the Whip. When published, the Labour Group minutes for the 14th January meekly reported, 'Members expressed a wide range of opinions regarding the current Iraq situation'. The Party apparatchiks responsible for penning the Group meeting minutes had vigorously underplayed our mood, and could not bring themselves to record our true disagreement with Tony Blair's warmongering antics. It seemed that Cardiff County Council's executives were not the only culprits over the embellishment of official minutes.

The first Economic Development Committee meeting of our final term directed considerable energy to the problems within Wales of promoting Information Communication Technology (ICT), and the dire shortage of Broadband facilities had long exercised the Committee's collective mind. Acknowledging that Broadband connectivity in Wales trailed England's ratio of some 65% availability to a miserly 35% in Wales, WAG had launched a £100 million programme in an attempt to close the gap and speed up the slow development. This was due largely to BT's total monopoly. Any upgrading of a telephone exchange would happen only when sufficient subscribers had signed up and BT's imposed targets had been reached.

Only mega-intellectual Prof. Phil Williams, Plaid Cymru's AM for South Wales East, and its rocket technology Astro-Physicist, could run rings round Andrew Davies's officials with his penetrating knowledge of 'gigs' and 'hertz'. He reeled off complex statistics and had often shared with me his frustration that the Assembly was making insufficient progress, and asked why Andrew kept refusing the offer of his paper that clearly explained the problems and solutions. I shrugged but suggested Phil should not give up. Too much was at stake for economic progress in Wales.

Although we grudgingly accepted that BT was not a public service company and had a duty to their shareholders, their monopoly status that allowed no competition to provide Broadband – other than at the company's pace – was seen as a serious impediment to business development across Wales. However, one good news story close to home emerged as enough citizens in Buckley, Flintshire – just up the road from me – had signed up so that the magical target for rollout of Broadband at that Exchange was soon to be delivered. 'Your determination's paying off, Phil,' I joked.

Phil was Plaid's elder statesman: gentle, astute and with prodigious energy. He invariably left the Assembly sporting a cycle helmet, lectured weekly at his university, wrote academic papers and was always working on some project or other. Almost being able to recite yearly Gross Domestic Product figures by heart, Phil was the bane of Committee officials as he was able to question their statistics in such detail that frequently challenged the officials' accuracy. I enjoyed watching a superior intellect in action. Never rude, always patient, he never sought to embarrass ministers but only to be a valuable part of the economic 'Team Wales'. He candidly admitted to me that the main reason for his decision to retire had much to do with his frustration of being unable to make a major impact on Welsh affairs. He was silent on the fact that he was the most cerebral AM and that his impressive background and scientific knowledge could not be bettered. Phil and I had discussed our respective retirement plans and his first goal was to install solar panels on his roof.

The day before, the 13th January, with the ink barely dry on Jenny Randerson's 'Letter of Comfort', building work commenced on the new Swansea Waterfront Museum and British troops arrived in Kuwait, although the Government stated that no final decision had yet been made to deploy them in Iraq. I stubbornly refused to give up on getting Russell Goodway to explain his Cabinet minutes. He had already ducked the question after his presentation to the Culture Committee on the 6th November 2002, and I suspected the reason for his reticence. I wrote and asked him if he would confirm that the three separate sets of Cardiff Council's executive minutes were a true record of the meetings they cover. On the 9th December Russell's private secretary wrote on very starched paper informing me that my letter was receiving attention, and a reply would follow shortly. Nothing was heard from the Lord Mayor or Private Secretary, and so I wrote again on the 9th January, and regurgitated the contents of my earlier letter. Still nothing from Private Secretary by the 20th January and so I wrote again. I told the Lord Mayor that my next step was to arrange a meeting with the District Auditor, to determine whether or not he could bring this matter to some speedy conclusion as I assumed 'that as Leader of the largest Authority in Wales, you will agree that it is important to determine whether Executive minutes of your meetings are accurate or not.'

Was there a funding link between the Welsh Millennium Centre and Cardiff's European Capital of Culture bid, and if so, why had two ministers, Jenny and Edwina, denied such a link? Why had the Lord Mayor informed an Assembly committee that Cardiff Council would not be paying any contribution towards the Wales Millennium Centre? Why was the Auditor General's staff so unsure about the accuracy of the internet Cabinet minutes? Why was it so difficult to answer simple questions? I mused. The silence was deafening. As the Lord Mayor was facing calls over alleged inaccuracies in his personal entry in a register of interests held by his own council, maybe he had much to preoccupy him.

On the 17th January self-appointed Press Assembly watchdog Paul Starling's column rattled Labour cages by printing remarks attributed to Mike German, suggesting that Rhodri lived in Cloud-Cuckoo land, was not fit to govern and pinched all the Lib Dems' best ideas. The article was brutal, even by Paul's colourful journalistic standards. On the 21st January Lorraine, Edwina and Rhodri were late to Group. When they arrived, Ron, Peter and I advised Rhodri that he should not ignore the column. I suggested that a complaint to the Press Complaints Commission might tame Paul, but Rhodri refused to react. 'German's taking the piss,' was Alun Pugh's view and, although we all agreed, Rhodri resolutely refused to retaliate and seemed content to allow the insults to go unchallenged. With Election Day closing fast I presumed that Rhodri, the experienced politician, recognised that backbiting and viciousness was an inevitable part of running a campaign.

I felt less like an impudent backbench ogre who constantly challenged Assembly expenditure when Lew Hughes, Deputy Auditor General for Wales, wrote to me on the 18th January. He explained that the Assembly was no longer picking up Cardiff City

Council's Christmas tree bill as the Harbour Authority had decided not to press for payment. The minutes unearthed by Leighton clearly read that the Harbour Authority felt justified in demanding payment from the Assembly for their £20,000 festive extravaganza. The Auditor General's probing at my insistence had led to a small but significant victory, as not all Wales should have to pay for Cardiff Council's Christmas baubles. Those decorations may have been a legitimate bill for the Assembly to meet, as the Alun Michael/Russell Goodway agreement left room for interpretation, but the Council, in my opinion, was morally wrong to even attempt to swing the costs on the Assembly. I shuddered to think how many more similar bills timid officials were accepting without challenge, but at least one claim had been foiled and the public purse the richer for it!

The pending war in Iraq and the ever-more acrimonious firefighters' dispute never left the Labour Group's agenda. The Fire Union's employers had upped the ante by insisting that the fighters could be uninsured whilst performing picket line duty. Yet again, Ann Jones begged for conciliation, but we were powerless to do anything as John Prescott's Government department made the decisions in London. I still thought that giving total support for the firefighters' massive £35,000 a year demand – when she hosted that Assembly reception – had put her in an impossible position. Alun Pugh announced that he would be moving his backbencher's bill to outlaw smoking in public places across Wales. Lorraine denounced this plan and said that it put her in a difficult position! Edwina sided with Lorraine and she expressed contempt for Alun's meddling, perceiving it as a workplace issue to be resolved by Trade Unions, and, as it was a 'non-devolved issue anyway', we should not interfere. No male AM spoke against Alun's proposal and I wondered why only the women seemed keen to protect their Party's notoriously male, smoke-filled rooms.

Ron coolly announced 100 days remained before the election, that Plaid were probably going to use their 'Minority Debate' to discuss Iraq and that we must urgently decide our collective stance.

Alun's smoking issue moved onto the back burner as we thrashed out a statement on Iraq that we could all support. 'The Labour Group of Members of the National Assembly for Wales supports our Prime Minister in looking for all ways possible to avoid war with Iraq when he meets President Bush at Camp David on Friday 31st January.' Clever! It kept all options open! Alun's back bencher anti-smoking in public places bill was debated. I spoke in favour by suggesting 'that the issue should be above party politics and that Alun's proposal will match the Chancellor of the Exchequer's goal to wean the Treasury off its own addiction to tobacco revenue'. Since Labour came to power, I sagely remarked that 'revenue has fallen from £10 billion to £7 billion, and I've had enough of smoke-filled rooms even if they are filled with my own party members'. Lorraine managed a weak smile at this remark, grudgingly added her vote for the motion and it was carried by 39 to 10.

Mike German was under fire from quarters other than Paul Starling and the Labour Group. British farming was due to lose up to £300 million a year, sparking huge discontent between different sectors and union leaders. If that was not enough, Mike's officials had ignored, or misinterpreted, a vital European agricultural directive that had been sent to the Assembly, resulting in incorrect statistics being laid in the Assembly library. This had led to further delay in paying subsidies to farmers, and the Opposition parties demanded punishment for his department's incompetence, namely his resignation. The 'mislaid' directive had sparked a media outburst and, as he was still a Cabinet minister, the Labour Government was taking hits as well. Mike's future needed full discussion by the Labour Group and on the 28th January it was doubtless his ears were burning!

As usual, Ron set the tone by reminding us that ministers are responsible for the actions of officials and the debacle over the lost statistic was a resignation issue. Full agreement to that, and Richard Edwards rightly remarked that if Christine Gwyther had dropped a similar brick, the Opposition would be demanding censure motions screaming for her head. Never short of an opinion, Lorraine demanded that 'Mike must go', as she could not 'forgive him smirking when Alun announced his own resignation.'

After expending clouds of hot air on the farmers and muttering rebelliously over Rhodri's suggestion that, if given the chance in plenary, Mike would be able to offer a full explanation for the controversy, we moved on to the firemen's dispute again. Ann Jones was more upset than ever and thought that the Government had messed up any chance of an early reconciliation, because in response to the threat to impose a pay settlement by changing the law, the firefighters walked out on another 48-hour strike. The *Western Mail* ran dire daily forecasts that war was just weeks away, and losing the Fire Union's support at this sensitive time seemed careless indeed! As usual, with predictable understatement, the minutes duly reported, 'Members believed that Mike German should accept responsibility for the clear mistake by his department.' He chose not to of course! Two days later the *Daily Post's* banner headlines crowed that the Rural Affairs Minister would pay compensation for late subsidy payments (on the 30th January).

At the first Culture meeting of 2003 on the 22nd January, Jenny read her statement on the Swansea Waterfront Museum. She carefully avoided my eye when announcing that 'as no member sought a debate on the issue' (Assembly financial support via a notifiable transaction), 'consequently, I, (Jenny), sent a Letter of Comfort to National Museums on 19th December.' She announced that Rosemary would be the chair and the minister would officially launch the project on the 10th February. Smiling happily, Rosemary confided that she and other AMs had attended the slate laying ceremony at the WMC the day before, with slate conveyed by horse and cart from Gwynedd. Bryn Terfel had accompanied the roof material on the last part of its journey with the aid of the South Penarth lifeboat. That explained Lorraine, Rosemary and Rhodri's late arrival at Group. Rhodri Glyn Thomas and Dafydd Wigley looked suitably embarrassed at this revelation, and I assumed they had attended the slate moving bash too when Dafydd muttered that invitations were the gift of the minister. Jenny shook her head vigorously at this suggestion. It would have been charitable to have invited the entire Culture Committee, but I could not blame Jenny for wishing to exclude me. I said nothing and the meeting moved on.

The meeting that Leighton and I had with Cardiff County Council's District Auditor and his colleague followed immediately after the Culture Committee ended, and I soon realised that the dash to make this meeting was not worth the effort! I formed the strong impression that Ceri Stradling was not keen to press officials too hard for information in case his probing infuriated the Lord Mayor. Far from exerting authority bestowed by his role as District Auditor to the biggest Authority in Wales, he barely exuded the confidence needed to monitor effectively Cardiff Council's accounts. We learnt nothing more about the controversial Christmas tree payments, the land deal that implicated the Finance Minister, or his opinion on the connection between Bute Square and the costly 25-year PFI scheme. He was anxious to maintain his commitment to confidentiality and this reason was offered in reply to most of our questions. Thus, we failed to learn anything of real interest that would allow us to make a judgement on the areas that concerned us. 'How far should your commitment to confidentiality go?' I asked. I suggested that the public was entitled to information on how their money was being spent. Gravely, the District Auditor assured us that other enquiries were ongoing. I said, 'Cardiff County Council minutes indicate that your probing of councillors' expenses has caused friction between your office and that of the Lord Mayor, who seemingly resents such interference. Do you have a view?' Wearily, he hinted that relationships were difficult but were not preventing him from doing his job, but he sought no further confrontation. By walking the District Auditor to the front door, I had hoped he might unwind and be more forthcoming, but apart from exchanging pleasantries, no clue emerged that he had the full measure of the task of scrutinising the Lord Mayor, his Council or the Council's accounts.

Mulling over the meeting later, Leighton and I had learnt little apart from deepening our suspicion that this public spending watchdog allegedly lacked the teeth or the courage, or both, to deal adequately with the Lord Mayor famed for his prowess as a formidable politician and supreme administrator. Had not Cardiff's leader originally defied the Auditor General for Wales and the permanent secretary in the battle to gain access to the Harbour Authority accounts? Any public watchdog effectively overseeing local Government affairs in Cardiff would need very strong teeth!

Showing much courage Sue Essex, Julie Morgan, Rhodri's MP wife and some 40 Labour party members staged a symbolic protest against the war outside Cardiff's Temple of Peace, dashing Tony Blair's hopes of uniting his party behind military action. Julie declared that 'Welsh women have a long tradition of letting our leaders know how we feel'. Cabinet colleague, Sue Essex believed that 'war should be the last resort'. Against such powerful opposition, Rhodri's refusal to commit himself either way at any time – allowing the Opposition to pour scorn on him for his questionable silence – was now very understandable. A huge row engulfed the new session's first Audit Committee held on the 23rd January. The AG's report on the National Council for Education and Training for Wales had been leaked prematurely to the press, breaking the embargo and causing WAG embarrassment. The largest Welsh Quango had come into existence in April 2001, when it took over responsibility for all post-16 education and training in Wales, excluding higher education. This Assembly-sponsored body received some £371 million for young people to gain qualifications and training opportunities and had been the brainchild of the 1999, Post-16 and Education and Training Action Group, working to ex-Minister Tom Middlehurst before he resigned. The Committee thought that this new body should exist only in shadow form until April 2002, giving it time to get the necessary systems and infrastructure into place. Someone had ignored this sensible 'staged approach' recommendation, and despite the complexities of taking over five Welsh TECS, all private companies, the new funding body, and the National Council, had gone for a 'business as usual' approach. It was the wrong decision as the Auditor General's report bluntly showed. Sir John's team identified 31 separate 'system failures' in a total of fourteen contracts that Assembly officials had refused to authorise retrospectively. Irregular expenditure also totalled £2.5 million. This was just one serious weakness he had uncovered in the organisational and financial arrangements. The Auditor General's banned confidentiality clauses had also been used frequently in staff departures and settlements. No wonder it was leaked. It provided the Opposition with wonderful political ammunition on how not to run a Quango. With an election weeks away, the opportunity to cause embarrassment was too good to miss.

The public gallery was full, and led as usual by the Permanent Secretary Jon Shortridge, five witnesses trooped in to face their inquisitors. Steve Martin, a thin, articulate, confident chief executive adopted an almost arrogant and patronising manner. Although no stranger to Audit Committee interrogation, he soon lost his composure when pressed to explain why so much had gone wrong under his watch. He became ratty and passionately declared he could blame ministerial demands for the blunders but, nevertheless, he was confident his judgement had been sound. No witness admitted responsibility for aborting the shadow year. Steve thought that the hurdles had been set too high and beyond even his self-perceived awesome administrative capabilities. Although bruising for the witnesses, once our evidence was assimilated, further changes were made to the Funding Council's structure, one being the reduction of Steve Martin's area of responsibility, which was split in an attempt to minimise further mistakes of such magnitude.

The committee was poised to move into private session to discuss the Assembly's new and costly computer contract, when Dafydd Wigley casually asked the Auditor General who should pay for the unexpected increased costs in the Health Minister's new NHS proposals. Jane's re-structuring of the NHS into 22 local health boards was promised as 'cost neutral'. Dafydd announced that the Auditor General's team had identified £8.8 million as being the true figure. Warning bells rang loud in my head. This was an untimely exploration of NHS costs, I thought. 'Who asked the Auditor General to examine the costs and when?' I queried. The Committee Clerk calmly handed Dafydd a note. '19th December meeting,' he replied evenly. 'That was the rushed meeting just before recess,' I countered. The cameras that recorded every word were still transmitting, and my discomfort grew. With the pending election, moving from 'no cost' to millions for an untested NHS administrative change was political dynamite. 'We should be in private session,' I complained. Refused! 'Are we quorate?' I demanded, as Ann Jones and Val Lloyd, our two Labour members, had left before Dafydd launched his exocet. The meeting was quorate! Janice Gregory was doing her best to follow my lead by asking why this item was not agendered, and surely it was unprecedented to discuss costs before expenditure had occurred? For the first time in the Audit Committee's history, political tactics were being used. I respected Dafydd Wigley, but I felt uneasy that we had been drawn subtly into a very sensitive situation beyond our control, and Dafydd was in the driving seat. The Labour Group was insufficiently numerate to call for a vote and Dafydd sat placidly aloof as the debate raged between us, the seriously depleted Labour AM membership, and the Chair. When Sir John Bourn suggested that perhaps an early debate on the proposed reorganisation costs might offer the opportunity to save public money, I winced. Dafydd had prepared the ground very well!

In my last attempt to deflect the costing issue before the election, I demanded that at least Jane Hutt's officials should be allowed to comment before further discussions. Alun Cairns piped up, 'The director (Ann Lloyd) can cope with the task!' 'Why is the meeting getting so political?' I was asked. 'Because there's never been a bloody election before now,' I snapped rudely. After bowing to Opposition AMs' demands to discuss Jane's NHS cost changes before March,

Janice and I rushed to the Labour Group Office – territory I rarely frequented, and we explained our failure to close down the 'cost neutral debate' with the apparatchiks. We knew that the Auditor General's figures would be correct and so how could Jane's 'cost neutral' promise ever be squared? Anxious that even the unflappable NHS Director, Ann Lloyd, might not be able to extract Jane from the Wigley elephant trap, my suggestion that she might just have to go sick and duck the Audit meeting was met with a chorus of approval. For a moment, my stock rose with the Party faithful.

On the 28th January, four days before the Bush-Blair Camp David Summit, the Labour Group's frustration grew after being gagged from speaking out against the war when the *Daily Post* printed the views of Welsh MPs, several of whom spoke candidly against it. Alun Pugh offered the chilling scenario that Bush had already made up his mind to invade Iraq. The Friday Summit was merely a fig leaf, as having already deployed half a million troops, Bush would hardly lose face by recalling them. Jane Davidson suggested a compromise that allowed us some freedom to state our personal views, and thus lessen the risk of falling hostages to fortune by Plaid Cymru during their Iraq Minority Debate. Even Karen had to accept the unfairness of being associated with Blair's desire for war, and whilst muzzled and unable to show our dissent, we risked losing our seats by a disaffected electorate. Another bland Labour Group statement depicting our concerns was finally drafted. At the 29th January plenary, Edwina told us that only last week the slate plaque had been laid to mark the final stage of building the WMC, and announced another major step forward as she had chosen the preferred bidders to construct the new Assembly building. Ron intervened but she coolly suggested that we put the past behind us. I grabbed the chance to note that 'it takes a woman of your calibre to deliver what has been a difficult project then ask for a summary of a tendering meeting, and ask had disability access been discussed?' The ever-canny Edwina refused to give tendering details and announced that the disability access issue had been resolved.

In Group on the 4th February Lynne Neagle in the Chair behaved like a bear with a sore head during an irritable and tetchy meeting. I blamed her foul mood on the arrival of her first baby. The Labour Group was still angry over Mike German's poor handling of farming payments as AMs were worried that the foul-up could rub off on them. The Opposition chose a debate to censure Mike for his departmental incompetence but the Labour Party apparatchiks wanted no hint of a rift in Government policy, 'fearing a later cynical attempt to attack Labour Ministers'. Events dictated that we had to sit on our hands and Mike German would keep his job. During the German discussions, the normally totally composed Chris Gwyther became incensed by this decision. 'He's a maggot and I would love to see him on a hook,' she said angrily. How she must have been wounded from censure motions and destructive barbs when the Opposition tried to get her to resign as Agriculture Minister. Her bitterness was understandable. How she kept faith so patiently with her fickle Party I will never know.

The agenda moved on to NHS affairs. When Jane Hutt was valiantly defending the latest dreadful NHS statistics by claiming they were not really as bad as they seemed, and we need to be confident about our achievements, an unimpressed Lynne ripped into Jane. 'There is a capacity problem and I've got my back to the wall to get re-elected. All the complaints are about the NHS; we need more money,' she snapped. Lynne's amazing outburst would have shaken lesser mortals, but not Jane. Nothing fazed or confounded her, even though she had a wafer thin majority and was vulnerable herself at the election. Several heads nodded in agreement with Lynne: our Labour Group Chair, powerful executive member and model Labour loyalist. She must have been very scared of losing her seat.

More frustration swept through the Group over Jane's complacency towards Kirsty Williams, the Lib Dem Chair of the Health and Social Services Committee, who had captured the headlines by demanding that all prescriptions should be free. Jane worked so hard and had set up so many scrutiny groups to tackle chronic problems such as bed blocking and residential care shortfalls, little wonder she remained calm under pressure. She was used to it! Ron immediately recognised this as a Lib Dem attempt to out-manoeuvre us so he growled, 'On the back foot again'. He was right of course. The suggestion was a real vote winner as the election clock ticked remorselessly on, and this time the business manager could not be blamed for failing to spot a potential elephant trap. Free prescriptions had always appealed to me and would curb the massive fraud that the Auditor General's review had exposed, as chemists were paid for each prescription issued and little incentive existed to challenge potential fraudsters. Jane Hutt's political acumen held firm when she sagely told us we should vote with the Lib Dems because everyone else would. Rhodri backed her by admitting that he was chronically asthmatic and as the motion was not mandatory, we should go along with it – so we did.

Ron suggested we needed a strategy to combat the negative aspects of poor NHS performance as people did turn out to support the big picture and liked big themes. We cheered up when Lynne calmed down and announced that a discussion on Iraq might be scheduled after the half term recess. Progress indeed! Ron Davies chaired the Economic Development Committee on the 30th January, having been nominated some time ago by the Labour Group to give cover for Chris Gwyther when absent. He took no prisoners by ruthlessly moving along the three presentations and cutting across any attempt for official or membership waffle or prevarication. We listened politely to the BT presentation, arranged to satisfy my concerns relating to BT's monopoly over Broadband provision across Wales. However, BT officials soon realised that they were in hostile territory. Dafydd Wigley grew angry when we were shown a map of Broadband connection links that favoured England and not Wales. Both he and Prof. Phil Williams, Plaid Cymru AM for South Wales East, nearly exploded when told that the National Government planned to auction a radio band: 3:4 GHz. Although the bid winner need never use it, it would only stifle competition and taking over this radio band would be, according to Phil, very detrimental for Wales. The arrival of Welsh devolution seemed to have been missed in Westminster. Most of the technical jargon of spectrum radio was lost on me but I grasped the point that rain affected radio transmissions. Rain-soaked Wales could ill afford to lose this proposed auction and I suggested that the Assembly should make a bid and shame Her Majesty's Government. Surprisingly, everyone thought it was a good idea!

On the 3rd February, battling back to Cardiff through sleet and rain, I encountered a lorry impaled on a crash barrier and then a Saab embedded in a hedge. I felt deeply for the victims and their families, having witnessed, as a police officer, the consequences of such accidents. It did, however, remind me to mentally calculate the miles I had still to travel before I retired. These minor accidents and the trivia of my journeys paled into insignificance when news broke that the American space shuttle had disintegrated the day before killing all seven astronauts.

A fat briefing document accompanied the Culture committee papers for the 5th February meeting. The Assembly Library had introduced a research service that had begun work by examining the Culture Committee's progress and the weighty tome produced an unsolicited opinion on its effectiveness. There was more to read but the researchers had made a promising start. Jenny Randerson was unimpressed by the research service's handiwork and peevishly complained that it was full of errors. Glyn Davies, our token Tory on the Committee, loved the briefing paper and brusquely announced that it was time ministers were called to account and that the service had not come soon enough.

Radio 4's 'Yesterday in Parliament' on the 11th February featured Tam Dyell, MP challenging the Speaker, holding an emergency debate on Iraq, as No. 10 had deceived the House with a spoof report. An intelligence document suggesting a 'smoking gun' theory that Iraq was on the edge of war was found to be partly based on a student dissertation, together with original spelling mistakes which had been lifted and used to beef up the Government's stance that war was inevitable. We, the Labour Group, had been right to express war concerns and the Labour apparatchiks had been wrong to demand our silence by putting off debating Iraq as long as possible. Had the Assembly united against going to war publicly and gone against the Prime Minister, would war have been avoided? Who draws the line between blind loyalty to the Party leader or standing up and being counted as an elected representative of the Welsh people? That's too political a question for me to answer!

Twenty four hours before the Speaker and 'Father of the House of Commons' were gearing up to clash over Tam's demands for an emergency debate, down the road in the High Court, Rod Richards's political career finally crashed after being declared bankrupt on the 10th February. The career of the Conservative Party's great hope for Wales, their 'Tory Rotweiler', lay in ruins. Having spiralled headlong from his career peak as Welsh Office minister, all bets were off for his continued role in politics. This was toppled further via his enforced resignation as the Tory Leader in the Assembly, and the party suffered more humiliation in September 2002 following tabloid exposure of an affair with an animal welfare lobbyist in 1999.

Although cleared of assault earlier, in the same High Court, luck finally deserted him when a tenant in his pub vanished, owing more than £10,000, and, despite selling the properties, his brewers finally sued Rod for bankruptcy. The *Western Mail* photograph depicted a haggard and prematurely aged Rod who reportedly told Martin Shipton 'without the cloud of bankruptcy looming, there is now light at the end of the tunnel. The miners will understand that.' How sad that such a stellar political career ended so ignominiously. The moving finger writ, and having writ, moved on, but fate had ensnared just two of the best political brains in Wales: Rod Richards and before him, Alun Michael. However, another brilliant politician was soon to go the same way, but the time had not quite arrived to chronicle the recklessness that brought dishonour to one of the best brains known in Welsh politics.

On the 15th February one and a half million protesters marched against the proposed war in London while Rhodri chose to watch the Wales v Italy game instead. The tabloid press was furious and railed against his insensitivity to Welsh soldiers and lack of judgement. This was unfair criticism of course, as he would be damned if he did and damned if he didn't! By the 23rd February John Marek's political career also faced termination when the Labour Party dropped him in favour of his former secretary in his Wrexham Constituency, Lesley Griffiths. Losing by four votes, John vowed to appeal to the Welsh Labour executive, claiming that he was the victim of a 'smear campaign'. Russell Goodway was in further trouble for apparently failing to explain more discrepancies concerning his business interests, and pundits suggested his chance of standing in next year's elections could well be affected. On 25th February, having hardly taken off my coat, John Marek strode into my office clutching a manila folder. He was cross with the antics of his Wrexham Labour colleagues and had a letter allegedly written by the official Labour candidate's husband. He was particularly hurt by an anonymous one that he believed had wrecked any chance of reselection. Could he start a judicial review? 'You are the only person here with experience of these things,' he muttered darkly.

I was hesitant. The law is an ass, and only lawyers win, was my cynical view, but I agreed to read the file as a priority once the Labour Group had finished its deliberations later that morning. Finally, the Group was allowed the freedom to discuss Iraq. Richard Edwards suggested that Tony Blair should be indicted for war crimes; a wild suggestion that made us all recoil in horror. Brian Gibbons was worried that the reason for war kept changing: first weapons of mass destruction, then regime change, and now to free the suffering people of Iraq. Which was it? I thought that having unwittingly been entrapped by Bush, Tony Blair could not lose face and was stuck with his decision, but at least he should be given marks for standing firm.

The US has weapons of mass destruction and cluster bombs too, someone remarked sneakily.

Ron lightened the gloomy mood by announcing the birth of his baby daughter on the 7th February and informing us she had already gained 1lb. The child's name was unknown to me so Ron wrote it on my papers: 'Gwenllian', Princess Daughter of Owen Glyndwr. He smiled proudly.

Having digested John's papers, I trotted up to his well-appointed office, drooled over the paintings again – unchanged from Jane Davidson's day – and told him bluntly, 'I am unsure a judicial review would stand up'. Doubtless, Labour Party rules would be all smoke and mirrors and open to wide interpretation. The 'anonymous' letter was not libellous, uncharitable and mean, but basically true – his nickname was 'Gulliver' as he did travel abroad frequently. His Assembly attendance was not brilliant and could be proved. They (the Party), would start digging and the lawyers always ran out winners. Pulling no punches I said, 'You have two options: do nothing and find another job, or stand as an Independent.' 'I propose to be back here in May,' he snapped angrily. He was grateful for my advice. I left his office knowing that Lesley Griffiths and anonymous Wrexham letter writers had a real fight on their hands.

Jane Hutt's visit to Holywell on the 27th February was only announced the day before her visit to my constituency, leaving me to scramble to return in time as she was expected to announce that Holywell would finally get the community hospital after a 27 year delay. This campaign was one of the first I had taken up when I became an AM, and I dearly wanted a good news story to end my political career on a high note. It seemed that Jane was going to oblige and I had to be there. Daffodils were handed to her to loud applause and smiles all round when the ministerial promise was finally made. It seemed that she had heeded my dire threat that if my people and those in the North East get nothing from the Assembly, a Labour election result could be tricky. Nothing like muttering about losing an election for coffers suddenly to become full!

Leighton waved a copy of the *Sun* at me as soon as I strolled into the office on the 4th March. On the 3rd March, the paper's photographer had caught Ron Davies 'committing a gay sexual act' at a public beauty spot days after becoming a dad. Sleazy looking photos depicted Ron in a bramble bush at Tog Hill near Bath under the exclusive, 'Another moment of madness, Ron?' 'He's been set up,' I babbled. At the Labour Group meeting, I went directly to an empty chair next to Ron. Only thirteen AMs were present and Ron immediately asked if he could make a statement. 'Total denial of the allegation. Left home 9.30am, Service Station 10.52'. This put him 50 miles from where the *Sun* said he was, and in London by 12 noon. By luck he could produce a petrol receipt proving it was impossible to be where the *Sun* had alleged. He waved a pristine looking receipt at us. After a shocked pause, Sue Essex thought it was dreadful and he should go for the *Sun*. The Group were supportive, possibly remembering how we had bestowed warm congratulations on his new daughter just the week before. I whispered, 'If you're watertight you must sue, or they will not stop pursuing you'. He whispered back, 'Just consulting a lawyer costs £500 and taking on a major paper would cost thousands.' Then, he envisaged being in and out of court for three years. He was handling his emotions well and continued, 'I walk my dogs in the woods every day: if the price of a public position is not being able to walk my dogs, that's hard.'

The Group moved to debate Iraq. Meeting disbanded, the Assembly's BBC Wales reporter Rhun ap Iorwerth pounced on me. 'What was the view of the Group?' 'Supportive, appalled at such tabloid abuse, and he claims he has an alibi,' I responded. 'No time was mentioned in the paper', replied the journalist, 'and that information was not revealed to us, but we expect further revelations'. Rhun smiled archly. I shrugged and walked away, but did Ron's neatly timed and spotless receipt seem too good to be true? No tabloid would run that story unless the evidence was indisputable. Once confronted, did Ron put distance between himself and the scene, need petrol and hung on to the receipt just in case it would be useful?

Events would confirm that the *Sun* contacted Ron for comment before running the article, and the photographer had confirmed capturing the Tog Hill incident at 11.00am. Later again, Ron admitted that the *Sun* journalist had indeed made contact before publication. Did Ron realise their timing was out by almost an hour and audaciously play an ace? If the *Sun* had made a timing mistake and thought his walk in the woods was at 11.00am, then the petrol receipt became a timely escape route to clear his name. Or was it? Sadly, the ill-conceived alibi became the final straw that metaphorically broke the back of a fine Welsh politician.

Ron's office door was open on my way to afternoon plenary, and I barged in to a deep conversation he was having with Ben Cottam, his researcher. 'Shall I walk with you to plenary?' I asked. He thanked me, but said he was not going. I hesitated, wondering if I should tell him to throw in the towel as I thought the paper would win. If Ron had admitted the truth, fallen back on his 'high risk compulsion phobia' immediately returned to therapy and pleaded forgiveness once more, I think he may have just survived. I lost courage to speak the unspeakable word 'guilty', nodded curtly and walked away.

On the 5th March, the next instalment of this unseemly saga was published. It was a disaster for Ron! Under the headline 'Ron in denial', the *Sun* printed a sordid picture showing him hoisting up his trousers following a male into woodland. The paper gave timings of his movements, including the confrontation at 10.11am with a *Sun* journalist, also captured on film. The *Sun's* cartoon was wickedly witty, as it showed teddy bears carrying picnic baskets entering woods, with speech bubbles saying, 'We'd better not be surprised 'cos today's the day Ron Davies is having a pick-up.' The lunchtime news reported Ron admitted taking only a loo stop at the scene and he was still defiantly rubbishing the *Sun* story. By Thursday, Ron was closeted in his office with his smiling wife, new baby, a TV crew and David Williams, the presenter of 'Dragon's Eye'. Had Ron the effrontery to use his family to mitigate his misdemeanours? I was shocked and rushed to Audit where I shared my concerns over what

I had seen to Dafydd Wigley, who expressed similar disgust. Thankfully, mother or child did not appear on the programme as 'Dragon's Eye' clinically exposed the latest twist to the saga that evening. Ron was unable to watch his own TV performance as his Welsh Labour Party bosses had summonsed him to Transport House and were allegedly mauling him. His reason for stopping at the beauty spot now changed from a 'loo stop' to watching badgers, having observed them before. That excuse was blown out of the water when the local badger group denied the existence of any setts in the area. Clearly unimpressed by his latest cynical ploy to hang onto his job, rumour began to flow that he must consider his position. 'Ron, you're gone' shrieked the *Welsh Mirror* headlines on the 8th March, and predicted that he had just 24 hours to resign or face being sacked. His Caerphilly constituency members had withdrawn their support and 'found his lies unforgivable'. Step down or be booted out was their ultimatum too!

'I have not handled this very well,' was the caption under a brutally detailed close up of Ron on the front page of the *Western Mail* on the 10th March, and we learnt that 'Ron Davies agrees to quit politics'. The *Western Mail's* Assembly journalist, Martin Shipton, was kind and trundled out worthy compliments gleaned from the great and the good in Wales. The *Sun* newspaper was less helpful. 'Sun "setts" on Davies', and 'Lying politician quits over badger lie' were the headlines. Dafydd Wigley, having worked closely with Ron in the run up to devolution, stood by his friend and said, 'It's very sad that it has come to this. What Ron Davies did for Wales as Secretary of State will stand in history as a massive contribution to developing our democracy.' The *Telegraph* was less charitable, with 'Badgered out of public life' as their headline. The article eruditely explained that the 'late earl of Aran introduced two Private Members' bills into the House of Lords. One concerned badgers, the other the rights of homosexuals. He allegedly commented, 'Do you know, when I spoke about badgers no one turned up, but when I spoke about buggers, the place was packed. 'Has it never occurred to you, Boofy', his interlocutor replied, 'that there are very few badgers in the House of Lords?' Warming to his task, the *Telegraph* scribe continued, 'the only other politician who has tried to combine the two subjects is Ron Davies, the much married Welsh Assembly member. Poor Mr Davies announced yesterday that he will leave public life altogether. There are now plenty of MPs interested in gay issues but expert badger researchers do not grow on trees (even in woods near Bath) and the combination of the two interests is rarer still. An earldom for Ron Davies!'

At Labour Group after Ron's resignation, feelings towards him were sharply divided. He was absent and I had not seen him since his TV preparation with 'Dragon's Eye'. Karen wanted us to offer him comfort, whilst Edwina Hart coldly announced that he was still on the payroll and should be forced to attend plenary to vote. Ben, Ron's man, had confided to me earlier that Ron had somehow got through his public valediction, but was now clinically depressed. I believed him. The tabloid coverage, the sleazy shots, the revelation of pictures too explicit even for the *Sun* to publish of 'fondling the genitals of his one-off partner' would have decimated a lesser mortal. 'He's clinically depressed and now under his doctor's orders,' I patiently explained to my colleagues. Edwina said nothing more, guessing that even Ron's most ardent enemies were in no mood to humiliate him further. Always astute, she probably realised that Ron's departure had plunged the Labour Party into an election crisis, because if Caerphilly fell, the slim Labour majority was lost.

On the way back to my office I encountered John's wife, Anne Marek. She looked dishevelled and upset. I followed her into John's office; her lair she used when working for him. She immediately blurted out that John had lost his appeal to the Labour Party. 'I'm not surprised', I said stoically. 'If John had won, Lesley would be shouting foul from the rooftops. Did he manage to get a comparison of the language used in the anonymous letter and those written by named constituents?' I queried. It had seemed sensible to identify the anonymous letter writer to strengthen John's claim of a 'smear campaign'. 'John's huge file was just ignored', she lamented, 'They are trying to dumb down this place. John, Ron and Cynog (Dafis) all leaving, and you.' She spoke my name with feeling. 'I'm a political lightweight', I grinned, 'No', she responded angrily, 'you are a free thinker and you have a brain!'

The Lord Mayor was accompanied to the Culture Committee on the 12th March by Lynne Williams and Yvette Vaughan Jones, who briefed us with the assistance of a polished PowerPoint presentation that highlighted Cardiff's plan to win the European Capital of Culture bid. Although littered with pretty pie charts high on goals and creative schemes, it was low on hard facts and financial detail. Jenny Randerson now agreed that £1.5 million had been given to Cardiff to secure their success, and although she had made a plenary statement of WMC and Culture bid funding, she refused to give further details until the final Culture meeting before the Assembly recessed for the May election.

In reply to my dogged questioning, I was told 'yes', extra Assembly funding had been found to support extra staff salaries and consultants fees and the bid deadline had been extended, and 'no', the business plan could not be released because of 'commercial confidentiality'! My attempt to probe further irritated Lorraine Barrett who sarcastically asked if anyone else could ask a question and thought my questions inappropriate? 'Are you going to declare an interest, Lorraine?' I quipped. There was laughter from everyone but Lorraine who sat stony faced, clearly unimpressed by my witty repose and desire for detail.

My questions were fair. Cardiff's bid was at risk on two counts: firstly by a shortage of a certain quality of cultural building, although new money was being frantically lavished on existing buildings to upgrade them to fit the bid. Secondly, Cardiff had no professional theatre company of its own and was reliant on the local Sherman Theatre, who in turn used professional visiting companies to stage theatre in the capital. Although not widely known, Terry Hands, Director of Delyn's Clwyd Theatr Cymru (CTC) in my constituency, was collaborating with the Lord Mayor who had earmarked an old chapel in the heart of Cardiff as a base for CTC.

They had their own Welsh speaking company of actors and regularly toured Wales. Terry Hands believed that it takes time and education to build up regular theatre audiences, but saw the advantage of becoming the capital's live theatre provider. But at what cost to Flintshire: who owned CTC? I knew that altering this Ebenezer chapel into a theatre had a cost, as did the entire possible collaborative venture, and no-one was saying who was going to pick up the bill. I asked the minister what help was to be given to audience education and if CTC filled the void in Cardiff, thus stiffening the bid, why not increase CTC's budget and award it 'National Theatre of Wales' status? Neither the Bid Team, Russell Goodway nor Jenny Randerson responded, nor could the business plan be released yet again because it was commercially sensitive. Jenny suggested that I should ask the Economic Development Committee to press for its release.

I was confused! Why was it 'commercially sensitive' for Culture Committee purposes, and yet allegedly available under another committee? Such obfuscation irritated me and so, knowing the answer, I mischievously asked the minister to confirm the amount of private sponsorship that had been invested to date in the WMC. Private funding was an essential part of the total cost when Jenny Randerson had made her financial WMC statement, and if such sponsorship was not realised, the Assembly must make up the shortfall. A year had passed and no sponsor had yet materialised. Jenny prevaricated brilliantly and made a fulsome, vague statement that sounded fine but meant little. 'Can we have what the minister just said in writing?' Rosemary Butler piped up and winked at me. I winked back, grateful that another AM shared my concerns.

Funding the WMC had not been simple or transparent. There was hardly any chance to debate it as Jenny's ministerial statement had offered only limited opportunity to ask questions. Plus Edwina Hart's verbal and written denial of any connection between Assembly funding for the Capital of Culture, in return for the land

needed to build the WMC, stifled the quest for information still
further. The Auditor General's staff had obvious confusion over the
accuracy of the Cardiff County Council minutes, and Russell
Goodway's blatant refusals to answer my direct questions or reply to
my letters on the contents of his executive's minutes lent weight to
my conspiracy theory. Jenny had assured Peter Law in plenary on the
18th April 2002 that private funding was going well, by March 2003
the private sector had contributed nothing and now the business
plan was too sensitive to see the light of day!

Why had Sir David Rowe-Beddoe been able to present a detailed
paper on the Centre's business plan on the 16th May 2001, whilst
admitting candidly that he was unable to promise that the centre
would succeed commercially, yet now that the centre was under
construction, Jenny was unable to release a business plan because of
commercial sensitivity? The facts did not stack up! Why was Jenny
postponing another financial statement until the very last Culture
meeting of the present session, thereby curtailing any real chance of
proper interrogation? Surely the timing was nothing to do with the
fact I would not be seeking re-election and my scrutiny
role would end. Anne Marek's sanguine comments haunted me.
'You are a free thinker and you have a brain!' Was everything being
slowed and dumbed-down until the departure of this 'turbulent,
free-thinking member with a brain'?

With the presentation finished, I joined Yvette Vaughan Jones
and Lynne Williams over coffee and hoped that they had not found
me too antagonistic, and must realise I was only doing my job. Both
women nodded wanly and when asked, promised me a copy of the
Capital of Culture accounts, albeit not the definitely 'off limits
business plan'. The accounts never reached me, I presumed they were
lost somewhere in Cardiff Council's shaky printing processes.
Later, as we sat together during the afternoon's plenary session,
Delyth, Jenny's deputy, admitted that Jenny had looked
uncomfortable as I made my points in the meeting. 'She lavishes
money on Cardiff without any consideration for openness or value

for money, yet is reluctant to keep the National Botanical Gardens afloat,' I reasoned. Delyth became defensive and felt that Jenny was tied down to honouring commercial confidentiality. I remained unconvinced! Advising me to press for the Capital of Culture Bid's business plan through the Economic Development Committee – having refused me the document in her own committee – made no sense at all, and loyal Delyth was lost for a reply! The money that was pouring into Cardiff was bugging me, particularly as Clwyd Theatre Cymru's fabric and facilities were so shabby: worn carpets, no air conditioning so professional productions closed down in the summer; the list of problems was endless.

Was it wise for a Labour Cabinet to give priority to this slate roofed ostentatious Opera House, when one of Wales's top businessmen could not guarantee its success and when Cardiff was already well served with five similar edifices? Should WAG have allowed a yearly £6 million maintenance millstone around taxpayers' necks for perpetuity? Could the rest of Wales legitimately benefit from this latest South Walian Cultural Palace? Other theatre and arts venues across the principality must scrabble for a meagre £2 million annual budget between them! Convinced that another expensive, financial, cultural 'cock-up' was about to be created, all totally unnecessary, I was terribly disappointed in the now hollow promise to close the North-South divide.

My detractors will loathe my persistence in challenging funding for the projects the Assembly had inherited: the Bay, albeit bequeathed from the Cardiff Bay Development Corporation and generously supported by Alun Michael's agreement with Cardiff City Council. There was also the new Assembly building, inherited from Welsh Office, and the WMC, also taken over from Welsh Office and the Swansea Museum. Both the Waterfront Museum and the WMC had been launched with no proper debate or full disclosure of the costs and risks. These were all Cabinet decisions and I was sorry that Jenny bore the brunt of my interrogations. I genuinely wanted Cardiff to improve its infrastructure, and enhancing the city's wealth through improved business and commercial ventures were goals I willingly accepted, but at what cost? Could not these vast sums have been collectively better spent for all of Wales? Should the Assembly have made improved transport links between north and south a higher priority?; should drug treatment or underage pregnancy schemes, or improving housing stock become priorities that are more meaningful? Should dilapidated schools have received money to mend roofs, eradicate buckets to catch the drips or ensure the availability of clean and comfortable lavatories? Of course the Assembly had given funds to these problems, but more could have been given when calculating the money spent and to be spent on the Bay, the new Assembly building, the Wales Millennium Centre and now the new Maritime Waterfront Museum in our first Assembly term. I think that the jury is still out.

The Standards Committee was the only mechanism left to learn if Cllr Russell Goodway had compromised councillor Codes of Conduct and had behaved unethically in his high office. On the 12th March 2003 I sent my carefully drafted letter, in which I lodged a formal complaint against Russell Goodway, heavy with highly detailed, complex facts that demanded total accuracy from me to His Grace Barry Morgan, Bishop of Llandaff, and Cardiff's Standards Committee Chairman. I suspected that Russell Goodway might escape censure under his own County Council code, as they had not been introduced until May 2002 after the 'rogue' executive minutes had been published. But no such time bar prevailed under Nolan Principles and as a councillor, they certainly applied to Russell!

I doubted that the complaint would be proven, as the system does not work like that, but I had to do something. The Bishop must have bounced my letter straight to Cardiff's Chief Legal Services Officer, Stephanie King-Davies, who responded to me on the 14th March. Her response was frosty. My complaint was not the only one in the pipeline because I learned that Russell Goodway was also under scrutiny by the *South Wales Echo*. This appeared on the 26th February, under banner headlines 'Dirty Tricks'. A campaign to plant a series of pro-Russell letters in that paper, boosting Goodway's public image, went seriously wrong. Mike Doel, Cardiff's chief corporate support officer, admitted writing the letter and sending it to a Party supporter to pass on to the paper's 'Viewpoint' page. The letter, apparently sent by mistake to the *Echo's* offices, was immediately pounced upon as a political irregularity of the Council that used its own postal system, and exposed the official close to the Lord Mayor as having shown political bias. The *Echo* felt affronted by the blatant attempt to manipulate its 'letters' page for a series of supportive letters to enhance Russell's political persona. The Lord Mayor correctly pointed out that most letters were politically motivated and the Lib Dems frequently operated the same ruse. 'It won't happen again,' was his final repost. Having embarrassed the Lord Mayor so publicly, it seemed that the *Echo* had established its own Standards Committee and written a damning verdict on the Lord Mayor's officials, a process that I suspected had been applied more vigorously by the *South Wales Echo* than I could expect from the County Council's own Standards Committee regime.

Irritated by Alun Pugh's unctuous public pronouncement that John Marek's Wrexham constituency party had followed the right selection rules and that every AM must abide by them, I sent him an uncharitable and cutting email. 'I acknowledge that you are a keen publicist and well-known to fire off press releases with the force and momentum of a Gatling gun, but John (Marek) is starting an appeal that could now be undermined.' Alun's reply was most polite. He replied, 'As a 30-year Labour member, he (Alun) would never stand against a Labour candidate and I should encourage this.' Martyn Jones, another Welsh Labour MP, also entered the fray by writing to the Flintshire Leader on the 28th March pleading that 'for your own pride and self respect, don't stand John'. Martyn Jones's advice arrived a tad too late, as on the 21st March John decided to sever his links with Labour and go it alone.

On the 30th March, John launched a new independent party, 'Forward Wales', that would field candidates in the forthcoming election. John proposed to stand in Wrexham, his current seat, and the other 'Forward Wales' election hopeful targeted Chief Whip Karen Sinclair's constituency that she shared with Martyn Jones, author of the 'don't stand John' letter. The press warmed to reporting the intriguing battle 'between the veteran ex-Labour man and his former secretary that turned a rock-solid Labour seat into a potential marginal.' John Marek won. The result was a travesty for Labour, but a victory for justice!

On Monday the 17th March, armed with daffodils from the garden and a cheque from my account, I met with a constituent, a Mrs Hughes whose feisty letter in the *Chester Chronicle* had made me angry. Yobs had stolen her little car – her only means of transporting her elderly mother – and burnt it to a shell. Although the wreck was recovered, the insurer's compensation was insufficient to buy a replacement so mother was grounded. Peter checked that the story was genuine and I offered to stump up the necessary to get Mrs Hughes mobile again. The press captured a grinning me handing over the cheque to an ecstatic Mrs Hughes. Had I stood again, I would have certainly secured one vote!

Anti-war protesters disrupted our Iraq debate but lessons had been learnt from the last invasion. Bobbies and security staff now faced the public gallery in greater numbers; order was quickly restored, and the debate continued. I delivered the speech written by Leighton, my loyal researcher. I thought it was rather good that, being one of the oldest AMs, and born during the Second World War, I could speak with authority. I spoke of the brutality of war and said that despite our Prime Minister's failings, he was a leader who had not been deflected from what he thought was right. 'Such tenacity in a leader is rare in politics. Gladstone was right when he said that Parliament's job is not to run the country, but to hold to account those who do,' I trumpeted. With a final flourish I roared, 'Parliament had finally got off its knees and backed its elected leader. I hope that we will do the same.' I hated supporting Tony Blair. The Whips had bullied and cajoled MPs to support the Prime Minister and no-one, according to Robin Cook and Claire Short, had thought the whole thing through. We AMs had been given precious little freedom to speak out, even though winning votes at the next Assembly election could well be lost by our silence. I had given a disgustingly hypocritical speech but with the final recess and an election upon us, I could forego my precious integrity for once and speak in tune with my Labour colleagues. The Labour Group had despised war but under scrutiny of the public, we chose to support the leader of our party and played the Westminster game. I was rewarded with the congratulations of no less than six AMs, including Lynne Neagle (not my greatest fan) and Delyth's researcher, who confided later that my speech had been brilliant. 'Far too emotional,' I muttered.

In Westminster, sixteen Welsh MPs chose not to support their leader and voted against the Government. David Hanson, my Delyn MP, as the PM's bag carrier, felt that he could do no such thing. Soon after, we met at my very last Delyn Constituency Party meeting on the 21st March. He looked tired, thanked me for my supportive email and agreed that it had been a difficult week. The day before, George Bush had declared that the operation to disarm Iraq had begun and Rhodri Morgan had infuriated most Welsh newspapers by refusing to give an opinion on the war. 'The rest of the world knows where its leaders stand on Iraq, but Wales stood alone in the wake of Rhodri Morgan's refusal to speak out' (the *Western Mail*, 2003).

My final constituency meeting as AM was addressed by an abrasive firefighter, whose case for a huge pay hike grew weaker by the minute, yet spared David from having to defend his boss too vigorously as Constituency Labour Party members (having endured the firefighter's unconvincing 45 minute presentation) were ready for off! Bryan Grew, the Group secretary, finally muddled through his paperwork and business was completed. I knew Bryan Grew did not recognise me as a Delyn member; he never sent me notification of a meeting and relied upon Peter to keep me informed, but other members regarded me more highly. My honesty and willingness to tell it how it was and not add 'spin' was appreciated, and my briefings on the money being lavished on Cardiff projects drove them wild. Peter York suddenly appeared, clutching a bunch of red roses and a gift-wrapped parcel: an inscribed clock when it was undone. It read, 'With appreciation of our first Assembly member Alison Halford', followed by the dates. Deeply touched, I staggered though an unrehearsed speech that thanked them for their comradeship, and I drove home with wet eyes. A Llandudno family would also weep that night as Wales suffered its first casualty of war; a young man called Llewellyn Evans. At the Labour Group on the 25th March Rhodri promised to write to the dead soldier's family.

The Welsh election campaign was launched the day before the first Iraq fatality on the 24th March, and Labour AMs seeking re-election fretted continually about the effect of war on their chances of re-selection, particularly as Rhodri admitted that capturing public interest against the backcloth of war would be difficult. Sue Essex had always been heavily against the war and gloomily agreed that AMs campaigning would be diminished. Max, Labour's Press Guru brought in to advise on the campaign, had ruled 'balloons are out.' Too frivolous in these desperate times! Write letters to the local press and uses phone-ins instead.' Max's anti-balloon advice was immediately punctured when Ann Jones, highly regarded campaign veteran, announced 'I've been handing 'em out for ages and I'm almost out of them!' We took comfort in the fact that the Assembly now had 413 extra teachers. This was a welcome good news story that was badly needed as Neil Fowler, former editor of the *Western Mail*, had mounted a stinging attack on the Assembly, gratuitously opining that the Assembly was 'not up to the task'!

The agenda for the final Audit Committee held on the 27th March was a mixture of taking new evidence and signing off previous reports. We ploughed through yet another 'cat and mouse' session with Ann Lloyd, the NHS Wales Director, on 'Procurement of Primary Health Care Medicine' even though a new incoming committee would take over where we had left off. Happily, we nodded through the report on 'Reducing Lost Income from Prescription Charges', in which the Auditor General's staff had calculated that fraud was costing the NHS £15 million a year. We congratulated ourselves for making recommendations to strengthen the NHS Counter Fraud Service that had reduced the losses dramatically by £8 million; equivalent to a 47% decrease in fraud activities. Ann Lloyd's task was also to explain that worrying mismatch between Jane Hutt's 'cost neutral' NHS re-structuring, and the Auditor General's suggestion that £8.5 million savings were required to achieve 'cost neutrality,' where could savings on this scale be found? she asked.

The item had been agendered despite Audit committee Labour AMs fighting back from being outfoxed by Dafydd Wigley just before Christmas. In the end, our fears of great damage being inflicted over Jane's restructuring were unfounded and the item became a damp squib. I secretly suspected that calling Ann Lloyd to give an opinion was now a complete waste of time. Plans were too far advanced to abort. Dafydd, who had raised the issue, was not seeking re-election, and a new Audit committee would take over again from where we had left off and would want to move on. As the Opposition were presumably seeking ammunition to taunt WAG just before the election, I was in no mood to adopt my usual inquisitorial role and refused to ask any difficult questions for the NHS Director to field. Ann Lloyd produced another bravura performance; she accepted that NHS restructuring faced financial uncertainties but was confident that the changes would be successful! Masterfully, she pulled the rug from under Jane's opponents' feet in one fell swoop! The issue that had worried me so much slipped quietly into the void!

The Opposition had been right, of course. Increasing NHS bureaucracy could never be cost neutral and, although the Group had cheered Jane's idea to disband Health Authorities, restructuring costs might still bite the minister. In Jane's defence new ideas must be tried, and seasoned hands will know that politics is all about timing, short memories and creating new schemes to distract the enemy, not to mention the public! Had Neil Fowler, ex-*Western Mail* editor, suggested that the officials and legal beagles that drew up the 'never signed contract' between the Welsh Office and the Richard Rogers Partnership 'were not up to the job', I would have wholeheartedly agreed once having read the Auditor General's latest report on the construction issues of the new Assembly building. It was now our task, as the Audit committee, to test his findings with the responsible officials before sending our recommendations forwarded to the Government to accept or reject. The facts were simple. Assembly lawyers, headed by the Consul General (the Assembly's highest earner), and by prestigious law firm Eversheds, plus Queen's Council, had jointly decided that the Assembly's case was sufficiently strong to fight the action brought by the Richard Rogers Partnership and seek damages of £6.85 million in a counterclaim. After Edwina Hart terminated the Richard Rogers Partnership's 'contract' in July 2001, citing loss of confidence in the architect's capacity to deliver on cost, when estimates began to rise dramatically the Partnership still demanded fees, and amazingly, wanted its designs returned. The Richard Rogers Partnership had quoted £13.1 million for construction in January 2001, which had relentlessly risen over the months to an estimate between £37 million and then to £47 million for construction, fees, VAT, furniture and fittings. Once Edwina had sacked the Partnership, the fee payments became the issue, as the unsigned contract was not clear on this point.

The Richard Rogers Partnership started an adjudication process that left the Assembly with the stark choice of capitulating or defending the action. Edwina's officials lost the adjudication and were obliged to pay £448,086 to the Richard Rogers Partnership, but the Assembly won the design copyright ownership dispute. The one clear element in this discredited contract was that the Assembly owned design and drawings copyright; why then had the Partnership demanded them back and refused to part with others still in their possession? To me, this looked like a selfish act of mindless arrogance.

Permanent Secretary Sir Jon Shortridge faced a sceptical Audit Committee. We had the task of apportioning blame and identifying the culprits who had cost the Assembly money paid to an architect who appeared to have got so much wrong! Jocelyn Davies, a perceptive Plaid Cymru Audit member, who was also well-briefed, worried over the Richard Rogers mechanism that allowed the Partnership to choose the adjudication method. A quantity surveyor had been selected to judge the case rather than the more conventional court! She surmised that 'in construction matters', the Rogers Partnership would allegedly have an affinity with any construction expert; even one maybe called upon to act as the adjudicator and agreement with the RR Partnership interpretation of the contract easier to understand. Although unspoken, the committee may have thought that the legally qualified surveyor might not have been the Assembly's best option. Jon Shortridge laboured for words but put simply, the Richard Rogers Partnership invoked that form of judgement and the Assembly was obliged to respond.

Jocelyn's point was the adjudicator, Harold Crowter Associates, was part of the professional building services profession. Who better to adjudicate on the architect's contractual dispute? If she was right, despite the formidable Edwina as the opponent, was it always to be game, set and match to the Richard Rogers Partnership? Not a brick had been laid, yet legal fees of £267,000 and £45,000 for the failed adjudication had been wasted. More galling still, although a new developer had been preferred, the Richard Rogers Partnership had been reinstated as partners in the project. Undeterred from cost to the public purse and the embarrassment already heaped on the Assembly, Lord Rogers threw down a further challenge by objecting to Jon Shortridge's comment to the Audit committee on the 19th December 2002.

In a letter to the chair, Dafydd, he demanded an apology, claiming that the civil servant's remarks were 'wholly unacceptable'. Jon Shortridge had merely responded to a question from a member relating to costs. He replied, 'If the true cost had been known at the time, its entry would have been rejected from the competition as non-compliant'. The press picked up on the letter. The headlines suggested that 'top official refuses to bow to intimidation.' Sir Jon justified his comments and squared up to his critic by responding bluntly, 'I should feel free to express my views as Accounting Officer without fear of intimidation'. His Lordship was informed of this stance by letter and, in a further press report of the 10th April, under the heading, 'Rogers in Welsh "intimidation" row', correspondence that had passed between the architect and the top civil servant was revealed to a very confused public.

The committee had been very sceptical about several claims made by the Partnership; namely that their new building would be mostly self-maintaining and ergonomically efficient. How then, was the glass roof to be cleaned after the Bay's numerous seagulls had left their mark, and at what cost was just one niggling question that remained unanswered? When journalists pressed me for comment, I merely spoke the truth: 'Jon Shortridge has the committee's full backing' and I described Lord Rogers's demand for an apology as the behaviour of 'an arrogant man. Rogers had made mistakes on the project and should be made to realise he was wrong'. I could have added that the Richard Rogers Partnership design overflowed the footprint of the land set aside for the new building as the first mistake and the land footprint had to be increased, at a cost, of course! Surely that alone made his plan 'non-compliant'. I could also have mentioned that the promised disability access appeared to have been originally dumped by the Partnership, despite pressure from the AMs, myself included, and had only recently been introduced after Edwina's intervention!

Two fundamental problems had beset the scheme; one was that officials lacked competence in negotiating with the Partnership and, according to the Auditor General's detailed reports, the original estimates submitted by the RR Partnership in the design competition had been proved as far too low. So, the dream of a modest £13.1 million building that would be in use by April 2001 retreated to summer of 2005. The final cost, including Merlin, the Assembly's new (under construction) computer system, was still not known! It seemed very clear that, following the disastrous Millennium Dome project, civil servants are incapable of protecting the public from horrendous overspends. Even the Assembly, determined not to make the same costly mistakes as their sponsors in Westminster, have still not learnt the lesson of entering into contracts with the private sector and coming out on top.

The meeting finished in closed session to consider the draft reports on 'Continuing Regeneration of Cardiff Bay'. The mists were clearing slowly but many questions remained unanswered. The downside: all we knew was that annual finance for the Bay and its environs would, like the poor, be always with us, and that the Auditor General had to be paid for his extensive investigations. The good side: that Assembly expenditure was subjected to regular and thorough scrutiny, both by the drearily uninspiring District Auditor process and by the more energetic Auditor General. Of all the Assembly committees, Audit had punched its weight.

The Auditor General's reports and recommendations produced hefty savings and fearlessly highlighted bad practice. True, so many poor performers had not been called before us to account for their shortcomings but much good had come from the years of probing and asking questions. As the meeting was ending, Ann Jones demanded to say a few words and promptly sang my praises for my excellent attendance and commitment to the work of the Committee. I was overwhelmed. It was a wonderful gesture. I had enjoyed the experience of testing my interviewing skills against the cerebral skills of Sir Jon Shortridge et al. He was always well prepared, always courteous and only once in the many months of relentless interrogation did he show the smallest sign of irritation. He dropped me a complimentary note some days later about my performance as an Audit committee member. It was cherished!

On April Fools' Day, the 143rd Group meeting of the First Session chewed over the leaking of a report about ELWa (Education and Learning Wales) that showed a lacklustre performance. Being the Assembly's largest and costliest Quango, only recently restructured, leaking the report was designed to embarrass WAG. Rhodri was gung-ho about poor delivery and blamed failure of officials rather than policy failures of Government. To quote from a statement from the Auditor General released on the 14th January 2003, Sir John Bourn said, 'Robust procurement procedures are basic to the proper conduct of public business, and I consider that these weaknesses were matters which management should have addressed from the outset. It is a matter of concern that a body charged with conducting public business should demonstrate these shortcomings.' The £2.2 million expenditure was not approved because of weaknesses in financial management – the expenditure was judged 'irregular'.

It was allegedly an open secret that the Chair, Enid Rowlands, and her chief executive Steve Martin did not enjoy a warm relationship, and one AM who had worked in the ELWa training field even alleged that office furniture had been thrown. Such was the level of animosity between the ELWa's bosses! That tantalising snippet gained momentum; when taking evidence on ELWa the Audit Committee raised a collective eyebrow as only Steve Martin, and not the Chair, submitted himself for questioning! Was the relationship so strained that sparks may have flown during the pressure cooker atmosphere of an Audit committee evidence session? Maybe the tittle-tattle was true, but the Auditor General had mauled ELWa's performance, and for the most senior management to absent herself, for whatever reason, was noted with some regret!

This being our last Labour Group meeting, Tom, Delyth and I were graciously thanked by Rhodri for our contribution over the years, whilst Lynne handed out gifts and fumbled a hesitant kiss when she handed me my pen-set. My departing speech was short. It was a 'white-knuckle ride, which certainly had its 'ups' and 'downs' and I wished them well for the future.' Lorraine was fulsome in her praise of Tom and Delyth. I did not get a mention! Leighton scored a huge coup by successfully tabling my last oral question to the First Minister on the last plenary of the Assembly term (still April Fools' Day!).

'What discussions had the First Minister had with the UK Government regarding the conduct of Cardiff county councillors?' First Minister: 'I'm not sure whether that is below the radar or above it?' I pounced. 'It might not be above your radar, First Minister, but Cllr Goodway has told his Cabinet colleagues a version of vital financial dealings with the Assembly, that cannot be confirmed by his own Monitoring Officer, the Auditor General for Wales or Assembly records. His version appears in three Cabinet minutes signed by him as representing the truth. Evidence suggests that the Lord Mayor has seriously misled his executive by making statements that appear untrue. The refusal to answer my letters and direct questions seems to me to bring Wales's biggest council into disrepute.' Final punch line – 'Do you agree with me that all councillors and elected representatives should act with openness and probity at all times?'

The Presiding Officer butted in. 'May I confirm that I did not hear an allegation of untruthfulness against another person…?'

Alison Halford: 'I chose my words extremely carefully and I am happy to stand by my supplementary question.'

Presiding Officer: 'I want to establish that you did not allege that someone has been untruthful, which would be contrary to Standing Orders.'

Alison Halford: 'Would it be helpful to read the question again?'

Presiding Officer: 'Order. This is a serious matter and we must abide by Standing Orders. If there is an allegation of untruthfulness, the wording must be amended.'

Alison Halford: 'My supplementary question was based on evidence suggesting that the Lord Mayor had seriously misled his executive by making a statement that appears to be untrue.'

Presiding Officer: 'Rephrase the expression containing the words "appear to be untrue"'.

Alison Halford:'I will say that it seems not to match the contents of the minutes.'

Finally satisfied, the Presiding Officer allowed Rhodri to reply.

First Minister: 'I am a great admirer of your skills that you acquired during your years in the police force Alison: in your ability to rephrase remarks when they are outside the rules and to obtain inside information on what goes on inside Cardiff County Council cabinet meetings, you have succeeded to a greater extent than I have in that regard.'

Being the consummate politician, Rhodri invited me to make representations to him before close of play on Thursday and I was just thankful that the Presiding Officer had shown tolerance. Delyth congratulated me for holding firm, and plenary cheered me for my persistence. I had little faith in the powers of the Standards Committee and thought that some airing of my concern over the peculiar ways of Cardiff's executive would not go amiss, particularly as Russell Goodway had ignored me. Owen John Thomas, a Plaid AM for the Cardiff area, grabbed the chance to raise his dissatisfaction with the Authority too! 'During the last four years, I have held 140 surgeries and have dealt with hundreds of problems concerning the council. One response took 80 days and a school matter took several letters and over sixteen months before even an acknowledgement was received.' It seemed that CCC had more than one critic.

My ego was further inflated by a clearly impressed Glyn Davies, who asked 'who was going to replace' me, when an email fizzled onto my touch screen: 'I'm ashamed of you and quite honestly I'm glad you are going. You are a disgrace to the Party.' Lorraine. Seat 53. 14.32pm. I was shocked. In no mood for such nonsense, the following day I asked her to justify her comments and either give me a full written apology before close of the day's business, or I would consider involving our Standards Committee.

This was a silly threat that I had no intention of pursuing, but I rather felt that Lorraine's email had been intemperate and deserved some apology. Lorraine replied, 'I was so angry that you chose to attack Labour colleagues so publicly, and to see the Tories and PC cheering you on made me feel ill.' I just could never do that to a Labour colleague, no matter whether I felt I had a case against them or not'. She told me that she had blown the whistle on the Vale of Glamorgan Leader, Shaun Sutton. Her evidence would have been used in court, but a deal was done with the courts and he got away lightly. She continued, 'That was the way she did things and not give the Opposition such a golden opportunity to have another go at Labour colleagues, just before an election. Also, I did not feel it was the right way to use First Minister's questions. You were joining in the laughter and that made me see red – literally.' She admitted that her remarks were made on the spur of the moment and may not have occurred if she had slept on them. Lorraine emailed me again, 'Because life is too short and because Karen asked me nicely, I am sorry if I upset you with my email… I was upset at your public comments attacking one of our party members. The Opposition do it enough without it being done by our own Labour members. Lorraine.'

It had never been my intention to damage a Labour member and, naively, I had not considered political fallout although I knew Labour held the majority in County Hall. Just a reply from Russell Goodway would have stopped me in my tracks. It seemed very clear that the Assembly and the Cardiff County Council, both united under a Labour banner, were co-operating to guarantee that Cardiff got far more than its fair share of scarce resources. WAG was made up of South Wales AMs and the Assembly had been exceedingly generous to the three major cities in the South. I was elected to represent my constituents in the north, and I asked no more than some assurance that the South was not always given the preferential treatment. There was certain blatancy too about favouring the south. Had not Paul Murphy awarded Newport 'city status', neighbouring his own constituency of Torfaen, and left Wrexham out in the cold?

Those heady days four years before in the Members' Tea Room when everyone welcomed me were long gone. I had not tried to make life uncomfortable for anyone, but only to be an industrious backbench AM, a useful committee member, share the workload of tabling questions, contribute to debates and scrutinise the work of the Assembly. The only thing Lorraine and I had in common was Party membership, and she and I were living examples of the North-South divide. Lorraine fought for all the expensive Cardiff concentric projects as they were in or close to her constituency, and her duty lay to her voters, whilst I was doing the same for my electorate. We were scrapping for a share of the same budget and Lorraine ran out the winner every time! April Fools' Day was proving to be very busy indeed. Four of my electorate, two governors and two headmasters travelled to Cardiff for a long awaited meeting with Jane Davidson, the Assembly's Education Minister, to plead for more funding for their dilapidated schools. Holywell High School was close to infringing Health and Safety rules, and for years, Mold Alyn High School used buckets to collect rainwater that came though the roof. Circumstances conspired to prevent the meeting starting on time at 12.30pm and when we trooped late and apologetic into her office, Jane offered us less than 30 minutes as she had to officiate at a Milling Area reception.

A smug looking official watched events unfold. The Delyn contingent were eloquent in making out their case for more funding; well rehearsed facts and figures flowed, after years of inadequate financial support either from Local Government or the Assembly, they were now desperate and would the minister help? No, she would not. In a few deft words, the minister demolished their arguments. The Local Education Authority was the problem, nothing to do with her. She charged down every argument, every plea! I was appalled at this insensitive and arrogant display towards professional people working hard for their pupils. The smug official sat smirking at our discomfort. I said quietly, 'Minister, can nothing be done? These people are desperate.' Having worked hard to arrange that meeting, I had no idea it would be such a public relations disaster. Jane rose imperiously, blamed the Education Authority again and swept out leaving my party shocked and speechless. 'Is there nothing you can do for us?' I begged the official. The man smiled unctuously but said nothing. 'We are wasting our time,' I snapped angrily and marched out, followed by my constituents. In shock, they caught the next train back to Delyn. Jane Davidson's behaviour spread like wild fire round Delyn schools and the meeting has been held up as an example of how not to treat principled people committed to schools fit for purpose.

Before the last plenary session started on our last official day of the first term, the 2nd April, most of the AMs gathered in the Milling Area to welcome Colin Jackson, the Olympic hurdler, and to celebrate his stellar career and retirement from athletics. He stood beside an almost life size portrait of himself and we clapped warmly when Rhodri, responding to Colin's speech, wittily regaled us with his marvellous international record that spanned seventeen seasons. 'What better way to celebrate our retirement as an Assembly on the final day, of the final year of the first Assembly after four years, than with one of the greatest sportsmen that Wales, indeed Great Britain has ever produced.' I drew Question five at my final time in the chamber and grabbed the chance to praise Edwina's generosity towards an All Wales Police Schools programme and, as she managed our finances so well, could not even more be saved if the Assembly gained control of the police? Edwina responded that she was minded to support that idea in principle. She favoured devolving police to the Assembly; the four Chief Constables favoured it, and should Lord Richard's Commission recommend it, surely the Home Office must listen!

John Marek called me to speak in the final debate of the Assembly, entitled 'preventing youth offending'. Having galloped nervously through my brief, I thanked him for calling me, told him that he had always been kind to me and 'as this is my last plenary, I wish you well in the future.' 'Thank you Alison,' he replied gravely.

He had been looking gaunt and distracted for days, and was deeply troubled as to whether or not this was to be his last plenary also. Peter Rogers claimed the very last 'Short Debate'. Ironic, I thought, that a Tory should end this historic session despite being so opposed to the Assembly. Peter charged into his subject. 'Is North Wales losing out to Cardiff?' and soon we were collapsing with laughter as he stumbled, his fury and passion rising as he ripped through his diatribe. Just as he launched into an attack on dreadful rail links between north and south, Peter Law drifted lazily into the chamber, took his seat and theatrically unfurled a large campaign type poster that depicted Peter, himself, and grinning broadly waved it at the podium. The other Peter broke down into laughter and we all joined in the mirth.

This camaraderie and sharing a joke was what the Assembly had been all about – no more 'Ya-Boo' politics; all pulling together to benefit Wales. Sadly, someone had been naive to think politicians could ever work in harmony for long. I left before the end of the debate, filled with sadness that another wonderful career was about to close, but not before I attended the last Economic Development Committee on the following day (Thursday the 3rd April).

By chance, I bumped into John Grimes the Clerk, and Sian, his deputy, in the canteen before the meeting. We mulled over Andrew Davies's paper on 'a science strategy for Wales'. I formed the impression that the Clerks saw the report as a missed opportunity, called it a 'Janet and John' paper and, reading between the lines, I assumed it was seen as a veiled attempt to offer policy in a half-hearted manner. I giggled at these sagacious remarks, as I happened to agree with all they had said. I really rated these two officials. They never fudged issues, had given full information when asked and did not flinch from my tough questions. Val Feld had believed in John when she had chaired EDC and I had thought him to be rather weak and 'waffly'. He proved me entirely wrong and I saw qualities and courage that I had missed before.

Delyth stood in for Ron Davies at this last Economic Development Committee. Ron's 'pay-off' and pension had been leaked and the *Daily Sport* vented fury that the shamed minister was to cost the public a bumper £40,000 redundancy and £18,000 a year pension. Not much to show for many years of flying high and competently in the political stratosphere, I thought, and certainly no ermine or other rewards. I endured a re-run of the Cardiff Capital of Culture presentation given previously to the Culture Committee. This committee was far more sceptical and asked tough questions about risk analysis and the real advantages to all of Wales and to Cardiff after 2008. What had Cardiff County put into the scheme and why hide behind the promise it will benefit all of Wales when this was not the case? Lynne Williams and Yvette Vaughan Jones responded spiritedly to our barbs and attempted to allay fears that the Assembly was being led by Russell Goodway's ambitious financial demands. We learnt that Cardiff County had seemingly had a re-think and had match funded Assembly money to such an extent that the Lord Mayor was allegedly furious over spending one pound more than that contributed by the Assembly.

My colleagues were not convinced by the presentation and the comparison between the scepticism shown by Economic Development AMs and the 'accept everything as fine' approach from Culture Committee AMs was remarkable. The science strategy paper was next for discussion and Delyth, although new to the discussion, united with Dafydd Wigley to plead for a policy that would enable the Welsh economy to move forward. The entire committee saw the value of science, but Andrew's difficulty lay with personalities. He distrusted the advice of the expert even though he was a Bangor academic, with the knowledge and wisdom to recognise a glaring weakness in Welsh policy and recommend solutions. We could only plead for Andrew to keep an open mind, as the three of us would not return to call the minister to account.

Another agenda favourite – shortage of Broadband provision across Wales – was debated again and Phil Williams blinded us once more with his deep understanding of how it operated. We agreed that some progress had been achieved but still more effort was needed. My request to Andrew Davies for Broadband installation in our constituencies, desperately needed for speedier communications, was rejected as £600,000 was considered too high a price for moving AMs into the 21st century.

Thankfully, Alun Cairns was less confrontational toward Andrew than he had been at the previous meeting when he virtually called the minister a liar over some steel deal. Alun was furious that Andrew had allegedly given £30 million to a steel firm without securing more jobs. He was behaving so aggressively, and faced with this onslaught, Andrew could only blink. I suggested that he should be called to order. Christine Gwyther in the chair pouted and looked displeased. Primly, she stated that Standing Orders had not been infringed. My interruption had quietened Alun down and the minutes diplomatically recorded that a member had asked for information. They noted, 'member's disappointment after a very positive discussion on 28th November. When the committee had given enthusiastic cross party support for the principle of a science policy, they had received such negative support from the minister'.

Canteen discussions were one thing but keeping discreet minutes was another, and the Committee Clerks were not quite telling it like it was this time, but I forgave them! Emyr Roberts, the civil servant – who had fielded much of my relentless probing into the Harbour Authority, the WDA, Objective One funding and so on – rose to leave as the minister no longer required him. Impulsively, I rose too and offered him not only a hand but also a timid embrace. By mutual accord, all the months of combating that difficult AM and, from my perception, a secretive civil servant, melted and our cheeks touched. Christine announced loudly, 'For the benefit of the cameras, Alison has just got up and snogged an official.' 'A gentle embrace, Chair,' I chided. Andrew Davies blinked in disbelief. 'Firsts never stop happening,' he stammered, bemused by my showing the perceived 'enemy Emyr' such affection. An even higher official, David Pritchard, always beside Andrew during EDC, also met my embrace and returned it in mutual consent. I was not 'snogging officials'.

I had been a difficult member; probing and asking tough questions, although I had always drawn back or asked for a note later rather than cause embarrassment on camera if a fact was not known. I suspect that I had ruffled feathers. The embrace recognised that I respected them and I hope that they respected me in return. We had served our respective masters to the best of our ability and invariably, we had performed our roles fairly.

Saying farewell to John and Sian was more difficult and as we hugged and a tear was shed, Alun's immaculate deeply cuffed shirt did not escape either as I turned to bid him goodbye. Ever the diplomat, Leighton noticed my red eyes when I returned to the office. 'It's good to cry. Shows feeling,' he murmured comfortingly.

My car was stacked with clothes, furniture, and a fig tree torn from its plastic pot. Still, a last meeting remained as the Auditor General wanted to brief us on winning a contract to take over from the Audit Commission in 2005, and inform us that his team would now audit Police Authorities. I was euphoric. It seemed that refusing to disclose documents, using verbal reports, those disingenuous confidentiality clauses and even opting to intervene in legal disputes such as the Jenny Trigger saga, would now be regulated and properly monitored. Calling Police Authority staff to account and banning the nonsense of the Clerk monitoring himself could now be possible. Had years of battling to make Police Authorities accountable not been in vain?

With more tear welling goodbyes and stopping only to pick up the dogs in Penarth, I pulled away from the murky waters of Cardiff Bay and headed north. 'Dragon's Eye' that evening made me wince. Leaving plenary for the last time, a mike was thrust under my nose and a battery of questions thrown at me. 'Most amusing incident?' 'David Davies's bottom.' 'Most stressful incident?', 'David Davies's bottom.' These silly answers and the rest were rolled out including 'and the most excruciating event?' 'Probably now', I muttered, 'I'm leaving with very mixed feelings!' The camera followed me as I stomped across the Milling Area, overweight and stooping, my poor posture captured on film for posterity. I was not the only slouch, as the post brought a letter from Carwyn Jones, thanking me for all my hard work and promising too that he would try not to slouch again.

I left my Delyn office for the last time on the 24th April, leaving Glen and Peter to finalise its closure and then I flew to Barbados on Concorde. I had survived four years of intense physical and mental pressure, more challenging than any time in my previous 30-year police career. I now know that politicians are a breed apart and that I could never really fit the mould. On the night the Welsh Assembly election was held, I watched waves breaking gently onto a moonlit, tropical beach. Raising my glass, I drank to absent friends.

Loose ends.

*'The Socialists can scheme their schemes and the Liberals can dream their
dreams, but we at least have work to do.'*
Iain Norman Macleod. Speech to the Conservative Party Conference, 1960

Much has happened since the first Assembly term finished and the
new one began. Two elections have been fought and several key
players in the first term have moved on in every sense of the word.

After the 2003 Assembly elections, AM Prof. Phil Williams,
(Plaid's cerebral and charming AM) would not have had the time
to install solar panels on his roof as he died in tragically regrettable
circumstances on 10th June 2003, aged 64. John Marek returned
as an 'Independent' member under the banner of the Party he
established, 'Forward Wales'. Ron Davies became a founder member
of the party.

The original Cabinet members of May 2003 remained in the
Cabinet but some portfolios changed. Andrew Davies continued to
hold the Economic Development portfolio and four years on, Wales
still has no official Science Policy. The 'Janet and John' paper that
found little support from Committee Clerks and the previous
Committee, seems to have been aptly named, and Peter Law went
on to sit as an independent AM after falling out with Rhodri
Morgan's Labour party.

The WMC opened with great ceremony, jazz bands, open air
concert and fireworks on the 28th November 2004 followed by the
official opening by the Queen. The cost to the Assembly
Government to ensure it continues to flourish is a well guarded
secret. In a letter dated the 13th December 2003, the Auditor
General promised a review of WMC expenditure if the Government
of Wales Bill was enacted. The Bill will take effect after the May 2007
Welsh Assembly elections.

The Assembly Building, the Senedd, fittingly opened officially on the 1st of March, St David's Day 2006. Before the extremely late arrival of the invitation to attend the opening, I had unwittingly booked to travel abroad. The feedback of the building from friends in the north was very fulsome and the protracted delay and hugely increased cost of construction seemed worth it.

Leighton Jenkins, my researcher, became office manager to Jeff Cuthbert AM, who replaced Ron Davies when his Caerphilly constituency lost patience with him. Leighton is now the Assistant Director-Policy Wales with the CBI, a well deserved career change and promotion that occurred in February 2007.

Before I finally stepped down, on the 31st April, and like a dog with a smelly bone, I pressed Stephanie King-Davies, Cardiff County's Chief Legal Services adviser and Council's Monitoring Officer, for some action over my complaint against Lord Mayor, Russell Goodway. She held both positions of Monitoring Officer and Chief Legal Services Officer, exactly replicating the unsatisfactory situation we had faced on the North Wales Police Authority. Surely, I asked, 'wearing two hats demised the possibility of effectively challenging suspected irregularities by elected representatives?'

King-Davies responded in her letter of the 8th April that 'I try to act without partiality and without favour to any member, or group of Members or to any officer.' Fine, I thought, but impartiality in her position is impossible to prove. Doubtless stung by my capriciousness, she laboured to explain that the Cabinet, whose activates were described so graphically in the trawl of County business on its official website, had no executive powers of its own, as it was not a Committee of the Council! This Cabinet was part of a trial adopted by several Local Authorities at that time and thus, this 'Shadow Cabinet' did not record an official record of the Authority. Amazing!

Whatever powers the Shadow Cabinet/Authority did or did not possess at the time remained unclear, as I have no record of any response to my bold letter dated 31st March in which I expressed 'surprise that the Cabinet has no legal status and certainly no clue was forthcoming in the official minutes that would reflect their impotence'!

Why was the Cabinet actually reviewing the relationship between the proposed WMC and the Capital of Culture bid if it possessed no authority to make progress? Why were discussions on the WMC not fully agendered and why was the item being 'considered as a matter of urgency' bearing in mind both items have been discussed for many years? I reminded Ms King-Davies that I had written to Russell Goodway three times seeking clarification and furthermore, he had visited the Assembly twice, and on both occasions, he had grinned and ducked my probing questions. The Lord Mayor oozed confidence and authority and certainly did not display any lack of powers, executive or otherwise.

Possibly stung by my written suggestion that 'there appears no real desire to investigate what appears to be a serious complaint regarding the integrity of the Lord Mayor' in her letter of the 23rd April 2003, she reported that she had commenced a formal investigation into my allegation. Frankly, I knew what the outcome would be. She had all the powers and I was yet again the pawn in a one sided system that was geared to protect the powerful.

Now free of Assembly responsibility, something pricked my conscience and I dropped Rhodri Morgan an apologetic little note dated 21st May, seeking forgiveness for being an ardent member of the 'Awkward Squad' during my time as one of his AMs. I did not expect a reply as I suspected I had been a very unwelcome thorn in his flesh and I was, after all, supposed to be on his side. His reply on the 25th July was gracious and very flattering: 'Your successor will have benefited from the hard work you invested in Delyn but your contribution to the Assembly went far wider than that, and will have played an important part in our overall success.' He continued, 'Members of the "Awkward Squad", as you put it, are essential in any political group. It means that ideas get properly tested and that no pieces of received wisdom are able to be perpetuated without challenge. Your contribution to the Audit Committee continues to be held up as an example to your successors to cite but one example.'

Greatly chuffed to read such glowing praise reminded me of an incredible suggestion floated by the Presiding Officer once I had left the Assembly. Troubled by the timid and wavering performance by the new Audit Committee members, who apparently seemed unable or unwilling to follow the 'tough, let's get the truth' performance of the original AMs, the Presiding Officer sought ways of stiffening their resolve and making them worthy members of this prestigious committee. The rumour reached me that the Presiding Officer sought my involvement in training up new members to make them fit for purpose! I was flattered when the plan was revealed but I knew that this courageous suggestion could never really work.

My experience was gleaned from 30 years of being a police officer, where interviewing skills had been honed by asking tough questions, remembering the replies, and most importantly doing the preparation. The other elusive ingredient missing from the new intake, that no tutor, however talented, could easily impart to the Audit AMs, was that 'Awkward Squad' mentality again. Seeking the truth and a refusal to be deterred from the right to challenge facts and not automatically salute the Party flag through misguided loyalty, was something I cherished, and I was not alone in that respect.

Rhodri's letter had made the point nicely. I just wanted to ensure that the millions paid by the public to the people who serve us, was not wasted. With so many levels of Government in Wales, its citizens are entitled to know their money is not being wantonly squandered by its officials and that their elected representatives are giving value for money too.

Pursuit of this heady goal goaded me into yet another letter in the quest for a result on the Goodway complaint. On the 15th September 2003, I apologised to the Archbishop (Chair of CCC's Standards Committee), but having heard nothing, could he ask the Committee's Secretariat to update me as it was worrying the issue was taking so long to resolve?

The silence remained deafening and on the 27th October, I asked Ms King-Davies for a progress report as 'I found the Archbishop's failure to respond particularly disappointing'. The reply came almost by return as on the 6th November 2003, Ms King-Davies wrote that she regretted that she had received no correspondence from me since April of this year. 'Since we have not been provided with a contact address, I am afraid it has not been possible to send you the details of the outcome of the investigation, I now enclose a copy of the report prepared by the Archbishop.'

A six page unsigned and undated missive was duly enclosed headed 'City and County of Cardiff – Report to the chairperson of the Standards and Ethics Committee.' I grasped the gist quickly. Any suggestion of alleged misconduct arising from the role of a member in minutes was construed as inaccurate. Under the heading, 'Recommendation' was found: 'That it be determined that there is no case to answer', no signature appeared of the Archbishop, nor for that matter, any other member of the Standards and Ethics Committee, although 'Stephanie King-Davies, Chief Legal Services Officer and Monitoring Officer' was typed in bold case. Had Ms King-Davies not advised me that the report was prepared for the Archbishop, I would have not even know that he or any other individual had been involved or that any independent scrutiny had taken place.

I was shocked to read that I had 'offered to provide further information and despite further letters, that information had not been forthcoming'. Councillor Goodway's response was 'I do not share her (the complainant's) view that the matter reported in relation to the WMC at the meetings to which you refer, was in any way inaccurate. I believe the reports made on each occasion were entirely correct. The opinion of the complainant seems to be based on a misinformation of the words of the minutes in question. In my view the complaint is based on a false premise and is not made out.'

Thus spoke the impartial opinion of an employee of Cardiff Council who happily acted in the conflicting roles of Chief

Executive and the Council's Monitoring Officer. Ms King-Davies ruled supreme. The 2004 Local Authority election removed Cllr Goodway from the role of Lord Mayor but he has not moved far from the political corridors of power with South Wales.

Before the 2005 general election, Peter Law was diagnosed as having a brain tumour and showed tenacity, humour and courage by fighting a dual winning campaign. He returned as the elected member for both the Assembly and as a Member of Parliament for Blaenau Gwent, having won the seat on a swing of 49%, defeating Labour candidate Maggie Jones, and gaining a majority of 9,121 votes. Having lost Labour's safest seat in Wales, Maggie was subsequently rewarded for this humiliating defeat by being made a life working peer in April 2006. Peter then served his constituents almost to the end when he succumbed to his tumour on the 25th April 2006, aged 58.

We had met at the funeral of John Marek's wife, Anne in Wrexham on the 20th March 2006. Peter had made the journey from the valleys by wheel chair and was greatly changed from the vibrant, bouncy man I had known when he and I served together. He recognised me instantly and the old friendly banter and joking started between us as if nothing had changed. 'Its Teflon Halford,' he joked, watched by his wife Trish. Rhodri Morgan defied his wife's plea that he should not attend Peter's funeral, by appearing amongst a huge turnout and deeply moving service that his valley had laid on in respect for their trusted and loved comrade. After his death, Trish swept into the Assembly as the AM for Blaenau Gwent with another handsome majority.

At the 2007 Assembly elections, Ron Davies wrote the 2007 'Forward Wales Party' manifesto and he stood against his former political agent in Caerphilly, but came third, losing to Jeff Cuthbert who held the seat for Labour. John Marek also lost in 2007, ironically to his former secretary, Lesley Griffiths, whom he had soundly beaten in 2003. Wrexham was the only Labour gain in Wales, that lost Christine Gwyther and Minister Alun Pugh, both beaten by narrow majorities. Welsh Conservative Glyn Davies failed to be re-elected and the final count was 15 Plaid Cymru AMs, 12 Welsh Conservatives, 6 Lib Dem AMs and 26 Labour AMs, 5 short of a majority. Independent Trish Law was returned to the Assembly in 2007 with an increased majority. Only Carwyn Jones increased his majority for Labour whilst in Delyn, my comfortable 1999 majority plummeted by a swing against of 3.7% compared to 2003. The Conservative challenger lost by only 511 votes, turning a safe Labour constituency into a Tory winnable marginal.

The Assembly had until the end of May to nominate a First Minister and form a Government and for a time, a 'rainbow coalition' between Plaid Cymru, the Welsh Conservatives and the Lib Dems was proposed. The topsy-turvy on/off, off/on proposed rainbow coalition machinations were in deep disarray as May drew to a close. First accepting a pact with Plaid, thereby elevating Ieuan Wyn Jones to First Minister, the Lib Dems 'bottled it', which 'shattered PC's hopes of taking over a Plaid led Government', and left Dai Lloyd, PC's chairman, seething at the missed chance after eight years in Opposition. However, Mike German must have rallied his powerful six AMs, as, on the 26th May, 'the wheels were very decisively put back on' in the Lib Dem camp and the coalition was being explored again.

By that time, with no rainbow coalition firmly cemented, Rhodri Morgan knew he was 'back from the dead' having read his 'political obituary' when the alleged rainbow coalition was on the brink of power. 'I read that I was toast when I was eating my toast', Rhodri told the Senedd. On the 5th June, for the third time, this seemingly indestructible 66 year old was leading his country again with a minority, when he and the Presiding Officer, still holding the same role, greeted the Royal Party that included Camilla, Duchess of Cornwall in the Senedd (Debating Chamber). Rhodri stated that 'there were simply no words that convey what an honour it is to serve your country as First Minster'. Today's significance is that this Assembly had the new powers conferred on us by the

Government of Wales 2006 – 'new and better tools to do more for the people we serve.'

Rhodri's new Cabinet rewarded the same ministers but yet again, new mixes of portfolios had been concocted. Edwina Hart took command of Health and Social Services, Carwyn Jones moved into a mixed bag of unrelated tasks: Education, Culture and Welsh Language. Dr Brian Gibbons, now relieved of Health, was given the Economy and Transport, whilst Jane Davison moved from long years with Education to take responsibility for Sustainability and Rural Development. Rhodri kept faith with Jane Hutt again and she was given Budget and Business.

Carl Sargeant, the only North Wales Cabinet representative, was made Chief Whip and Deputy Business Manager, a position that allowed him to attend Cabinet meetings. His local newspapers were fulsome in their congratulations that a Connah's Quay town councillor and former process operator in a chemical factory had done so well.

Cynics suggested that Rhodri's choice of six minsters holding such poorly matched portfolios, gave him room to bring in a minister from another party without having to fire a Labour crony. Rosemary Butler, who had lost the election to Deputy Presiding Officer by one vote to John Marek in 2000, succeeded unchallenged into this role for the Third Assembly session.

Rhodri sought permission to form a pact with Plaid Cymru from his Westminster colleagues on the 14th June and some flexibility was offered to him. Although the Lib Dems clearly regretted missing the chance of forming some part of a rainbow coalition Government, the All Wales Accord scheme still had not happened and Rhodri Morgan opened negotiations with Plaid Cymru in a desperate attempt to hang onto power.

An Editorial in the *Daily Post* on the 5th October 2000, would have made uncomfortable reading for the party leaders in 2007: 'For the best part of 18 months, politicians in the first National Assembly for Wales have been fighting like ferrets in a sack.'

After approving Labour's devolution plans by the narrowest of margins in a referendum, a bemused Welsh electorate has been reluctant to witness a succession of second-rate operas, played out in the name of democracy in Cardiff Bay. Alun Michael tried to bind things together with his own brand of dodgy sticking plaster and string and called it 'inclusive politics'. It was so inclusive, the three Opposition parties tested their collective clout against Labour's minority regime and booted him out. In-fighting was in vogue, about buildings, about anything. Leaders came and went amongst the Tories and Plaid Cymru – and it had to stop, because it was turning the fledgling institution into a laughing stock. 'People aren't interested in who is in or out of the Cabinet but they are interested if their kids need jobs, the school roof is leaking and waiting lists for hospitals are too long.'

In an interview on the 11th June, Alun Michael placed the blame squarely on Ron Davies and the media for the Assembly's political stability. Answering a question: 'Having been accepted as a ruling party, is it legitimate for the Opposition to oust Labour as soon as an opportunity presents itself?' Alun responded, 'These are the dangers of an unstable structure that was put into place by Ron Davies. The politics of consensus that everybody signed up for before the first Assembly elections need two things: Opposition parties that are willing to be constructive whilst holding the Government of the day to account, but not to be purely destructive, and new journalism that does not only reward people for knocking six bells out of each other, but tries to make politics of consensus interesting to the public.' Alun continued, 'I tried to persuade Ron Davies to go along with a different approach – two member constituencies which largely would have meant that each constituency was represented by people of two different parties, provided a degree of stability and the difference of constituency AMs and regional AMs would not exist and it is a problem.'

Hindsight is a very exact science and whether Ron's selection plans were catastrophically wrong and the Opposition genuinely believed they were holding the Government to account and were not being destructive during the first shaky Assembly term, is a difficult one to call. On the 19th July, Rhodri announced a new cabinet having formed a coalition with Plaid Cymru. Their leader, Ieuan Wyn Jones became both deputy leader and Economic Development Minister. In August 2007, a favourite Labour 'think-tank' accused Labour of being in denial and far from closing the wealth gap between East of England and all of Wales, Wales had dropped still further down the league. Wales's low economic output means that it still qualifies for European funding.

Eight years on it is very clear that the Welsh Assembly has failed to boost the economy across all Wales, and several of the brave promises we cheered to the rafters in the beginning, have not materialised. Ron's plea that devolution was a process, and not an event, seems to be never-ending, but at least Wales is governing itself and is entitled to do so!

Printed in the United Kingdom
by Lightning Source UK Ltd.
124251UK00001B/151/A